D1609925

WP 0485022 X

A HISTORY OF CZECHOSLOVAKIA SINCE 1945

Original title:
GESCHIEDENIS VAN TSJECHOSLOWAKIJE NA 1945
Translated from the Dutch by Evelien Hurst-Buist

A HISTORY OF CZECHOSLOVAKIA SINCE 1945

HANS RENNER

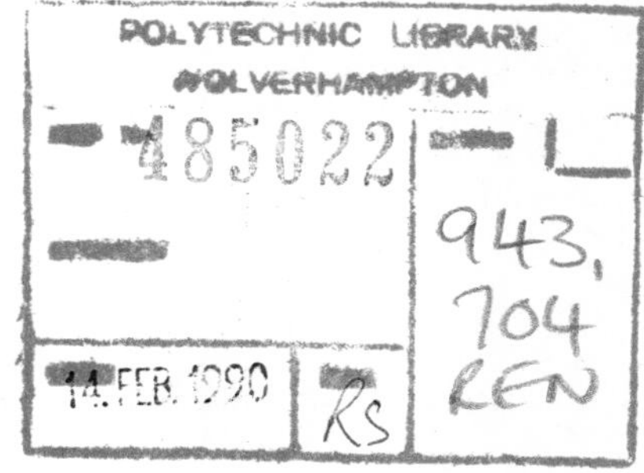

ROUTLEDGE
London and New York

First published 1989
by Routledge
11 New Fetter Lane, London EC4P 4EE
29 West 35th Street, New York, NY 10001

Typeset in 10/12 point Baskerville by Witwell Ltd

Printed in Great Britain
by TJ Press (Padstow) Ltd, Padstow, Cornwall

British Library Cataloguing in Publication Data

Renner, Hans
A History of Czechoslovakia since 1945
1. Czechoslovakia. Political events,
1945–
I. Title. II. Geschiednis van
Tsjechoslowakije na 1945. *English*
943.7'04

ISBN 0-415-00363-6

Library of Congress Cataloging-in-Publication Data

Renner, Hans.
[Geschiedenis van Tsjechoslowakije na 1945.
English]
A History of Czechoslovakia since 1945/
Hans Renner; translated from the Dutch by
Evelien Hurst-Buist.
p. cm.
Translation of: Geschiedenis van
Tsjechoslowakije na 1945.
Bibliography: p.
Includes index.
ISBN 0-415-00363-6
1. Czechoslovakia-History-1945- I. Title.
DB2216.R4613 1989 89-6040
943.7'04-dc19 CIP

To Justa Renner-van Niekerk
in gratitude

'I do not know why it is, but whenever I walk through the streets of Brussels, I am reminded of Prague. This is what life in that town would have been like, if the communists had not seized power in Czechoslovakia.'

J.R. (1988)

CONTENTS

- Does not produce works acceptable to the authorities
- lecturer at Dutch uni - researched opened / freedom

PREFACE

This book sets out to give a picture of the contemporary history of Czechoslovakia. Most of the subjects discussed here touch a raw nerve in its present-day communist rulers. As I am not part of the group of historians who, either voluntarily or by order, produce works acceptable to the authorities, I did not have to take account of political guidelines or any other impediments. I was able to write completely independently, in accordance with the rules a historian should observe, and with my own conscience.

Compared to the hundreds of independent historians in Czechoslovakia who have been affected by a ban on publication, and with whom I feel a bond, I found myself in a privileged position. In the first place I conducted my research openly and in complete freedom as a lecturer at a Dutch university, supported and respected by many people. I did not have to fear confiscation of my manuscript during an unexpected search of my home, or, even worse, of interrogation or prosecution on the basis of the written text. Second, in contrast to most Czechoslovak historians, I had easy access to various sources and publications. I was able to consult official Czechoslovak books, journals and papers, just as easily as material published in the west, including numerous works by the hands of Czechoslovak dissidents.

In one respect, however, I found myself in a less enviable position. I conducted all the research from outside the country which I had left as a student in 1968. Since then I have no longer been directly involved in the developments in Czechoslovakia, I have not been able to sample the atmosphere directly, nor have I been an eyewitness of anything that has taken place there. But maybe this situation also has a positive side. A contemporary historian should both be involved in the subject, and try to keep a certain distance from it. Since 1968 the political situation in Czechoslovakia has forced me to keep my distance; though only a distance in miles and in time.

H.R.
Groningen
spring 1988

ACKNOWLEDGEMENTS

I am greatly indebted to my mentor, Prof. Dr Z. R. Dittrich, Emeritus Professor of East European History at the University of Utrecht, for his critical comments on the manuscript, his warm interest, and his valuable advice.

Words are not adequate to thank Justa Renner-van Niekerk for her part in this book. Not only was she the first critical reader of the manuscript, but also the editor of the book in the broadest sense of the word, and more besides. This study is dedicated to her in gratitude, all the more so because the contemporary history of Czechoslovakia has long since become her own history.

Chapter One

THE COMMUNIST TAKE-OVER

February arrived. Who had won and who had lost? Had the non-communist parties lost and the Communist Party of Czechoslovakia won? It was the idea of democracy that had lost, and it had lost completely. Political parties stopped being part of the political structure in the traditional sense of the word. In fact, they stopped being parties at all. The so-called 'opposition parties' lost all significance, because the Communists would not allow them any freedom, and the Communist Party also became meaningless because it had never been a political party with a truly living organism in the first place, but a party with a closed structure under the direct control of Moscow. All opportunities for political life were lost, opportunities we used to have in the past.

Ivan Medek (1979)

BENEŠ AND THE SOVIET UNION

'East and West – Czechoslovakia at the Crossroads?' is the title of the last chapter of the memoirs of president Dr Edvard Beneš, which was completed in 1947, less than a year before his death.[1] During his war-time exile in London, Beneš, who, after the foundation of the Republic in 1918 had left his unique stamp on Czechoslovakia's foreign policy, became convinced that a friendly, loyal attitude by his country towards the Soviet Union, would offer the best guarantee for an undisturbed development of democracy in the future.

The picture that Beneš painted of the post-war world was very positive. With the optimism so typical of him, he relied on the allied powers and their social structures to live together in peace, and with co-operation and mutual respect.[2] The Czechsolovak statesman was not the only one to cherish illusions about a harmonious model of the future world. President Roosevelt had a similar belief in 'one world'. This would be created after the defeat of fascism, as a result of the joint efforts of all peace-loving nations, united in a universal world organization. It would be an international platform, where various political questions were to be solved.[3]

In Beneš's vision of the new world, and the new Europe in particular, Czechoslovakia was allocated an important role. This state would function as a bridge between east and west by offering mediation and co-operation to both sides. This was one of the reasons why, during the war, Beneš pursued a foreign policy that looked towards the Soviet Union. A concrete result of this policy was the 'Treaty of friendship, mutual assistance and post-war co-operation', in December 1943. Beneš personally devoted himself to this cause, despite repeated warnings, especially from the British, but also from some Czechoslovaks in his own camp.

Nevertheless, he believed that his policy was right. He did so not only because, as the war progressed, it became more and more clear that the influence of the Soviet Union in middle and eastern Europe would much increase after the German defeat, but also because the traumatic experience of the 1938 Munich crisis, when France and England handed their small ally over to Hitler without a fight, was still fresh in his memory.

The events of Munich led him to conclude that the western democracies were unable to offer sufficient guarantees against a possible future German threat. In the light of this the orientation towards the Soviet Union meant a necessary change of direction of Czechoslovakia's pre-war foreign policy. But Beneš had another important reason for striving for a good relationship with the Soviet Union. Russian help, diplomatic and otherwise, was vital to him, if he wanted to solve the problem of nationalities in Czechoslovakia – a source of trouble throughout the centuries – once and for all. In Beneš's view – and he was not alone in this – there was only one possible solution: expulsion of the minorities (the Germans and the Magyars) to the neighbouring countries.

It cannot be denied that the direction of Beneš's foreign policy towards the Soviet Union pushed Czechoslovakia even further into the arms of Stalin. The 'obsequious attitude' of the president regarding his eastern neighbour is criticized by a number of authors.[4] Other authors show understanding for the difficult situation in which the Beneš government-in-exile found itself.[5] Without doubt Beneš's position both during the war and after, was not an easy one. He had to take the powerful group of communist exiles in Moscow into account, and later the Red Army, which liberated the largest part of the territory of Czechoslovakia. He considered extensive concessions to Stalin to be inevitable, all the more because he believed Stalin's promises that the Kremlin would not interfere with Czechoslovakia's internal affairs, an undertaking to which the Soviet Union had committed itself in accordance with article 4 of the 1943 Treaty.[6]

How right the Czechoslovak policy was seemed to be confirmed by events in nearby Poland. Beneš and his minister of Foreign Affairs, Jan Masaryk, were witnesses at close quarters of Stalin's treatment of Poland which was in response to the legitimate Polish government-in-exile who refused to give in to the, in their eyes, excessive demands of Moscow. Eventually Stalin deprived the Polish democrats of any influence on developments in their country by setting up a puppet government. It goes without saying that the Polish state of affairs offered a highly unattractive alternative to the Czechoslovak non-communist leaders.

As regards the developments in the Soviet Union itself, Beneš was optimistic: he was convinced that its leading bureaucracy would not escape becoming 'bourgeois' to some extent, which would, in the long run, automatically lead to democratization and liberalization of the system, especially if this were amenable to the west. It could almost be said that in his reasoning Beneš was at least four decades ahead of his time.

As to his assessment of Soviet foreign policy, however, the premier Czechoslovak politician had remained stuck in the past. Beneš, a very popular figure in the international political arena before the war, still looked upon the Soviet Union as the Soviet Union of the 1930s. There was a great difference, though, between the behaviour of the Soviet Union during the time of minister Maxim Litvinov – the politician who tried without success to create a system of European collective security against Hitler – and its behaviour after the victorious battle of Stalingrad. In the weakened and devastated Europe of the 1940s the Soviet Union had become a completely different power, although still ruled by the same leader, Stalin.

In the course of 1947, Beneš increasingly began to doubt Stalin's credibility. A few points which he hastily added to the manuscript of *Memoirs* bear witness to his doubts.[7] The Czechoslovak leader was beginning to realize that he had been mistaken about Stalin. His expectations of his future world view had not been fulfilled either. Instead of there being trust and loyal co-operation, the climate of the Cold War encompassed the world, characterized by the Truman and Zhdanov doctrines.[8]

This reality of two hostile blocs opposed to each other in sharp ideological and political confrontation, allowed no space for the 'building of bridges' that the Czechoslovak president had had in mind for his country. The chances for democracy in Czechoslovakia diminished considerably. As the Soviet Union considered middle Europe a strategically important area, necessary for its security, and a definite sphere of influence, Moscow chose for total subjection of the middle European states as the best means of control. It was not merely interested in a loyal attitude from a friendly, yet democratic Prague government. Or, as a famous Polish historian once said, commenting on the power politics of the Soviet Union: 'For Moscow, however, they were not bridges, but bridgeheads'.[9] Stalin's concept was such that a form of voluntary 'Finlandization', especially in view of the strategic importance of the country, was not to be granted to Czechoslovakia.

DEMOCRACY AT RISK

The preservation of democracy in Czechoslovakia failed disastrously not only because of a foreign policy that was strongly directed towards the Soviet Union, but also because Beneš and the other Czechoslovak leaders did their utmost to find favour with the Kremlin regarding home affairs as well. In practice this resulted in attempts to remain on good terms with the Communist Party of Czechoslovakia (CPCz) by making concessions in politics, economics and social affairs, which was all to the satisfaction of the communist leader Klement Gottwald and his followers, and yet to the detriment of the democratic and humanitarian principles, for which Czechoslovakia had been famous between the two wars.

Backed by the authority of the Soviet Union, and taking advantage of the democratic parties' sympathetic attitude towards co-operation, the CPCz took the initiative as soon as it had set foot on liberated soil. The communists also managed to exert decisive influence on the government programme of 5 April 1945, which was proclaimed in the east Slovak town of Košice. The contribution to this programme by non-communist parties was significantly less pronounced.

In accordance with the Košice programme, the Czechoslovak political system was dominated by the National Front (NF), a co-ordinating organization in which all political parties had seats and worked together, and in which the communists had a leading position. The fact that it was very difficult to go into opposition within the NF, that no parties were allowed outside it, and, above all, that parliament was only allowed to play a minor role, meant a serious restriction on the democratic system in itself. An essential requirement for the subsequent, successful coup by the CPCz had now been fulfilled.

The same was true of the nationalization of industry, laid down in the Nationalization Decree of 28 October 1945. At the start this was restricted to firms with more than 500 employees. Oddly enough, this time it was the social democrats who pushed it through. The influence of the communists in trade and industry increased considerably by these measures and others, such as the compulsory purchase of enemy and collaborators' possessions, which also affected a large number of smaller businesses. The CPCz itself considered the nationalization as one of its major political successes. In 1945 no other state, apart from the Soviet Union, had carried out expropriation to such a degree as Czechoslovakia.

After the war the main goal of the CPCz was to gain as much political power as it needed to establish a communist monopoly. A step in the right direction was the substantial election victory of May 1946, gained in the first - and at the same time last - free elections, when the Communist Party got as much as 38 per cent of the votes.[10] It became a major party with easily the largest number of members.[11]

It is hard not to believe that the other parties seemed to have underestimated the power of their rival. Whereas the CPCz acted as a closed bloc, this could not be said of the Czechoslovak non-communist parties. In the tradition of the First (pre-war) Republic, these parties were primarily pressure groups, who each looked after the interests of their own followers, and were each others' rivals. They did not have a common strategy and were unprepared for the subsequent power struggle. The parties soon fell back into opposition with each other, and their pre-war political squabbling, without realizing that the political situation was quite different from that of the First Republic of T. G. Masaryk. A politician of that time summarized the situation pointedly: 'The greatest flaw of the non-communist coalition was that there wasn't one'.[12]

The democratic parties contributed to their own downfall in another way as well. Their leaders were all too easily persuaded by the communists to take measures that caused irreparable damage to the pre-war political structure of the republic. And this disruption of the mechanisms of parliamentary democracy was exactly what the communist leaders intended.

An example of this is that the democratic parties dropped their old coalition partner, the Agrarian Party - also the largest party in the First Republic - without any scruples, by simply banning it after the liberation. The reason for this ban was said to be that some members of this party, especially within the leadership, had propagated fascism before the war and later had collaborated with the enemy. In itself this was true, but whether this was sufficient reason to have the whole party, with its large following from the rural population, pay for it according to the principle of 'collective guilt', is another matter. All in all, the liquidation of the Agrarian Party remained a dubious matter, from which in the end only the communists were to profit.

The same was true of a provision in the programme of Košice, which affected about a quarter of the population in Czechoslovakia: the expulsion of over two million Sudeten Germans, and the sequestration of their possessions. The true facts about the procedures surrounding this expulsion are still regarded as taboo, although contemporary historians defend it on the grounds that it was a historic necessity to ensure lasting peace in eastern Europe, and, specifically for Czechoslovakia, an inevitable measure against any possible German aggression in the future.[13]

Although the decision to expel the Sudeten Germans can be understood in the light of the time, bearing in mind the Nazi atrocities and the previous history, the manner of the expulsion amidst national feelings of resentment and blazing emotions should be condemned unequivocally. It did not do Czechoslovak politics any good to be seen carried away by a mass psychosis and not making any attempts to strive for reconciliation, however difficult that might have been. The expulsion, which started straight after the war and was completed in 1947, got out of hand, and cost the lives of numerous German citizens.

The prime minister of Czechoslovakia after the elections of 1946, Klement Gottwald, and his party managed to turn the expulsion of the Germans in the Czech border region into considerable political gain. First, the CPCz succeeded (like its Polish counterpart) in getting control over the evacuated areas. The communist minister of Agriculture, in charge of land distribution, made sure that the CPCz held absolute sway over the Sudeten area. In a true 'gold rush' manner numerous applicants were helped to new property by means of political corruption. This reprehensible practice meant that to the new occupants were handed over, along with a house and piece of land, their membership card of the communist party.[14]

Second, by means of fierce anti-German campaigning[15] and other nationalistic propaganda the CPCz gave part of the population the impression of being the most consistent guardian of national interests. The communists presented themselves successfully as champions of national unity and advocates of strong ties with other Slav peoples, above all with their most powerful Slav neighbour, the Soviet Union. Such and other slogans did not fail to have an effect on the Czechoslovak population after the terrible war-time experiences with Germans.

Third, under the pretext of the fight against the Germans and their collaborators the communist leaders also attacked numerous political opponents. 'The Red Army freed our nation from the Germans, we have to free us of the enemy within our own ranks ourselves', Gottwald said in an appeal to the Czechs and Slovaks.[16] From now on the CPCz would determine who the enemies of the people were, what measures were to be taken against them and when they were to be taken. In view of their aims, this mainly involved people who were avowed critics of the party and not afraid to denounce the increasing pressure of the Soviet Union.

In this way, the disgraceful evacuation of Czech border country, and the measures against the anti-communists, who were labelled as 'collaborators' and 'enemies of the people', led to actual and unlawful repression taking place in Czechoslovakia for the first time, and even *before* the communist take-over. Dependent on the nature of the regime this repression has continued: up to this day it is still more or less a fixed constituent of the Czechoslovak political system. There was one exception: the Prague Spring, the short-lived period of liberalization by Alexander Dubček in 1968.

THE STRUGGLE FOR POWER

The strategy used by the CPCz to obtain absolute power in the country underwent important changes during the years 1945–8.

Initially, after the election victory of May 1946, Gottwald and his followers hoped the Party would succeed in obtaining an absolute majority in the next elections of spring 1948, with or without the help of left-wing groupings of other parties. In this way the opposition would have been quietly disposed of.

When the leaders realized that such a victory was not feasible under the circumstances, they decided to try to seize power by any possible means and at any price. In the autumn of 1947 preparations for a coup were well under way. At that time Czechoslovakia was the last country in eastern Europe with its democratic forces still intact.

The Party began to concentrate on extra-parliamentary action, which in party-jargon was called 'mobilization of the masses' and included the so-called 'organized expression of discontent of the masses'. This involved amongst other things organizing large demonstrations that were supposed to express the wish of the people, issuing innumerable resolutions with categorical demands, the continuous visits to parliament, government and other state organs by workers' delegations, and other suchlike 'spontaneous' actions.

Not only did the CPCz control the street scene, it also controlled the police and the mass media. It used blackmail and violence against politicians of the democratic bloc, eliminated the non-communist leaders in Slovakia, mobilized its supporters in the army and trade unions, built up a network of fellow travellers within other political parties, and armed its People's Militia.

Meanwhile their political opponents were still campaigning for elections that were never to take place.

On the other hand, it was extremely important to the communist politicians not to be seen pulling down the democratic façade of Czechoslovak politics before the take-over. Even the militant wing of the Party understood the advantages of an elegant coup, as can be seen from the following fragment from the address by Václav Kopecký, at the plenary meeting of the Central Committee (CC) in November 1947:

> We have a lot of power. To use this power straight away, however, might be explained as a dictatorship. We will determine ourselves when to use this power, in such a way that nobody can accuse us of having abandoned the democratic way.[17]

The 'nobody' Kopecký was worried about, referred in the first place to the Czechoslovak people themselves. In view of their strong, democratic traditions – especially in the Czech countries[18] – it was not likely that a violent Petrograd-style communist *putsch* would be accepted, nor would there be any understanding of, let alone enthusiasm for, the Marxist-Leninist doctrines of 'necessary transition of the national and democratic revolution into a socialist one' or the 'historic inevitability of the class struggle'. A coup in the 'democratic way' would at least provide the communists with more credibility.

The time for the decisive showdown was now not far off. On 20 February 1948 an acute cabinet crisis was at hand and the democratic ministers resigned from the government convinced that president Beneš would not accept their resignation, which would mean the fall of the Gottwald government and early elections. This resulted in an open attack by the CPCz.

Paradoxically, the communists initially played the Beneš card, too, in their attempt to persuade the president who was by then seriously ill, to accept their proposal of replacing the outgoing ministers with Gottwald's own candidates. The main difference between the two opponents was that if Beneš would not agree to the demands of the CPCz, the latter had two more trumps left to play: the use of violence and military assistance from the Soviet Union.

The non-communist leaders, on the other hand, clung to Beneš and the democratic rules, yet would be powerless in the case of a possible violent confrontation. The following is an example of how people thought and acted in those days. Asked for the reason why the democratic parties, on their part, did not organize manifestations of the 'will of the people' as the communists did, former minister H. Ripka explained:

> We did not think it necessary because every child at that time knew that it would have made no impression on the communists, who were deaf and blind to any argument, and who knew too well how they had organized the 'spontaneous' will of the people, who were not even all their own followers, but sometimes frightened members of a crowd commanded by communists organizers. No genuine expression of opinion by a mass meeting would have impressed them. In any case they would have seized the opportunity to accuse us of organizing a *coup d'état,* and would certainly have used weapons to disperse a crowd that would without doubt have been many times bigger than theirs.[19]

One might wonder what the democratic leaders did intend to do against the continuing communist pressure, apart from resigning and awaiting the results of new elections. The answer remained forthcoming. The non-communist politicians had simply not thought out an alternative. Another thing was that the Czechoslovak army - the only power which might have set things right - stayed in its barracks, this being the doing of the Defence minister, the communist sympathizer general Ludvík Svoboda. In this way the mobile units of the People's Militia and of the communist mobile police had a free hand.

After strong pressure from the communists, president Beneš gave in on 25 February 1948. He accepted the resignation of the democratic ministers, thereby giving the coup the semblance of legality. The idea of the 'peaceful and constitutional solution of the government crisis' was born and from then onwards got a fixed place in the official Czechoslovak historiography.[20]

In reality the CPCz may have engineered a constitutional solution to the crisis, but this was achieved with the frequent use of anti-democratic coercive measures and blackmail. Klement Gottwald's referral to this, two months after the coup, puts this matter beyond any doubt:

> We knew the president insofar that we knew that if we showed strength here [the February crisis], the president would rate it at its true value, balance the pros and cons against each other, and take it into account. We counted on this state of affairs, but we were also prepared for another solution. And I think that the realization that we were prepared for another solution also played a role in the president accepting our proposal.[21]

And it was this fear of 'another solution' which Gottwald was speaking about, that made Beneš finally give in. In the context of the February events this would probably have meant a civil war and direct Russian military intervention. As one of his old political friends lamented in those days: 'In great crises Beneš is small'.[22] The tired president, who had only a few months left to live, did not want to have all that on his conscience.

The above remark could give the impression that the communist coup was in fact Beneš's fault. Yet it would be going too far to blame him for the February coup, or even the entire post-war situation in the republic. For that matter, the defects of the political system and the weakness of the democratic parties have already been recorded.

All the same, Beneš did not have the moral right towards the Czechoslovak people to accept the resignation. On 25 February 1948 he failed not only as the guarantor of Czechoslovak democracy but also as the main symbol of independence, which is how he was seen both during the Nazi occupation and after the liberation. A categorical *no* to communist demands with the logical consequence of resignation, would have partially exonerated him in the eyes of historians.

But Beneš, co-founder of Czechoslovakia, national leader and democrat, remained in office while his country rapidly slided into a dictatorship and had in fact lost its independence. If only because of this, his post-war leadership of Czechoslovakia cannot escape criticism. He resigned on 7 June 1948, having already attended the funeral of his Foreign secretary, Jan Masaryk (whose death still remains a mystery), and died on 3 September of the same year, just in time to get a state funeral.

In summary, we may say that Beneš and the democratic parties had partially themselves to blame for the problems of 1948. Their pro-Moscow foreign policy (ever since 1943) and their shortsighted and rather unconvincing domestic policy made it very easy indeed for the CPCz. In the light of the international political situation of the time, it remains very doubtful, however, whether a 'wiser' policy could have prevented the Czechoslovak drama of February 1948.

EAST AND WEST

This brings us to the role the Soviet Union played in post-war Czechoslovakia. In contrast to the situation before the war the Soviet Union now had a common border with the Republic. It had also annexed Czechoslovak Sub-Carpathian Ukraine (Podkarpatská Rus). From a geopolitical viewpoint alone, Stalin was now able to exert pressure on his neighbour, whenever he thought it expedient.

The allied forces had vacated the country at the end of 1945, it is true, but Czechoslovakia remained surrounded by Soviet troops. They were encamped in Hungary, the eastern parts of Austria, in the Soviet occupied zone of Germany, and in Poland. Admittedly, the moving to and fro of the Soviet occupying forces over Czechoslovak territory could hardly be regarded as interfering in internal affairs. Yet it was a means of political blackmail, especially when the Soviet government demanded transportation of troops at politically sensitive times, such as just before the elections.

The limited nature of Czechoslovak sovereignty was apparent from Stalin's action in one of the rare occasions when the Prague foreign policy conflicted with Moscow interests. This particular occasion concerned the attitude of the Czechoslovak government towards the Marshall plan. Briefly: in July 1947 the Gottwald cabinet declared itself unanimously in favour of participation in the American aid programme, and accepted an invitation to attend talks in Paris. Barely two days later a Czechoslovak government delegation headed by Gottwald was informed by Stalin in no uncertain terms that it should forswear the Marshall plan, which it promptly did.

How can this rapid change of mind regarding the American programme be explained? There is the strong impression that it was caused by a misunderstanding. Both the communists and non-communists in the Czechoslovak government, which would definitely benefit from the aid, misinterpreted the Soviet reaction. They supposed the Kremlin would not object to Czechoslovak participation in the programme.[23] The Soviets, on the other hand, failed to give any guidelines to their Prague ambassador, with the result that the latter could not give a clear answer to the Czechoslovak government on this matter.[24] In this context it is interesting to note that Moscow had earlier blown the whistle on the Poles, who, like the Czechoslovaks, had initially been interested in Marshall aid.

Gottwald's interview with Stalin in the Kremlin had put a damper on the government delegation. It had not expected such a hard attitude, at least not the two non-communist ministers, P. Drtina and J. Masaryk. Back in Prague Masaryk was very sceptical about the talks they had had in the Kremlin and said in his own typically frank way: 'I went to Moscow a free minister and I'm coming back a servant of Stalin'.[25]

Even Gottwald, who was used to quite a lot during his wartime exile in Moscow, seems to have been greatly impressed by Stalin's response to his political blunder. 'I've seldom seen Stalin so angry', was his reaction afterwards.[26] Gottwald took care not to make any more blunders. From then on he did his very best not to give Stalin any more reasons for criticisms of his policies, and once in power himself he obeyed the instructions of his generalissimo indiscriminately.

During those critical days in February 1948 Moscow became engaged in Czechoslovak affairs even more. Stalin sent Valerian Zorin, his deputy minister of Foreign Affairs, who was an expert on Czechoslovak political relations, to Prague. He had served as ambassador in Prague until 1947, and was well informed about what was happening both in- and outside the CPCz.[27] In private talks with a number of leading democrat politicians the Soviet diplomat clearly hinted at the consequences if the CPCz were to be kept out of the government. Moscow itself would then feel obliged 'to safeguard Czechoslovak independence'.[28] At the same time the Soviet Union warned the rest of the world that it would not allow anybody to become involved in Czechoslovakia's internal affairs. As we shall see, the western powers did not have any intention of doing so.

Unfortunately, the exact proceedings of the talks between Zorin and Gottwald are still unknown to historians. It has been firmly established, however, that Zorin brought the leader of the CPCz a personal message from Stalin, in which he offered the communists Soviet military help.[29] It did not have to come to that, but it was essential for the further developments in Czechoslovakia, that Gottwald could fully count on the unqualified assistance of the USSR. The communists were now assured that their seizing of power would be guaranteed.

The non-communist politicians, on the other hand, knew that there was to be no rescue from the west. After the Marshall plan had been turned down, the United States had virtually written off the republic.[30] President Truman confirmed this indirectly during a meeting with Jan Masaryk in autumn 1947, pointing out that Czechoslovakia should not count on any other than moral support, not even in the case of Soviet intervention.[31] The Czechoslovaks were given the same response by the British prime minister Attlee during their visit to London to gauge the British attitude.[32]

The knowledge that the west was not able, or rather did not want, to do anything for Czechoslovakia, did not make it any easier for the democratic leaders to take action against the communist political offensive of February 1948. It is not surprising that for some Czechoslovaks the frustration about their own impotence turned into the feeling that the west had abandoned them and that the ghost of Munich had resurfaced.

Yet there was an essential difference with the year 1938. Then the responsibility for the Czechoslovak tragedy rested largely with the western allies, in this case France and Great Britain, who failed their middle-European democratic partner in every respect.

It is not the intention to defend the American or British post-war foreign policy towards Czechoslovakia either; they did not exactly show much empathy for the complicated situation in which the republic found itself. The following is certain: ten years after Munich the western powers no longer had any obligations towards their old ally, the country of president Beneš. Moreover, they were wary – in view of the international situation and their own capabilities – of giving any guarantee to independent Czechoslovakia.

To put it differently: in 1948 the western powers dropped Czechoslovakia in the same way that they had dropped the rest of eastern Europe in the period 1944–7. It was cold comfort for the Czechoslovaks in that their own case differed from the preceding cases of communist subjugation in one respect: their remorse and compassion were greater. But greatest of all was their fear of further Soviet expansion. The 'Czechoslovak affair' forced the west to think, and, with its deterrent effect, had a salutary influence on the rest of non-communist Europe.

AND THE PEOPLE?

In the free elections of 1946 the communists managed to secure 38 per cent of the national vote, the highest percentage ever obtained by a communist party in free elections. How can this voting behaviour of the Czechs and Slovaks be explained? And how is it possible that at the beginning of 1948 the CPCz counted almost one and a half million members, who, we may presume, were on the side of their Party during the coup and who supported it actively? What did the rest, the great majority of the population, do during the crisis? While investigating this subject, these questions arise time and time again, and demand further clarification. I will now examine these matters in more detail.

First the question of the 38 per cent communist vote. We have already seen how the CPCz was a master at playing on national sentiment. Like many a big party holding a persuasive campaign at election time, the CPCz had a highly pragmatic programme. In practice this meant that it hardly mentioned the concepts of 'socialism' and 'socialist society' in its campaign.[33] To the voters, it presented itself as a Marxist party emphasizing nationalism rather than class-struggle and other doctrines.[34]

In short, after the war the CPCz was very popular. Another reason for its appeal was that, as opposition party before the war it had sharply denounced the 'capitulation' of the government parties and Beneš during the Munich crisis, and had pronounced itself in favour of armed resistance against Hitler. Voters were now repeatedly reminded of the Party's firm attitude and of the fact that 25,000 of its members had paid with their lives for the German occupation. In addition to this, the communists played an important part in the resistance, while most Czechoslovak territory had been liberated from the east, by the Soviet Union, 'the fellow Slav ally and superpower'.[35]

Many Czechs and Slovaks expressed their gratitude for the Russian sacrifices with their votes. All this was greatly reinforced by the fact that both Czechs and Slovaks were traditionally pro-Russian. In contrast with the Poles, Hungarians, Romanians and Fins they had not had any bad historical experience with Russia.

Two groups of Czechoslovak society were particularly susceptible to the policies of the CPCz. First, the younger generation of Czechs and Slovaks which had grown up during the war, and second, a considerable part of the Czech workers. This leads us to the question of the enormous success of communist membership recruitment.

That the younger Czechs and Slovaks sought - and found - alliance with the CPCz is not surprising, in view of the political situation of the time. Frustrated by the Munich trauma and the German occupation, many younger people had lost confidence in the values of the old political system. They rejected the pre-war system, which, in their eyes, had failed because it had not been able to guarantee the integrity and establishment of the Czechoslovak republic.[36] Their political inexperience and their predilection for radicalism formed an easy target for communist propaganda.

The relatively strong flow of workers towards the communists cannot just be explained by labelling the CPCz as a traditional labour party. In the highly developed and industrial Czech territories the Social Democrats and, to a lesser degree, the People's Socialist Party (later renamed the Czechoslovak Socialist Party) also depended for their support on this group of workers.

The secret of the rapid success of communism with the Czech workers (after the war one in four became a member of the Party and they formed 58 per cent of the membership),[37] was not in the first place due to the programme. Rather, it should be attributed to two factors. First, in industry, where communists held leading positions, they could influence and harass non-communist workers and put them under a lot of pressure, not only by means of the mighty pro-communist trade union, ROH (Revoluční odborové hnutí: Revolutionary Trade Union Movement), for instance, but also by means of blackmail. In this way many workers had joined the CPCz long before February, for opportunistic reasons.

Second, it was party policy to endow the working class with the status of a strong social group and an important political force. Also, after the Second World War the Czech workers were in great need of self-esteem. During the German occupation their attitude was not known for its steadfastness, to say the least. Nazi Germany realized very well that it would be to their advantage to maintain social stability in the 'Protectorate of Bohemia and Moravia', with its arms factories indispensable to the German war machine.

Under Reichsprotektor Reinhard Heydrich (German governor in Prague) the great mass of the Czech workers was easily bribed, with increased rations and all kinds of privileges.[38] One could hardly speak of any resistance or sabotage. Reports from Prague to Berlin said that they were *im algemeinen ruhig und arbeitsam* ('generally calm and hardworking'), while the Czech intelligentsia blamed them for their corruptibility and 'stomach-patriotism'.

The German headquarters thought about the Czech workers in the same vein. Note a confidential remark of the Führer, at a time when the Nazis were still doing well:

> The Czechs could soon be turned into fanatical sympathizers of the German 'Reich', if one were to give these 'Feinschmecker' double rations and did not send them to the camps in the East. They would then feel morally obliged to work twice as hard in the arms industry.[39]

From a psychological point of view, a warm reception by the CPCz to the workers was an excellent means for a rapid cure of this kind of 'Protectorate-complex'. The Party, which blamed the 'treacherous bourgeoisie' for the collaboration, proved to be the best protection against a dented past and on top of that a chance for those who wanted to devote themselves actively to an attractive career.[40]

In short, it may be said that the reasons for joining the CPCz were varied. Some people were full of the ideal of realizing a new and better society. Others were attracted by demagogical statements and popular proposals, and yet others expected material benefits or attractive jobs. There were also people who chose for the communists simply because they wanted to belong to the strongest and most powerful side. They all had one thing in common: as members of the same party they were all responsible for the killing off of Czechoslovak democracy, or what was left of it after 1945.

Finally, a few remarks about the attitude of the non-communist majority of the population in February 1948. Of primary importance here is that during the occupation Czechoslovakia had lost a considerable number of its intellectual elite, which had a very bad effect on the intellectual resistance of the population, who should have been involved in yet another struggle for independence.

With a few exceptions, (e.g. the vehement protest by Czech students), the reaction to the February events can be described as resigned. After Munich and the German occupation the communist coup was the third blow for the Czechoslovaks to cope with within ten years, while they had not yet recovered from the previous two. They trusted and counted on Beneš and the democratic leaders, but these gave in. In this situation the Czechs and Slovaks could not be expected to climb the barricades, quite apart from the fact that barricades, armed resistance and heroic uprising did not fit in with their historical tradition. What did? Apparently what did fit was their talent to adapt themselves from pure self-preservation to the enforced reality while awaiting better times or the right occasion to take fate into their own hands.[41]

Chapter Two

BETWEEN REVOLUTION AND REVOLT

> Yes, say what you will - the Communists were more intelligent. They had a grandiose program, a plan for a brand-new world in which everyone would find his place. The Communists' opponents had no great dream; all they had was a few moral principles, stale and lifeless, to patch up the tattered trousers of the established order. So of course the grandiose enthusiasts won out over the cautious compromisers and lost no time turning their dream into reality: the creation of an idyll of justice for all.
>
> Milan Kundera (1978)

THE GOTTWALD ERA

Kundera, at the time of the revolution not yet twenty years old, also belonged to the generation which the Party proudly called the 'Gottwald Youth'. It was predestined to carry the revolutionary banner into the communist era. It was a generation of enthusiastic Party members, many of whom truly believed in the ideals of communism. They were soon to be confronted, however, with a totalitarian system of the worst kind, one they had never had in mind.

The so-called 'period of the struggle for power' had ended in February 1948. The CPCz had won its 'struggle for the character of the republic'. A process of consolidation of power followed, while at the same time society was reorganized along Soviet lines. The systematic destruction of 'capitalist remains' on the one hand and the blind copying of the Soviet example on the other, were the two main characteristics of the communist policy after the take-over.

The CPCz started an aggressive recruitment campaign to further increase its ranks. Within half a year, from February to August 1948, the number of CPCz members rose from 1,409,661 to 2,674,838,[1] a number representing no less than 21 per cent of the total Czechoslovak population. The aim of this action was the 'liquidation of the influence of other parties', as the then general secretary of the CPCz, Rudolf Slánský, explained.[2] After the enforced merger of the Social Democrats and the Communists in July 1948, and the replacement of the leaders of non-communist parties by second and third rate puppets, the CPCz encouraged people to defect to their ranks in order to unsettle the bedrock support of the democratic parties. At the same time thousands of members of these parties were sent to prison as early as 1948.

In order to bring about a rapid metamorphosis of Czechoslovakia into a totalitarian society of the Stalinist type the CPCz leadership was assisted by a great number of advisers from the Soviet Union. In some cases they operated completely independently from the Prague authorities and exercised direct influence on Czechoslovak affairs according to the orders from Moscow. This was especially true of their activities within the Czechoslovak security forces and the army, but also of some strategically important economic areas, such as the Czech uranium mining industry.[3]

It is possible that there were communist politicians who watched these developments with concern or who even attempted to achieve more freedom of movement - however modest - for their country in the negotiations with Moscow. If there were any, they were few and far between in the higher party echelons, as it was completely in the politicians' own interest to conform rapidly to the offical party line, which is succinctly summarized by the ideologist Václav Kopecký: 'February is our little, half October and Hradčany (the Prague castle, centre of political life, HR) is our small Prague branch of the Kremlin'.[4] The results of this political attitude, entirely in accordance with the Soviet aim of a comprehensive surveillance of eastern Europe, did not take long to materialize.

Two examples by way of illustration: one from an economic viewpoint regarding the change of market of Czechoslovak exports, the other showing one of the results of the 'struggle on the cultural front'.

I During the first Five-Year Plan (1949–53) the Czechoslovak economy was not only completely nationalized, but also reconstructed. All this had disastrous consequences, which can be felt to this day. Stalin's 'iron and steel concept', adopted from the Soviet Union, exclusively promoted heavy industry while at the same time destroying the traditionally well-developed branches of light industry. According to Soviet economists at the time Czechoslovakia was to fulfill the function of the heavy industry workshop within the Comecon, founded in 1949, and to concentrate entirely on the production of heavy machinery and other raw material-consuming capital goods. As the country is relatively poor in mineral resources, it became dependent on the Soviet Union for its supply of raw materials. The same was true of the export of the products, whilst the prices were also dictated by Soviet economists.

The following table clearly shows economic dependence and indicates the change in Czechoslovak foreign trade areas during this period.[5]

Czechoslovak export in % to	*1937*	*1948*	*1950*	*1953*
Entire group of socialist states	16.3[a]	39.7	55.6	78.5
Of these: Soviet Union	1.6	16.2	27.6	35.5
Other Comecon countries	—	16.4	26.8	36.4
Other socialist countries (Yugoslavia, China)	—	7.1	1.2	6.6
Other countries	83.7	60.3	44.4	21.5
Of these: western industrial countries	67.3	45.5	34.8	14.9
Developing countries	16.4	14.8	9.6	6.6

[a] The Soviet Union, Baltic republics and European countries which were later to form the east bloc.

The composition of Czechoslovak exports also underwent radical changes. During the period 1948–53 the share of capital goods rose from 20 to 42 per cent, while the export of industrial consumer goods fell accordingly from 31 to 12 per cent.[6]

II The total *Umwertung der Werte* (revaluation of values) which struck Czechoslovak cultural life, meant a drastic expurgation of Czech and Slovak literature. The head of the communist inquisition in Prague was Václav Kopecký. He banned the 'remains of bourgeois ideology' so forcefully, that, of the big private book collections confiscated by the state, half of all titles, some 7 million copies, ended up in the paper mill. A mere 3 million books were thought to be ideologically harmless and taken to public libraries, the rest went to various warehouses not open to the public.[7] As regards the liquidation of Czechoslovak literature, the communists even outdid the National Socialist 'Kulturpolitik' of the German occupation. The literature confiscated by the Nazis in the years 1941–4 (from bookshops, publishers, colleges, public libraries, and so on) consisted of a 'mere' 2,100,000 books. Also, these copies were not destroyed, but stored.[8]

With the works of hundreds of Czechoslovak writers banned and destroyed, the authorities called on the public to get rid of their bourgeois books at home as well. At some schools fanatical teachers even ordered their pupils to search for 'unwholesome literature' in their parents' bookcases and to bring these to school for the wastepaper collection. The empty library shelves were now being filled with new books, in the style of 'socialist realism' and written from a Marxist-Leninist point of view, and with new editions of older Czech works, sometimes partly re-written or otherwise adapted to the new cultural policy. Translations of Soviet novels or other reading matter from the Soviet Union were also in common use. Because of their educational and propaganda value, such books often appeared in enormous quantities. Editions of several hundreds of thousands were no exception, as the principle of profit had also become a part of the capitalist past.

In the case of political writings the numbers were even higher. Between 1950 and 1954 the Czechoslovak book market was swamped by a total of 2 million volumes of Gottwald's collected speeches, 3 million issues from Lenin's oeuvre, and as many as 4 million books by Stalin.[9]

Yet all this was not the worst thing that befell the Czechs and Slovaks. Far more drastic were the years of merciless terror, resulting in numerous casualties, and leaving a deep scar on the consciousness of the population. Exact figures of the number of victims cannot be traced back. According to estimates made during the Prague Spring, at least 130,000 people ended up in prisons, camps, uranium mines and other penitentiaries,[10] where they were humiliated and tortured, and fell ill; many thousands lost their lives. In 1951, between 25,000 and 30,000 convicts, the majority of them political prisoners of the regime, worked in Czechoslovak uranium mines, under inhuman conditions.[11]

The churches were hit very hard, especially the Roman Catholic church. All bishops were imprisoned or interned in camps. The religious orders were practically abolished, and some 8,000 monks and nuns were interned in special labour camps or arrested. They all spent an average of 5 years in these institutions.[12] The same fate struck a considerable part of the secular clergy and tens of thousands of Catholic laity, among them almost all prominent Catholic intellectuals. In many cases these people had spent years in German concentration camps, before they finished up in communist camps and prisons.

For example, the Catholic art historian and archaeologist, Professor Růžena Vacková (1901–82), who lost part of her family during the Nazi terror but who herself survived the concentration camps, was arrested in 1951 on false charges of 'espionage for the Vatican and the USA' and condemned to twenty-two years imprisonment. She was not released until 1967, and was not the last political prisoner from the Stalin-Gottwald period: some clergymen regained their freedom during the government of Alexander Dubček in the spring of 1968.

Apart from the Church and the non-communist intellectual elite, the terror was also directed against ex-officials of other parties, officials of the old state apparatus, the military who had fought on the side of the allied forces in the west during the Second World War, and people from the national resistance. Those who formed the economic backbone of the old order, were also hit, such as entrepreneurs, farmers and small traders. The families of these 'class enemies' also suffered by being forced to move or their family property (or what was left of it) being confiscated, or in other ways. Their children were excluded from higher and in many cases also secondary education. (At the end of the 1950s and the beginning of the 1960s this practice was less stringent but by then it was too late for hundreds of thousands of children.)

The communists' reign of terror under Gottwald compared to which the repression by the present regime is mere child's play, was nevertheless not limited to fighting the 'class enemy' outside the Party. As in other east European countries, the terror also spread to their own ranks. After the split between Stalin and Tito one 'conspiracy centre' after another was exposed and rounded up, according to the Soviet example and with the help of Soviet advisers. Initially Gottwald had hoped that the CPCz could escape this *danse macabre*, as before the war it had been a completely legal party, whose leaders knew each other thoroughly during years of political co-operation. Therefore, he reasoned, the leadership of the CPCz could not be a breeding ground of conspiracy (in contrast to its Hungarian and Polish sister parties).[13] This turned out to be a mistake, however. As early as autumn 1948 the first wave of arrests of highly-placed communist officials took place, as the result of the direct intervention of the Kremlin.[14] In the wake of Gomulka's fall in Poland (September 1948) and of the Hungarian trial and execution of Laszlo Rajk (September 1949), a series of show trials were being prepared in Czechoslovakia, too.

Gottwald did not resist, nor did he do so when Stalin's envoy to Prague, Anastas Mikoyan, asked for the arrest of the second man in the CPCz, Rudolf Slánský.[15] On the contrary. He and members of his politburo lent their full co-operation to this affair with the 'Czechoslovak Rajk' Slánský, an affair which also bore a strong anti-semitic stamp. Slánský was hanged with ten other top men in December 1952. In other trials too, Gottwald and his closest assistants were personally involved. It was their Czechoslovakia which saw not only the erection of the largest group monument of Stalin in the world in 1956, but also came first in something else: the biggest purges and the highest number of mass trials, death sentences and executions in the whole of eastern Europe.

Information about the number of death sentences carried out as a result of political trials under Gottwald is not always in agreement. Some mention 187, others say 280.[16] Among those hanged were also the popular member of parliament of the

People's Socialist Party, Mrs Milada Horáková, and the writer Záviš Kalandra. The number of people who died in prisons and camps ran into many thousands. By comparison, during the twenty years of the First Republic of president T. G. Masaryk, much criticized by the communists, all in all some nine people were executed; and these were exclusively heavy criminals and multiple murderers. It is common knowledge that Masaryk had great difficulty in condoning the death sentence. He pardoned 406 condemned people. In the Austria-Hungary of emperor Franz Josef, too, the practices of the Gottwald regime would have been inconceivable. In the period 1874–1917, that is during 43 years, a total of 24 death sentences were carried out in the Czech countries.[17]

THE CONTINUITY OF POWER

The death of Gottwald in March 1953, less than two weeks after the death of his master Stalin, did not mean a relaxation of the regime in Czechoslovakia. While in Moscow Stalin's right hand man, Beria, and some high officials of the ministry for State Security were being arrested and executed, the persecutions and arbitrariness in Prague continued almost unabated under the new strong figures in the Party, first secretary Antonín Novotný, and president Antonín Zápotocký. Under their regime Gustáv Husák, the 'Slovak bourgeois nationalist' (under arrest since 1951) got life in 1954, along with many others. Also amongst the prominent victims was Marie Švermová, widow of a close wartime assistant to Gottwald. While the late comrade Jan Šverma was suddenly called out as national hero number two, and squares, bridges and factories were called after him, his wife was sentenced to life imprisonment for 'conspiracy'. And still the end of the trials was not in sight. Even after Nikita Khrushchev had held his famous de-Stalinization address at the XXth Party Congress in Moscow in 1956, executions were still taking place in Czechoslovakia.[18] By that time the CPCz leadership was well acquainted with the Stalinist abuses.

It is clear that the Czechoslovak party leadership saw little good in the new course of Khrushchev. Novotný and all the other members of the old Gottwald team had personally been too much involved in the conducting of the political trials, as they had been in the strong repression to which the country had been exposed since the communist take-over. Of course the same was true of the Stalinist Matyas Rákosi in Hungary and Boleslaw Bierut and his group in Poland. Yet the situation in which the Czechoslovak leaders found themselves was in many ways more favourable than the situation with the Stalinist party leadership in Hungary or Poland. In fact, Gottwald's death came at a very good moment for the Czechoslovak party leadership. With him the most powerful man, and the first one to be blamed for the Stalinist trials and persecutions, disappeared from the political scene. The succession of Gottwald passed off without any internal wrangling; after the Soviet example a sort of 'collective leadership' was installed, by distributing Gottwald's functions, and with this the Kremlin seemed to be satisfied.

In any case Khrushchev left the Prague leaders alone. To use an east European saying: The Russian wolf had eaten and so the Czechoslovak goat was spared. The same could not be said of Hungary and Poland. Because of his misgovernment, Rákosi, for instance, had a hard time in Moscow in June 1953, which resulted in embarrassing self-criticism after his return to Budapest.[19] Naturally this did not do his authority any good. Khrushchev also repeatedly lashed out at the Pole Bierut, among other things, for detaining Wladyslaw Gomulka.[20]

The relationship between Khrushchev and Novotný, on the other hand, was excellent. Even at their first meeting the Czech ex-proletarian found great favour with the impulsive Soviet party leader (who attached great importance to a good personal relationship).[21] Novotný managed to keep Khrushchev's trust by always showing himself a reliable partner. The de-Stalinization was the only point in which the Czechoslovak Party leadership did not follow Khrushchev. Prague continued the old hardline policy and preferred not to know anything of a 'new course'. Admittedly, prisoners – especially communists – were being released on a small scale and quietly, but political rehabilitation was out of the question. Each protest and initiative for liberalization were immediately suppressed by the regime. In this way the atmosphere remained reasonably calm in Czechoslovakia in 1956. Novotný had his Party and his country well under control, while Hungary was struck by a bloody uprising, and in Poland too, far-reaching events took place.

This policy did not do Novotný any harm. All CPCz Presidium members in Czechoslovakia (apart from A. Čepička, Gottwald's son-in-law) survived the year 1956 politically in that they managed to retain their positions. This contrasts sharply with the two neighbouring countries, where the leaders dropped out of the picture almost completely, Rajk was given a belated state funeral, and Gomulka, who had earlier fallen into disgrace, became first secretary of the Polish United Workers' Party.

The following table shows the continuity of power in the highest Party organs of Czechoslovakia and compares it with the changes at the top in Poland and Hungary during the same period. The base point is the year 1954, when - in the party congresses of the three countries - the power of the Stalinists was once again confirmed.[22]

	Number of Politburo members[23] *in 1954*	*still in office after 1956*	p	d	nm	*still in office in 1960*	p	d	nm
Czechoslovakia	9	8	1	—	—	7	—	1	3*
Poland	13	4	8	1	5	4			
Hungary	9	1**	8	—	10	1			

*(1958) **(1957)
p = purged; d = died; nm = new members

The Prague Stalinists managed to maintain their position because in their country a number of things had proceeded in a very different way from that in Hungary and Poland. By 1956, no powerful opposition movement of workers and intellectuals had been created in Czechoslovakia, unlike Poland and Hungary. This requires some explanation. The Czechoslovak communist regime had been confronted with a wave of industrial unrest, which arrived too soon, in early June 1953, even before the workers' uprising in East Berlin. The immediate cause was the currency reform of 31 May 1953 which was announced suddenly, and which was to come into force the day after, Sunday 1 June. Especially workers in the most important branches of the heavy industry, who earned relatively good money and had savings, were the victims of this 'crushing blow against the former capitalists', as the reforms were presented. The prices of food and consumer goods rose drastically.[24] Unofficial strikes and demonstrations were the result. The biggest demonstrations, of some 20,000 workers, took place in Pilsen, where the Škoda factories were. The authorities suppressed the industrial unrest with the help of police units, and arrested about 500 workers and other employees all over the country. Many of them were given long prison sentences as a deterrent measure, while thousands of strikers were hit by other reprisals. After this confrontation it became quiet at the Czechoslovak workers' front. This remained so in 1956, when the workers in Poland and Hungary began to rise.

However, this was not the case with some prominent Czechoslovak intellectuals. Encouraged by the events of the XXth Party Congress in Moscow and the example of rebelling colleagues in Poland and Hungary, a critical mood took hold in 1956. The criticism came to a head at the Second Congress of Writers in April of that year. Jaroslav Seifert, František Hrubín and others exposed the abuses of the Stalin era as well as the situation at the time in Czechoslovakia, and argued in favour of more freedom. Although the reaction of the regime was unfavourable, it was afraid to make an issue of it. Only after the uprising in Hungary had been put down, did the Czechoslovak authorities feel master of the situation again, and took the necessary countermeasures. Seifert and numerous other liberal-minded writers received a strong attack, were expelled from the leadership of the Czechoslovak Union of Writers, and replaced by faithful Stalinists.

The criticism from the writers did not pose a real threat to the party leadership of Novotný, since in Czechoslovakia there was no strong urge for a change of course in the Party itself - in contrast to the neighbouring countries to the north and south. A few hesitant attempts to incur change in the Party did not pose any serious threat or problem for Novotný. Neither was the leadership under threat from 'national heroes' of the type of Gomulka or Imre Nagy, who were suddenly pushed forward by a group of opponents. But there were no opponents. To its own advantage, the Czechoslovak leadership kept operating as a monolithic bloc, and not divided into a 'Stalinist' and a 'liberal' wing.

THE 'DIVIDE AND RULE' POLICY

There was another important reason for the political stability of the communist regime in Czechoslovakia. More than anywhere else, the Party applied a 'divide and rule' policy towards the population, which had a strong effect. By means of a systematic smear campaign, the Party managed to stir up an anti-intellectual mood, and even feelings of hate towards the Czechoslovak intelligentsia among the workers.[25] Again, this is a specifically Czechoslovak phenomenon. No other communist east-bloc country in the 1950s suffered from such a powerful 'anti-intellectual' complex as the CPCz.[26]

The communist society of the 1950s treated the terms 'intellectualism' or 'intellectual' with as much scorn as fascism did with the terms 'democracy' or 'democrat'. The designations 'ty inteligente' or 'ty intelektuále' (you intellectual), for instance, were among the most common terms of abuse of the class-conscious parts of the population. The discriminatory attitude towards the intelligentsia in general was shown at the time in popular sayings such as: 'Vidíme to zase, co inteligent – prase!' (It must be so, all the time, every intellectual – a swine!).

The discrimination against the intelligentsia, one of the characteristics of the communist system in eastern Europe after the Second World War, was the result of a rigorous application of the Marxist-Leninist doctrine regarding the place of intellectuals in socialist society. According to this theory, in every social order the intelligentsia does not form a separate class, but a social stratum. Members of this group belong to the two main classes. In capitalist society the intelligentsia can be found in two camps; both on the side of the capitalist exploiters (reactionary intelligentsia in the service of imperialism), and on the side of the proletariat (progressive intelligentsia). If only because of its distribution over both classes, the intelligentsia will never function as a leading force in society. This means that after the socialist revolution, when power comes into the hands of the working class, the character of the intelligentsia should change. The new ruling class should beget its own socialist intelligentsia, which should be closely related to it as regards class origins. This implies that its members should be recruited mainly from amongst former workers or children of workers' or peasants' families.

Thus, a new revolutionary task awaited the victors of 1948 after the take-over: the re-education of the intelligentsia. In one sense the situation was now more complicated, because the intellectuals in Czechoslovakia had traditionally formed a broad social group, unlike the relatively small elite in Poland or Hungary. Within the leadership of the CPCz, therefore, the numerous and predominantly non-communist intellectuals were seen as a dangerous obstacle to the realization of a communist society. The bringing into line of the intelligentsia took place all over eastern Europe, but nowhere did the discrimination, and even persecution take on such unprecedented proportions as in Czechoslovakia. On the one hand there was a hysterical anti-intellectual mood, on the other, strong preferential treatment of the workers, varying from supplying better stocked shops in the working-class neighbourhoods to higher salaries. As to this favourable treatment of the workers, it was undoubtedly true that the experience of the workers' uprising of 1953, and the fear that such a conflict might repeat itself played an important role.

The non-communist intelligentsia, partly corrupted by the Party, partly gagged and frightened, kept quiet and rapidly adapted to their new role. They showed their solidarity with the working class by a new outward appearance and a 'proletarian' behaviour. They forswore the tie, this 'banner of the bourgeoisie' and wore open collars. They discarded the hat and went for the cloth cap. At work they wore blue overalls, in the canteen they used only soup spoons rather than fork and knife, and on Sunday they took part in 'collective activities'.

THE HARD LINE

Khrushchev's disclosures about Stalin, and his criticism of the outrages and mass repression during Stalin's rule, however, created a stir in CPCz ranks. In Khrushchev's opinion Stalin was personally responsible for the abusive regime in the Soviet Union. To many Czechoslovak communists, the question now arose who was really responsible for the lawless practices in their country. Neither Antonín Novotný, the first secretary (and, since 1957, also president) nor the other leaders, could give a satisfactory answer to this, if they did not want to end up in the dock themselves. For this reason an open discussion of this subject, or criticism of the system that had been installed in Czechoslovakia since 1948, remained impossible.

This had certain consequences. Feelings of certainty about the correctness of the course followed came under attack and increasingly made way for doubts. And those who had had doubts before, had them confirmed. If one wants to discover the roots of the communist reform movement in Czechoslovakia, one will have to look at this period.[27] Zdeněk Mlynář, one of the prominent reformers in 1968, said:

> At the end of 1956, after all I had been through, I found myself mentally incapable of taking part in party political activity. Too many elements of my original faith had collapsed, and I did not know what ought to be or might be preserved after all that. Of course my political activity had always been motivated exclusively by ideological convictions and therefore my inability to act politically followed from my inner uncertainty. Moreover, I was a party member who had just barely escaped punishment by the party, and therefore there was nothing for me to do inside the party but remain silent.[28]

For the time being this silence continued, and the XIth Congress of the CPCz, held in 1958, perpetuated the hard line policy. With the slogan 'For the completion of socialist construction in Czechoslovakia' the Congress called for ideological vigilance, and the struggle against 'revisionism' (referring to the allegedly aberrant policy of the Yugoslav CP). One of its main objectives was:

> The removal of the remainders of the exploiting classes, i.e. to bring about the gradual liquidation of the kulaks as a class in the countryside, and also the liquidation of the remainders of private enterprise in the towns by consistently pushing them back and containing them.[29]

The campaign against the remaining private farmers and small businessmen was intensified. Between 1958 and 1960 the number of private farmers was reduced from 542,000 to 256,000. This meant that over 1,100,000 farmers and almost 90 per cent of Czechoslovak farmland had become part of the socialist production sector.[30] The authorities could be content: 'The CPCz has completed its task as a leading force in the agricultural revolution, based on the principles of Marxism-Leninism.'[31] Even more striking results were to be seen in the liquidation of the remaining one-man businesses. They disappeared almost completely in this period. At the end of 1960 the country of Antonín Novotný counted no more than 6,601 small businessmen (mainly craftsmen, such as tailors, cobblers, and village blacksmiths), covering 6,553 businesses.[32] Compared to the GDR, for instance, or Hungary or Poland, this was a negligible number. The socialization of small businesses in these countries had not been carried out to the same extent as in Czechoslovakia.[33]

At the same time as these campaigns, a wave of reprisals against the traditional enemy, the former 'bourgeois class', which had taken place since 1957, increased hand over fist. Again, numerous arrests were made. Moreover, those people who had belonged to the upper layers or middle groups before 1948 and who had meanwhile found an - albeit modest - white-collar job, were dismissed on a massive scale. This formed part of the so-called 'administrative reorganization'. They were relegated to the bottom rungs of the social ladder. In most cases they were only offered hard manual labour or other unqualified work.

These and other measures were thought necessary by the regime not merely because of the approaching proclamation of Czechoslovakia as a fully fledged socialist state. The struggle against the 'last bourgeois vestiges', like the repeated warning of the dangers of 'revisionism' and 'sectarianism' for the communist movement, were the best means of removing any grounds for criticism in advance. Under the guise of strengthening party unity, both ideologically and organizationally, the leadership could maintain its control over the comings and goings in the CPCz. In this way the ranks remained temporarily closed and people's minds stayed focused on the near future, when, according to Novotný and his followers, the CPCz would be faced with new problems: the laying of the foundations of communist society.

Later, under the Husák regime, the communist propagandists would point out that Novotný had given the false impression at the time 'that all conditions for a socialist construction had been fulfilled and that society was on the brink of communism'.[34] But in 1960, when the party leadership, copying Khrushchev, announced to the world that socialism in Czechoslovakia had 'finally and completely' won, the official attitude was still completely different. There was talk of a 'historic victory' and it was seen as a 'magnificent confirmation of the correctness of the policy of the Czechoslovak Communist Party' which would directly lead the Czechs and Slovaks to a 'happy communist future'.[35]

After the Soviet Union, Czechoslovakia was the second country to boast about having reached a new, higher stage of development on the way to communism. In this way Novotný hoped to make his name as a successful international communist politician and able statesman. The country got a new constitution in 1960 and from then on was called the Czechoslovak Socialist Republic, the ČSSR. In the constitution the leading role of the CPCz was assured in terms even more explicit than those found in the Soviet constitution of the time.[35] Article 4 read:

> The leading force in society and the state is the vanguard of the working class, the Communist Party of Czechoslovakia, a voluntary combative union of the most active and conscious citizens from the ranks of the workers, peasants and intelligentsia.[37]

Moreover, the Marxist-Leninist doctrine was proclaimed state ideology, something we do not find in the Polish or Hungarian constitution:

> The entire cultural policy in Czechoslovakia and the development of civilisation, education and teaching are carried out in the spirit of the scientific world-view of Marxism-Leninism, and in close connection with the life and work of the people.[38]

The 'comradely co-operation' of the ČSSR with the Soviet Union and the other states of the east bloc was also constitutionalized. All this, and above all the fact that Czechoslovakia was a faithful and trouble-free ally of the Soviet Union, convinced Khrushchev of his assessment of Novotný's leadership qualities. Seen in this light, the dogmatic course of Prague was not a major concern for the Kremlin.

Chapter Three

THE *ANCIEN REGIME* IN DECLINE

Sometimes, reading all these speeches, I am really, I tell you, surprised by many things, by the way people look at a situation. I say one thing and someone else says something different. I criticize something and someone else praises it. Damn it, who is right? Is he right or am I right? I look at it again and then I see: yes indeed, I am right!

Antonín Novotný (1967)

DELAYED DE-STALINIZATION

The renewed attack by Khrushchev on the personality cult surrounding Stalin, started during the XXIInd Congress of the CPSU (Communist Party of the Soviet Union) in October 1961, greatly embarrassed the Prague leadership. Khrushchev used the criticism of Stalin to secure his own position. This time, however, the criticism was more dangerous for the Czechoslovak Stalinists than five years before, not only because it was fiercer, but also especially because this time the critical speeches were brought to the public immediately, from the Moscow conference hall by the Soviet press.[1] In the Soviet Union the embalmed body of Stalin was removed from the mausoleum, his monuments were pulled down - in so far as that had not yet been done already - and Alexander Solzhenitsyn was able to publish his famous novella *One Day in the Life of Ivan Denisovich*. Under the zigzag course of the impulsive Khrushchev the country embarked once more on a 'liberal' period in the years 1961-2.

Novotný faced a difficult task in Czechoslovakia. He had to react appropriately to the second wave of de-Stalinization in the USSR, not only because this would be explicitly required by some high-placed Soviet officals,[2] but also because he could not afford to ignore the Soviet developments in front of his fellow-Partymen. The Stalinist Novotný hesitated. He is supposed to have confided to one of his intimate friends that he was afraid of a popular uprising if 'we were to take Stalin away from the people'.[3] In reality his own position was at stake. The situation in which Novotný now found himself was not an easy one. He could neither act rashly, lest the surge of de-Stalinization swept him away on account of his own Stalinist past, nor could he afford to procrastinate too long, lest his political opponents closed their ranks on him.

Contrary to the situation in the mid-1950s, the early 1960s provided Novotný with a dangerous rival: Rudolf Barák, the young and ambitious minister of Home Affairs and a member of the Politburo. Barák enjoyed considerable popularity in some Party circles and - what is even more important - he had his own following. In addition, he had been able to collect a lot of incriminating material against his most senior boss in his function as chairman of a commission that had looked into the procedures of the trials in the years 1955–7, and in his function as a minister in charge of security.[4] Apparently Barák intended to overthrow Novotný at a suitable moment, counting on the help of Moscow. The file on Novotný was his undoing. The Party leader was informed about Barák's activities and dealt summarily with him. Barák was arrested in February 1962 and later sentenced to fifteen years imprisonment - in accordance with the order of the Politburo - not, of course, for suppression of archive documents nor for preparing a take-over, but for embezzlement of public funds.[5]

The Party leader tackled the problems of the Stalinist trials and purges very cautiously, having first released the remaining communist prisoners from the 1950s. One of the last among them was Gustáv Husák, who was discharged from prison in the great amnesty of 1960. Novotný insisted on the guilt of Slánský, however, to whom he ascribed the same dark role which Beria had played in the Soviet Union. As regards this comparison with Beria, Novotný was definitely right. Slánský and a few other top-ranking communist officials, who were executed, were more than anyone else responsible for the unleashing of the terror. This did not alter the fact that they had been sentenced unlawfully in a show trial, on the basis of false accusations.

Even Gottwald received mild criticism for his part in the 'personality cult' as the Stalinist atrocities were euphemistically called after the Soviet example. A few weeks before the XIIth Party Congress of the CPCz in December 1962, his body was taken from the Prague mausoleum where he had lain embalmed (in a similar fashion to Lenin and Stalin) and was cremated. At the same time Prague experienced another big sensation: the monstrous Stalin monument overlooking the Vltava was suddenly concealed from the public by a wooden structure, and shortly afterwards blown up in the early morning.

At first sight, this 'pyrotechnic de-Stalinization'[6] seemed to be the end of the matter. But other developments indicated that something more was afoot. Numerous prominent communist victims demanded rehabilitation and voices in the Party demanding order in the House were getting louder. By order of Novotný, a new committee was formed (the so-called Drahomír Kolder committee, of which Alexander Dubček was also a member) to review a number of important trials. Its findings were never published in Czechoslovakia, because it termed the sentences as 'completely unlawful'.[7]

By clever manoeuvring Novotný managed to shift the responsibility for these developments to a few top people of the Old Guard under Gottwald. Viliam Široký (prime minister and Presidium member) and Karol Bacílek (ex-minister of State Security in the early 1950s, first secretary of the Slovak CP and also Presidium member) were expelled from their posts in September 1963. The post of Široký went to Jozef Lenárt, while Alexander Dubček became the first man in Slovakia. Heads also rolled in the Party secretariat and in the government.

Novotný's position was safe. He remained at the top and in control of his own Party leadership, purged of a group of Stalinists he could no longer use and which had started to make life difficult for him. In many respects the situation in which the Czechoslovak Party leader and president found himself resembled Nikita Khrushchev's position in the Soviet Union after having pushed aside the powerful 'anti-party group' of Molotov and his followers in 1957–8.

The years 1962 and 1963 (in particular the period after the XIIth Party Congress) represented an inconspicuous but extremely important turning point in the history of communist Czechoslovakia. The assumption that the reforms began in January 1968 with the arrival of Alexander Dubček is therefore too simplified. The process of reform started much earlier, in the years 1962 and 1963. As regards the lingering affair of the rehabilitations, the communist victims finally obtained partial political reinstatement in 1963 (any rehabilitation of non-communists was out of the question). It was nevertheless important for the future course of events in Czechoslovakia that enough influential groupings within the CPCz came upon the scene, as they saw errors not only in the personal responsibilities of the leaders, but also in the existing political and economic system. They were people who in the course of the years had reached important positions in the Party hierarchy and in various political and scientific institutions, and who, until recently, had formally supported the official Party line. For quite some time they had had objections against the system and were merely waiting for a suitable occasion to air their criticism. These people, who (as one of the reformers from the beginning V. V. Kusín said), in 1956, still 'raised their hands to vote for the expulsion of their more courageous comrades',[8] were to become prominent reformers themselves in the years to come.

OPPOSITION ON THE WAY

Both the earlier reformers and sympathizers with the Prague Spring, as well as the 'normalizers' of Husák, are in complete agreement that the first critics of the system came almost exclusively from the ranks of communist intellectuals.[9] They belonged for the greater part to the younger generation who after the war had welcomed communism with enthusiasm and high hopes. This was the generation of, for instance, the future economists Ota Šik (1919) and Radoslav Selucký (1930), the writers Ladislav Mňačko (1919) and Pavel Kohout (1928), the journalists Jiří Lederer (1922) and Jiří Hochman (1926), the chess grandmaster and publicist Luděk Pachman (1924), the philosophers Karel Kosík (1926), Radovan Richta (1924) and Ivan Sviták (1926), the Party functionaries Jiří Pelikán (1923) and Zdeněk Mlynář (1930) and thousands of others.

In the name of the revolution they had first of all destroyed democratic values, called for rigorous expropriation of private property, called people who disagreed reactionaries and lackeys of imperialism and praised all things Soviet to the skies.[10] Now, in the mid 1960s, these people who were now in their forties and had been a member of the ruling CPCz for fifteen to twenty years had become a lot wiser. Their disillusionment was complete. The frustrations caused by the Stalinist excesses and the slow progress and meagre results of the de-Stalinization all played a role in this. They had, according to one of them, novelist Milan Kundera, 'an urge to slash the canvas of their youth to shreds'.[11]

It is true that they had lost their youthful illusions about the nature of Soviet communism, but they had not lost their belief in a reform of the communist system in Czechoslovakia, which had long been in a state of severe crisis. It was a system that had failed their expectations and had proved unable to solve any social problem whatsoever; whether this concerned the deep economic depression, the question of the incompetent bureaucracy, the low work ethic, the growing discontent amongst the Slovaks with Prague centralism, the strong rejection of and even enmity of the Czechoslovak youth towards the CPCz, or the case of the gypsies. Worse still, the Prague regime was unable to master such simple problems as constructing a motorway from Prague to Bratislava, or solving the chronic shortage of table vinegar during the summer months.

The reformist critics of the system formed the pivot of opposition within the Party, growing too strong for Novotný in the second half of the 1960s. This opposition was by no means united in its political opinions or visions of reforms. What kept it together was discontent with Novotný's policies.

The reformist economists criticized the highly centralistic manner of conducting the economy. This criticism gained in strength as the lingering crisis reached a peak in 1963.[12] It is true that the so-called 'New System of Economic Management' (Nová soustava řízení národního hospodářství), of which Professor Ota Šik was the spiritual father, was approved by the Central Committee in 1965, but the resistance of the Party dogmatists was so strong that even its name could not be allowed. Before 1968 it was officially called 'The Perfected System of Economic Management' (Zdokonalená soustava hospodářského řízení) or 'The

Improved System of Economic Management' (Zlepšená soustava plánového řízení hospodářství). It is no wonder that, besides the reformist economists, many pragmatic technocrats saw in Party leader Novotný and his followers the main obstacle to saving the Czechoslovak economy from its lingering crisis.

There was also an anti-Novotný attitude - which was publicly aired in various ways - among Czechoslovak writers. Like their far less influential non-communist colleagues, they were hoping for a thorough democratization of the whole of Czechoslovak society, in every area of which, up to then, the Party had held a monopoly position. In June 1967, at the Fourth Congress of the Union of Writers, the rebellion of 1956 recurred, but in a considerably more vehement form. The anti-Israel campaign, with which the regime reacted to the Arab débâcle in the Six-Day War, just after the war, added extra fuel to the fire. In protest against this anti-Israel policy, the famous Slovak author Ladislav Mňačko left the country and settled in Israel. At the Congress the writer-communists Pavel Kohout, Ludvík Vaculík, Jan Procházka, Ivan Klíma, Milan Kundera, the non-Party writer Václav Havel and others subjected in their speeches the actual functioning of the system and the failing cultural policy to a devastating criticism.[13] There was nothing left for the Party delegation, headed by ideologist Jiří Hendrych, but to leave the hall. Novotný answered this open protest of the 'conscience of the nation' with a series of repressive measures which a number of members of the Central Committee of the CPCz did not approve of. The gulf between the dogmatic leaders on the one hand and the more moderate ones on the other was increased by the 'writers' incident'.[14]

The ranks of the Slovak Communist Party, too, expressed their dissatisfaction with Novotný. Both progressive and conservative Party officials were hurt by the arrogant attitude of the Czech Novotný towards their country. His insensitivity towards Slovak problems caused immense harm to the relationship between the two peoples in Czechoslovakia.[15]

Besides the young progressive communist officials from the Party apparatus and the ministries, the opposition to Novotný included a remarkable number of the older communists from the 1920s and 30s. They were among the 52,000 members the CPCz had before the Second World War. Almost half of them perished in Nazi concentration camps, while of the 27,000 survivors of the horrors of war, 75 per cent became victims of the Stalinist trials and purges.[16] Among them were members of the International Brigade who had fought in the Spanish Civil War, communists who had lived in exile in the west or had fought against Hitler on the side of the Allied Forces, Party members of Jewish extraction and the 'bourgeois nationalists' of Slovakia. They were unable to stomach the fact that the head of 'their Party' was somebody who had been actively involved in the terror, while they were still awaiting their complete rehabilitation.

As the criticism of Novotný became stronger and louder, more and more members from the highest Party echelons joined the ranks of the opposition. They were spurred on by opportunist considerations or personal rivalry with the Party chief rather than by fundamental disagreement with his policies. Outside the Party it was mainly students who ventilated their dissatisfaction in public repeatedly and who, within the period of a few years, had changed the Charles University in Prague and other institutes of higher education into bastions of 'anti-Novotnism'.

As for the internal relations in the Party, the prospects for the reformists and other opponents from the mid-1960s onwards were not at all bad. Since many of them held important posts in the power structure, they had considerable influence via the Party apparatus, the ministries or the many institutions controlled by the Party (e.g. the Union of Writers, the Academy of Sciences, the universities, and the research institutes). Although outwardly the Party still seemed united and the power of Novotný unaffected, in reality the unity was artificial. A more and more powerful and critical reform movement was slowly becoming apparent underneath the surface. This also explains why, reluctantly, but more and more noticeably, liberalization won so much ground in the Czechoslovakia of the 1960s, under the same Novotný who not so long before had headed one of the most orthodox regimes in eastern Europe.

The previous chapter dealt with the great degree of continuity between the Stalinist era of Gottwald and the regime of his successors after 1953. Towards the end of the nearly fifteen-year-long regime of Novotný we find continuity still strong in another sense: the continuation of the Khrushchev line, even though the latter had been sent packing in Moscow in 1964 and the troika of Leonid Brezhnev had tightened the reins, while Wladyslaw

Gomulka in Warsaw had long since given up hope of changes for the better. As regards Budapest, here the tactician János Kádár had had had to mark time, checking the strong resistance of the dogmatists in his own party and adopting a more conservative image towards the outside world in order to win the favour of the new Russian leadership.[17] Only then could he recommence his slow, cautious and above all 'silent' operation of reform.

In Czechoslovakia things were different. Late 'Novotnism' was a peculiar phenomenon in eastern Europe at that time. It was an oasis of 'liberalism' and in many ways comparable to the Hungary of the 1980s. The irony of the matter was that Novotný could not take any credit for this. The president and Party leader was definitely not in favour of reforms and the process of renewal. On the contrary, if it had been up to him, he would have crushed his critics. But there were reasons why he did not dare take such a step. It was not because of unwillingness on his part to deal with the critics. But the communist dictator, once so powerful, was less and less able to master the growing discontent, particularly in the higher ranks of the CPCz, via the usual Party channels; so much of the immediate environment of the first Party secretary and president had been gnawed away by the communist reformist spirit.[18]

REBELLION IN THE HIGHEST PARTY RANKS

During the autumn of 1967, a group was formed from the highest ranks of the communist hierarchy, the central apparatus, the Slovak Party organs and the Party leaderships of some of the provinces, to get rid of Novotný. It was a monstrous alliance, held together by the anti-Novotný mood of these communist politicians, with or without backing from the lower echelons of the Party. Besides politicians whose views were decidedly reformist (Josef Smrkovský, František Kriegel, Ota Šik, Josef Špaček) this ever growing opposition group included members of the mighty 'Ostrava-group', Oldřich Černík and Drahomír Kolder, also Party secretary Lubomír Štrougal and an extensive political spectrum in Slovakia, including the moderate Alexander Dubček, the hardliner Vasil Bilak and the fierce, but not yet powerful Gustáv Husák. Husák certainly gave the impression of being progressive by his repeated outbursts against Novotný. Some prominent Party officials who until recently had been seen as belonging to the Party leader's camp, deserted him. The most prominent among them was Jiří Hendrych, ideologist and opponent of criticism in the cultural area.

The Party Presidium became divided, with the pro- and anti-Novotný groups balancing each other. Even the old corrupt practices of the Party leader could no longer prevent the formation of an anti-Novotný coalition. It was an open secret in Czechoslovakia that Novotný regularly handed out bulky envelopes filled with money to members of the Presidium (and also to others). This was a reward for their loyalty, and all of them - including Dubček - had always eagerly accepted it.[19]

In the Central Committee Novotný's position was even weaker. Here the 'anti-Novotný' faction could count on a majority. In the lower party ranks there was confusion, as nobody knew what was happening 'up there'. Up there, in the Prague Castle Hradčany, at the end of October 1967 a meeting of the Central Committee of the CPCz took place - following tradition - behind closed doors. According to an official statement this meeting would be devoted to 'theses about the position and role of the Party in the present stage of development of our socialist society'.[20] In one respect this meeting can be called historic. It developed into a straightforward rebellion against the Party chief, a phenomenon unheard of in the post-war history of the CPCz.

The Party secretary of Slovakia, Alexander Dubček, was the first to raise this matter. A furious Novotný went onto the offensive and accused Dubček of 'narrow and nationalist interests'. The latter, however, met with support from many other functionaries. One of the staunchest supporters of Dubček was his Slovak colleague and personal friend (later a fierce opponent), Vasil Bilak.[21] The discussion took an unexpected and unwelcome turn for Novotný because he himself came under discussion for the first time.

The Party rank-and-file members and the Czechoslovak public were - as usual - completely unaware of these developments. Public attention was focused on something completely different: the aftermath of a student demonstration in Prague, which happened to coincide with the opening day of the Central Committee meeting. Although the demonstration had a totally peaceful character, the police ruthlessly dispersed the students, causing injury to many of them. After initial silence from the press (which was normal with such affairs) it suddenly paid a remarkable amount of attention to the event.[22] The Prague Charles University was also in a state of commotion. Such a critical attitude by the mass media, such an open flood of protests from the academic community that did not meet with immediate counter measures, would have been totally unthinkable only a few months earlier. The Prague cinemas even ran a short documentary dedicated to the consequences of the police action, in which the viewers could hear some injured students talk about their experiences with the police.

But this was only a taste of what was in store for Czechoslovakia in the spring and summer of 1968. For the first time it was possible to do one's own thing, without any form of sanction whatsoever. The serious division in the highest Party organs paralyzed the resoluteness of the power base. For some politicians the critical notes that now sounded in society came at a very convenient moment. They helped to further undermine Novotný's shaky position. Novotný could not give any tangible proof that he was still a forceful figure, neither to the worried sympathizers around him who were beginning to have doubts about his position of power, nor to the Kremlin. The Soviet leaders clearly showed Nototný their displeasure with him during his stay in the Soviet capital for the occasion of the celebration of the 50th anniversary of the October revolution.[23] And what the Party leader and president needed most at that time was their support in order to maintain his position.

THE LAST MONTH

A. J. P. Taylor once stated that July 1914 is probably the most studied month in world history. In the history of communist Czechoslovakia this honour can no doubt be conferred upon August 1968, when the Soviet intervention, which brought an end to the Prague Spring, took place. In view of the stormy and often sensational events in which the Prague Spring abounded, all this attention is easy to understand. There is, further, enough interesting source material available to make the study of this period worthwhile for historians. The month preceding the birth of the Prague Spring, however, draws considerably less interest. And yet the events of December 1967 – the last month of the political life of the first secretary, Novotný – had the same influence on the development of the Prague Spring as the murder of the Habsburg heir to the throne in Sarajevo and its aftermath had on the outbreak of the First World War.

To begin with, the 8th of December saw an unexpected emergency visit of Brezhnev to Prague. Afterwards, it was officially announced that it took place at the request of the Presidium of the Central Committee of the CPCz and of the Czechoslovak government.[24] Later it turned out that not even all members of the Presidium had been informed about the arrival of Brezhnev and that the Central Committee and the government knew nothing about it. In reality Brezhnev had come on Novotný's own request.

There is conclusive evidence of this through a rare personal testimony by Brezhnev. The Soviet party leader let slip a few things during his conversation with Waldeck Rochet, the secretary general of the French Communist Party, in the Kremlin in July 1968.[25] On the basis of Brezhnev's remarks it is possible to make a partial reconstruction of this event.

It is beyond doubt that Novotný, driven into a corner, expected a helping hand from the Kremlin leader. To his surprise, Brezhnev did not commit himself. Apart from that, it was the first time that Novotný told Brezhnev about the internal troubles in the Party leadership. He was quite optimistic to Brezhnev about future developments, and did not consider his position at risk. Brezhnev soon knew better: 'I also spoke with other members of the leadership. I found clear evidence that the situation was worse than Novotný suspected, that it was a question of separating the functions of first secretary and president'.[26]

One of those whom the Soviet guest had consulted, for as long as an hour, was Alexander Dubček. Brezhnev said of him: 'With Dubček we had very friendly relations'. The Soviet leader made it clear to him and the others that he did not want to get involved in the Party affairs of the Prague comrades in the Presidium. He hinted that he would have no objections to separating the two highest functions, but: 'In no way did I touch upon the question of who was to become the First Secretary. I pleaded neither for Novotný, nor for anybody else'.[27]

So far Brezhnev. Insiders claim that he stated to his Prague audience something one does not expect the representative of a superpower such as the Soviet Union to say: 'Eto vashe delo' (That is your own affair).[28] These words were to be quoted repeatedly during the Prague Spring.

Many authors dealing with the Czechoslovakia of this period are of the opinion that Brezhnev purposely dropped Novotný, because he was no longer useful to the Kremlin. Thus Jiří Valenta concludes, in his interesting study about the intervention of the Soviet Union in Czechoslovakia:

> In fact, Brezhnev surprised the Czechoslovak leaders with his flexible attitude. After he became aware of Novotný's weak position, he reportedly told the Czechoslovak leaders, Eto vashe delo [. . .] and left. Undoubtedly, Brezhnev was unwilling to back a sure loser, probably being convinced that Dubček, who had spent part of his youth in the USSR and was an experienced party official, was a reliable successor.[29]

And indeed the non-interference of the Kremlin in the internal disputes of the Czechoslovak Party leadership was tantamount to a death sentence on Novotný's political leadership. This does not imply, however, that Brezhnev consciously aimed to give the Czechoslovak number one the boot. We have seen, after all, how he and the Moscow Politburo played a waiting game, apparently until there was more clarity in the situation.

This waiting game was due to several factors. For instance, Novotný and his followers maintained excellent relations with some Soviet top men (not with Brezhnev, however).[30] Also, the most important Kremlin-observer in Czechoslovakia, the Soviet ambassador Chervonenko was an exceedingly bad source of information on the situation in the ČSSR. This dogmatic politician, who was well-disposed towards Novotný and supported him, probably underestimated the weakness of the position of the Party leader. He was far too late with informing his superiors in Moscow about the tensions in the Presidium of the CPCz.[31]

The final decision about Novotný therefore had not yet been taken during Brezhnev's trip to Prague.[32] Nor did Brezhnev think the moment opportune, since, fundamentally, he had no cause for concern. Even if Novotný were to be replaced in the end, all of those eligible to be his successor were more or less acceptable to the Soviet leaders. Of course his successor had to be a member of the Party Presidium. But whether he would be a supporter of Novotný (e.g. Jozef Lenárt) or someone from the anti-Novotný group (O. Černík, A. Dubček, or D. Kolder) or the number two in Czechoslovakia, J. Hendrych, who had turned his back on the Party chief, remained to be seen as all of them up to now had been known to be faithful comrades. Moreover, it was even conceivable at the time that Novotný could hold his own in both functions.

The situation in the Czechoslovak Party leadership had not become any clearer after Brezhnev's departure. This had unpleasant consequences. Novotný's critics felt encouraged by Brezhnev's neutral attitude and felt they had been given the green light to get rid of Novotný. The Party leader and president thought he did not have to yield to the pressure of the opposition, not even after the stormy meeting of the Central Committee just before Christmas. During this December session Professor Ota Šik delivered a devastating judgement on the Party politics of Novotný. He did so in terms which made all other criticism since the emergence of the reform movement pale into insignificance. This prominent professor in economics also demanded the immediate resignation of Antonín Novotný from the most important function in the state, that of first secretary of the CC in the CPCz.[33] As Šik got a lot of support for his proposal, the position of the Party chief from then on became untenable.

There were two things Novotný could do in these circumstances. The most obvious was to resign as Party leader. In that case he might be able to play a key role in the appointment of his successor behind the scenes. At that time the Slovak Jozef Lenárt, the Czechoslovak prime minister, had the best credentials. He enjoyed Novotný's confidence and was acceptable to the other group.[34] In addition, Novotný might be able to secure the position of president for the future.

The other possibility implied Antonín Novotný not only staying in power, but also strengthening it: by applying force. His supporters in the army and the security forces, as well as a few faithful supporters in key posts in the government and Party apparatus, urged this solution on him. The lists with names of over a thousand prominent opponents who would have to be arrested - amongst them politicians, military men, writers, journalists, Party historians and artists - had been prepared. Furthermore, the most untrustworthy members of the Presidium and the Central Committee were being surveilled and their telephones bugged by the security forces. Since the autumn of 1967 these included Alexander Dubček and Josef Smrkovský,[35] a famous advocate of democratization.

In the highest Party circles the general mood was one of anxiety and fear. The political opponents of Novotný seriously reckoned with a military coup, about which they were almost powerless to do anything. Yet the 'Night of Novotný', which was to have taken place between Christmas 1967 and early 1968, did not come off. This was partly due to the situation in which the military also became divided in a pro- and anti-Novotný group, and to the fact that some generals took measures in time to pre-empt a possible action in favour of Novotný. And it was partly due to Novotný himself. He had no experience of this kind of thing. He was no partisan leader or cunning military man, but an 'apparatchik' who had only seen the army march past from the grandstand. He was not cut out for the part of leader of an army coup with unforeseeable consequences.

Moreover, (and that may have been the deciding factor for Novotný) he did not know how the Soviet Union would react to such an intervention. Without doubt the KGB had informed the Kremlin of the plans of the Czechoslovak comrade-conspirators. Some even claim that Brezhnev personally ordered Novotný by telephone to immediately halt all preparations for such an armed action.[36] Whether this really happened in this way, is of course doubtful. We only know for certain that Moscow did not give the go-ahead for such an operation. If they had, the year 1968 would have started in a completely different way. However it may be that, in Czechoslovakia it remained a 'putsch-to-be that never was'.[37]

Thus in December 1967 Novotný was not allowed what the Soviet leader would demand of Wojciech Jaruzelski in December 1981: a military coup with large-scale arrests of the 'rebels'. It could also be put in a different way: in the Poland of 1981 the Kremlin followed the tactic of the 'military solution of December 1967' to avoid the alternative, a Russian military intervention. This was the lesson that Brezhnev had learnt from December 1967 and August 1968 in Czechoslovakia.

The events of December 1967 had important consequences for the dynamics of the further developments in the republic, more far-reaching than some think possible today. Thanks to Brezhnev's 'judgement of Solomon' and Novotný's obstinate refusal to give up the function of first secretary, militant feelings within the Czechoslovak Party leadership rose to an even higher pitch. Early in December 1967 Novotný could have passed his most important position on to one of his confidants without any great problems. At the beginning of January 1968 he no longer had this opportunity.

Chapter Four

THE PRAGUE SPRING

The reform movement of 1968 was emphatically democratic, both in its impressive measure of consent and in its upsurge of political participation; the only remaining question was that of the institutional guarantees for the newly-won freedoms. The abolition of censorship in May 1968 pointed in that direction, and a further decisive step forward would have been taken at the party congress three months later, which was to legitimize dissent for the first time since the Russian Bolsheviks had ruled it out in principle in 1921. The trend was thus clear at the time the Soviet intervention abruptly interrupted it, leaving open the tantalizing question of whether 'socialism with a human face' was a viable promise or a contradiction in terms.

Vojtěch Mastný (1978)

THE NEW PARTY SECRETARY

On the night of 4 to 5 January, the Party Presidium decided that the Slovak Alexander Dubček, 46, was to become Antonín Novotný's successor. Within a few months Dubček's name was to be inseparably linked to the Czechoslovak reform process, the Prague Spring. And Dubček himself was to be worshipped as a hero by the population. However, seeing Dubček as the obvious person for succession because of his strong reformist profile and his past as a champion of reforms in the ČSSR, is reasoning with hindsight. Alexander Dubček did not have such a progressive past. Yet this 'Dubček-myth', in which the progressive Dubček figures as the sole conceivable replacement for the Stalinist Novotný stubbornly persists.[1] In reality, the choice of Dubček that night, was an uncertain affair up to the last minute. The recommendation of Dubček to the Central Committee was the result of complex political horse trading between the compromised Novotný and his opponents in the Party Presidium. One of the insiders later described the changing of the guard in the Party leadership as follows:

> Many were proposed for the function of First Secretary; Novotný was against some of the candidates, the Slovaks against others. There were several quarrels, and finally Dubček remained as the sole candidate who was thought to be viable. The Slovaks voted for him, as did the Czechs, and Novotný was afraid to oppose Dubček. [. . .] And so everybody finally agreed that Dubček was the sole candidate. But as far as I know, Dubček did not want to accept this. Later they told me how Dubček resisted that night of Friday to Saturday, when the Presidium session was concluded. Černík promised him heaven and earth, and begged him to accept the function; they would all support him; in short, they literally pushed Dubček into it. He was not at all prepared for such a function and all of a sudden he could not get out of it.[2]

The outsider Dubček had been 'pushed' into that position, not because of his aura of a reformist, nor because he was someone with a clear perception of how to help Czechoslovakia, but because at that moment in time he was the most obvious compromise figure. His election was a surprise for everyone. Moreover, in the Czech countries Dubček was completely unknown. For this reason, the people received the news with a fair amount of scepticism. They did not believe any improvements would be made. On the contrary. The anti-Slovak policy of Novotný undoubtedly played a role here. The Czechs were afraid that the new secretary would give preferential treatment to 'his' Slovakia at the expense of the Czech territories.

Another factor the papers focused on in particular was Dubček's Soviet past. As a child, for thirteen years between the two world wars, he had lived in the Soviet Union with his parents, two idealistic communists. Whilst there, he attended a Russian secondary school, and returned again in the 1950s to study at the Higher Party School in Moscow. One could hardly imagine better credentials for a Soviet satrap. As no other notable changes of personnel within the leadership took place during the first few weeks after the change of power,[3] the toppling of Novotný was considered to be just a minor 'palace revolution' without far-reaching consequences.

From the start Dubček's position within the Party Presidium was not an enviable one. Although some new faces did enter this body on the 5th of January, and some of these politicians did actually support Dubček, the rest, amongst whom was Novotný and his clique, remained in their posts.[4] This was to the satisfaction of the Kremlin, who considered the Czechoslovak affair closed. For the time being the separation of the two most important functions formed the only noticeable difference from the situation before 5 January. It was of great importance to future developments, however, that the new Party leader had sided quite unmistakably with the reformists in the Central Committee and that he - in contrast to his predecessor - sincerely intended to search for the causes of the crisis in the system.

After Dubček's assumption of power the polarization and the consequent indecisiveness in the Party leadership continued and remained unabated. From the Presidium (where each group did what seemed most opportune to them under the given circumstances) came a stream of contradictory statements and guidelines. This created confusion in the lower Party echelons, resulting in increasing unrest and calls for more information. More and more articles critical of the policy of Antonín Novotný appeared in the press.[5] This unexpected state of affairs provided great opportunities to the reformists. But there were drawbacks. The unstable situation could easily lead to the collapse of the old system, which indeed did happen at fast speed. Such a sudden break was a highly dangerous development for Dubček and Czechoslovak society. In view of the international political constraints that Czechoslovak policy had to reckon with, a certain measure of continuity with the old system was to be preferred. Every great leap forward, however desirable it might be, was tantamount to a 'salto mortale', with a fatal result.

When speaking of 'continuity', I do not imply that Dubček should have continued on the same lines as Novotný. In the circumstances, that would have been neither possible nor desirable. I do imply that on no account should the new Party leader have let the initiative for the reform of the system slip out of his hands. In other words, it should have remained a 'revolution from above': a controllable process with a well-balanced number of reforms. Because Czechoslovak society was, in January 1968, relatively apathetic from a political point of view, and no social unrest had taken place unlike in the Poland of *Solidarność* in the years 1980–1, the opportunity for such an alternative was still present.

But more was needed in order to be able to pursue such a cautious policy in a post-Stalinist satellite state in the Brezhnev era – for instance, a leader with a lot of political experience, cunning, the ability to act quickly, and the necessary toughness; all qualities which the kind and decent Dubček did not have. Furthermore, especially in the beginning, Dubček lacked the necessary room for manoeuvre, due to the relative stalemate in the Party leadership. This resulted in an unexpected upsurge of activism in society, which, in turn, diminished the chances of a successful and controllable 'revolution from above' (i.e. acceptable to Brezhnev) considerably.

The *Novotnovci* – as Novotný and his followers were popularly called – did not yet want to acknowledge defeat. The President and politicians from his camp travelled all over the country to explain their point of view at Party meetings and mass meetings in factories, and to mobilize support so as to strengthen their positions. Their reformist opponents did the same, wasting precious time while a power vacuum developed, which provoked the radicalization of society. Up to the middle of February 1968 we can still speak of a 'revolt at the top'; after this date we cannot. In the second half of February and early March the floodgates of criticism opened at annual meetings and conferences of the local organizations of the CPCz. The tide of criticism had now reached the bedrock of the Party and could no longer be stemmed. Soon it had reached every layer of society.

To tackle this situation the 'old-new' Party leadership of Dubček did not have any concrete plans which, in view of the strong division within the Party Presidium, was in fact impossible.[6] With hindsight it does not take great wisdom to see that in these few crucial weeks Dubček and his followers lost control of society. One should rather ask oneself if Dubček ever stood a chance of getting a grip on affairs in Czechoslovakia. Carefully formulated, the answer is that he probably did stand a chance during the time when Novotný was still president, but probably not at the height of the Prague Spring and in the summer months, and certainly not thereafter.

THE BREAKTHROUGH OF THE PROGRESSIVES

The days of Novotný's presidency were numbered after the mysterious flight from Czechoslovakia of one of his closest friends, major general Jan Šejna. He was chief of the secretariat of the ministry of Defence and, in addition, secretary of the Party Committee at this ministry. In these capacities Šejna knew all the top military secrets of the Czechoslovak army leadership. He disappeared suddenly on 25 February 1968, and, via Italy, ended up in the United States with his new employer, the CIA. His flight caused, understandably, great consternation in the Warsaw Pact and represented one of the greatest catches in the history of the American intelligence service.

The inquiry into the causes of Šejna's journey to the west revealed some sensational facts, in which the name of Antonín Novotný was frequently mentioned. In the press, reports appeared about Šejna's part in the preparation for military action.[7] The Šejna affair, more than anything else, worked as a catalyst in the process of the liberation of the Czechoslovak mass media and the arousal of public opinion. Censorship or not, the journalists felt like real journalists again; they chased news stories, and published them too. The age of Czechoslovak *glasnost* at its best dawned. People now heard about the terrible corruption and intrigues that had taken place under the Novotný regime, in which the ex-first secretary and serving president and his family had been involved.

There was a wave of criticism from all sides. Serious charges were made against Novotný and a whole range of compromised Party and state officials; people no longer trusted them and demanded their resignation. This happened at numerous meetings in various institutions and organizations, in thousands of open letters and resolutions, in radio broadcasts and in the press.[8] The great exodus of Novotný's followers in high positions had started. It was amazing how easily and swiftly this happened. The 22nd of March finally saw the event everybody had been waiting for: president Antonín Novotný, the symbol of the old regime, resigned. His departure was the best proof for the man in the street that things were really changing in Czechoslovakia. For him, too, the Prague Spring had become noticeable.

The National Assembly (the Parliament) chose general Ludvík Svoboda (b. 1895) as Novotný's successor. This presidential election took place in a completely different atmosphere from the one people had grown accustomed to, if for no other reason than the fact that organizations and groups in society could nominate their own candidates. As the Soviet Union and the other allies were by then making serious objections to the Prague course, Dubček and the other progressive leaders considered general Svoboda the most suitable candidate because of the reputation and the prestige he enjoyed with the Russians. During the Second World War he had been commander of the Czechoslovak armed forces in the Soviet Union, and he had been awarded the highest Soviet honours. The Kremlin seemed to accept the nomination of Svoboda,[9] which could not be said of other candidates such as Josef Smrkovský or Čestmír Císař, who, incidentally, was popular with the young people.

In the eyes of several older Czechs and Slovaks Svoboda's past was not undisputed. They had not forgotten his role during the communist take-over in 1948, which had been tantamount to treason. Ludvík Svoboda had later also become a victim - albeit to a lesser degree - of the Stalinist purges, and had disappeared from public life for a few years. It was due to Khrushchev's personal intervention that Svoboda had been rehabilitated.[10] In March 1968 Svoboda sided with the reformists[11] and after his election he made a deep impression on the population with his official visit to the grave of T. G. Masaryk, founder of the Czechoslovak republic, whose name had been reviled by the old communist regime.

What the Czechoslovak population and the reformists in particular did not suspect at all was the boomerang effect which awaited them with Svoboda. The general turned out to allow himself to be used for Dubček's reforms with the same ease as he later was to allow himself to be used for Husák's 'normalization' policy.

At the beginning of April, things started to change in favour of the reformists in many important state and party posts, and in state organizations and institutions. Among the champions of the democratization process in the new government of prime minister

Oldřich Černík were, for instance, Josef Pavel, minister of Home Affairs, himself a victim of Stalinist trials; Jiří Hájek, minister of Foreign Affairs; Miroslav Galuška, Culture and Information; Vladimír Kadlec, Education, and Josef Borůvka, Agriculture. One of the five vice-premiers was Ota Šik; also of a progressive stamp were the vice-premiers Gustáv Husák and Peter Colotka. Josef Smrkovský, who was the second most celebrated leader after Dubček, because of his informal speeches and warm relations with the population, became chairman of the National Assembly, and the old Spanish civil war fighter František Kriegel became chairman of the National Front, an umbrella body in which several social organizations and all political parties were united.[12]

The reformists also won influence in the Party Presidium and the secretariat of the CPCz. Strong supporters of reforms in the Presidium were, besides Dubček, O. Černík, J. Špaček, F. Kriegel, J. Smrkovský and B. Šimon, who was a candidate member. The dogmatists V. Bilak, J. Piller, E. Rigo, Fr. Barbírek, O. Švestka, D. Kolder, J. Lenárt (candidate) and A. Kapek (candidate) also had a place in the Presidium. In the Party secretariat the newcomers Č. Císař, Z. Mlynář and V. Slavík were, in addition to Dubček, among the fervent advocates of the reformist course.

Conversely, the Party secretariat also saw the entry of A. Indra, who soon turned out to be one of the bitterest enemies of the reform process and a mainstay of the Brezhnev policy in Czechoslovakia. He and his sympathizers did not want to reform the system at all but seized their chance to take the empty places of the Novotný cadres. So, on the one hand, Dubček's position in the Party leadership was substantially strengthened, but on the other, the divisions in the Presidium and the secretariat remained. Instead of having to deal with the Novotný group, the Party leader now had to face a fierce and in some respects even more dangerous Bilak-Indra-Kolder group.

THE ACTION PROGRAMME OF THE CPCz

This Magna Carta of the Czechoslovak reform movement, which was regarded by some to be the Communist Manifesto of the twentieth century, was approved by the Central Committee on 5 April 1968 and published a few days later.[13] The Action Programme was surprising in its openness with which the numerous problems in Czechoslovak society were discussed and with which the political mistakes of the past were admitted. As far as both form and content were concerned, it exuded a different spirit. It was expressed in understandable language, stripped of perfunctory, empty optimistic phrases and other meaningless slogans. One got the impression that this was a party with a different voice from that of Gottwald, Zápotocký and Novotný.

The Action Programme pointed out the reprehensible, dogmatic approach to the social problems in the past, the serious distortion of the political system, the power concentration, the suppression of democratic rights and freedoms of the people, the bureaucracy, the breaking of the law, the arbitrariness and the misuse of power. The programme also exposed economic and social wrongs: the too hasty expansion of heavy industries, expensive investments, slow growth of wages, stagnation in the increase of the standard of living, backward infrastructure, poor functioning of public transport, disastrous shortage of housing, insufficient building of new houses, and bad quality of products and service.

In its turn, this political system affected the ethical norms and values in society, and caused moral and political defects in human relations, and political apathy: 'some people became demoralized, others lost perspective'.[14]

The programme emphasized the necessity of political reforms. From now on the Communist Party in the ČSSR was to fulfill a new function, one in accordance with the real relationships in Czechoslovak society, in which class differences would be erased. From now on the Party would play a guiding role in society, exclusively on the strength of the results of the policies carried out, and would be subject to the democratic rules of the game, both internally and externally. This meant that various social organizations (such as trade unions) and political parties could develop far more autonomy within the framework of the National Front.

The document also held out the prospect of a new electoral law, a satisfactory settlement of the relations between the Czechs and Slovaks - a federal form of government for the republic - a new constitution, and a rehabilitation law for the victims of the political trials and purges. The Action Programme explicitly mentioned freedom of assembly and association: 'The implementation of the *constitutional freedom of assembly and association* must be ensured this year so that the possibility of setting up voluntary organizations, special-interest associations, societies, etc., is guaranteed by law and the present interests and needs of various strata and categories of our citizens are tended to without bureaucratic interference and without a monopoly by any individual organization'.[15]

In addition, the CPCz promised to guarantee freedom of speech; to protect the citizens against the Czechoslovak Secret Police (Státní bezpečnost), in saying that: 'The party declares clearly that this apparatus *should not be directed towards or used to solve internal political questions* and controversies in socialist society';[16] to simplify free travel abroad, i.e. the west: 'In particular, this means that a citizen should have the legal right to long-term or permanent residence abroad and that the people should not groundlessly be placed in the position of emigrants [. . .]';[17] and to bring about an increased import and sale of foreign literature.

An important part of the Action Programme was devoted to economic reforms. The principle of Professor Ota Šik, that socialism, too, cannot do without the spirit of enterprise, was at its centre. In future, businesses would get enough freedom to develop independent initiatives. A democratization of economic life also demanded the foundation of democratic institutions within business communities, i.e. workers' councils. These were to have substantial powers. The managing director and the leading officials of the business would be nominated by the council and would be accountable to them for the policies pursued. The Party also unfolded a new vision on the activities of trade unions. They were to return to their original function as guardians of the interests of their members by being, from then onwards, 'independent democratic organizations with their own political line'.[18] It was remarkable that the possibility to found small-scale individual enterprises - one of the demands of the Czechoslovak liberal economists - had also been included in the programme. It was, however, limited to the sphere of service industry.

This was the platform of the new system that was soon to bear the defiant name of 'socialism with a human face'; a system that intended to join socialism with democracy - and this was repeated over and over again - under specifically Czechoslovak circumstances. Whether specifically Czechoslovak or not, the criticism the programme had of the policy of the CPCz was just as relevant for other communist and workers' parties in the eastern bloc. In this light, the Action Programme was completely unacceptable to Brezhnev and the other party leaders of that time (with the partial exception of Kádár). The explicit assurance of allegiance to the alliance with the Soviet Union could not alter that, nor could the promise of a more active Czechoslovak part in the activities of the Warsaw Pact and the Comecon.

To its own detriment, Dubček's leadership was too late in coming up with the Action Programme. Dubček, Smrkovský, and some other politicians originally wanted to appear before the Party members and the people with a simple programme, consisting of a few points and more a proclamation in which they wanted to explain the new policy. The elaboration of these points into a comprehensive programme would come later. This did not happen, however. First, a large editorial committee, consisting of several study groups, was nominated to draw up the text of the political document, just as it used to be done under Novotný. Then, 'several comrades turned it into a great work in which they wanted all kinds of things mentioned', as Smrkovský later recalled.[19] There was nothing left for the Party leaders but to agree to the rules of the game, against their better judgement. They were forced to wait. In particular, the debates on the constitutional position of Slovakia seriously delayed the publication of the document.[20]

After two months of groundwork, when the Action Programme was finally ready, it had already been overtaken by the developments in Czechoslovakia. This is what had happened according to Antonín Ostrý, a reformist communist intellectual:

> By then January had loosened the chains. Everybody could freely look for who had been guilty of what and in which way, and everybody was free to think of ways, means and ideas to improve and alter the situation. In the period in between there were too many strategists. When the Party finally disclosed its own strategic plan, many people had in the meantime identified with their own plans – even more so because the Action Programme showed clear signs of being eroded by compromises, which were the result of fear for a broad and vigorous wave of opposition as well as the opposition of the powers which did not want any big changes at all.[21]

These 'powers' referred to Bilak and his followers. All of them voted in favour of the Action Programme in the Central Committee. A few members of the group, such as Pavel Auersperg and Jan Fojtík, had been closely involved in the drawing up of the document, and Drahomír Kolder was even chairman of the political committee in charge of supervising the implementation of the programme.[22] Yet it turned out that these comrades - for whom the programme went much too far - were only waiting for a suitable moment to turn against the reforms.

On the other hand, there were progressive Party members, intellectuals, but also a section of the workers, who held far more radical views than the more moderate Alexander Dubček and his sympathizers.[23] For them and for many non-Party members the reforms in the programme were restricted to the absolute minimum. They supported Dubček where possible, but expected more. Furthermore, they had doubts about the feasibility of the new course. They feared that the reform process might be slowed down or even halted altogether by the conservative wing of the CPCz and the ever-increasing pressure from abroad. For this reason they urged a rapid and firm enforcement of the proposed reforms.

All in all it can be said that the Action Programme was favourably received by most of the Party members and in wide circles within the Czechoslovak population. A representative survey, held in Bohemia and Moravia straight after the publication of the Action Programme showed that 76 per cent of the Czech population (88 per cent of the Party members and 72 per cent of the non-Party members) approved of the policies of the Party, while 12 per cent of the population disapproved.[24] According to a survey in Slovakia in June 1968, 77 per cent of the Slovaks spoke out in favour of the Action Programme, something over 5 per cent were not prepared to support the programme, while 14 per cent did not know.[25]

The reformist leaders surrounding Dubček realized that new policies would only be possible if the dogmatic Party officials, who still held important positions, were to step down. They proposed to hold an extraordinary Party congress at short notice which would choose a new Central Committee, from which the dogmatists would be pushed back, in accordance with the new political course of the CPCz. At the time of the publication of the

Action Programme, in early April, Dubček himself was still convinced that this step was not necessary. According to him the current CC of the CPCz had enough power to successfully complete the process of democratization.[26] Later, under great pressure from the Party, Dubček changed his mind.

During the May session of the Central Committee (29 May–1 June) it was decided to convene an Extraordinary XIVth Party Congress on 9 September 1968. The elections, held in June and July of that year, in which 1,600 delegates were appointed in a secret ballot, proved a great victory for the supporters of Alexander Dubček. About 80 per cent of the delegates represented the reform movement, 10 per cent belonged to the radical-progressive wing of the Party, and another 10 per cent represented the conservative ranks in the CPCz.[27] This was supposed to become the new balance of power in the Central Committee and in the Party Presidium. The Extraordinary Party Congress was also expected to approve the new Party statutes which would considerably enlarge internal democracy in the CPCz.[28] The future of the reform course seemed safe.

THE GLOW OF FREEDOM

The Czechs and Slovaks did not have to make much of an effort to gain their freedom. They did not have to tear it off bit by bit from the communist authorities as the Poles were to do in the seventies and in 1980–1. Everything happened automatically in 1968: there was no bloodshed, no sacrifice, no hard action, no strike. The freedom seemed to return just as easily as it had disappeared twenty years before, without any notable resistance from the population.

People's fear disappeared, and society changed beyond recognition. Probably most striking in the Prague Spring was the role of the mass media. In early March 1968 censorship was almost completely suspended and two months later it was lifted altogether. New perspectives opened up for the mass media. They began to inform the people about the doings of the political leaders, expressed the desires, criticism and other feelings of society, analysed the developments of the past, commented on and criticized recent events and future plans, and stimulated open debate on various current problems.

Czechoslovakia experienced a real explosion of information. Public interest in news coverage and involvement in the developments were enormous. The press in particular was of great importance. The circulation of the papers rose as never before. While in January 1968 the one million inhabitants of Prague daily bought 118,000 papers, in the second half of March the number of copies sold was 557,000. The newspaper presses could not handle a larger print run than that at that moment.[29]

The most influential paper during the Prague Spring was the weekly of the Czechoslovak Union of Writers *Literární Listy* (Literary Leaves). It turned into a platform where, from a radical position, the reformist course was carefully guarded and ardently defended by prominent Czech intellectuals, amongst whom were many well-known authors. The latter in particular enjoyed great popularity and esteem with the population for their brave stance under the Novotný regime. The (originally literary) journal reached a circulation of 300,000 copies. Other papers with marked radical and progressive leanings were the weeklies *Reportér*, the organ of the Czech Union of Journalists, *Student*, of the Union of University Students, and *Kultúrny Život* (The Cultural Life), the Slovak counterpart of *Literární Listy*. Daily newspapers that deserve mention are: *Mladá Fronta* (The Young Front), the Trade Unions' paper *Práce* (Work), and *Zemědělské Noviny* (Agricultural News).[30]

Without the free press, radio, and television, the Czechoslovak reform process would have been completely different from the one the world came to know about. The free mass media were unequalled in giving concrete form to 'democratic socialism' by taking the concept 'democratic' to mean the fundamental right of virtually unrestricted freedom of the press, and freedom of opinion. It is a fact that they mobilized millions of citizens in favour of the reform policies and made them politically aware. But at the same time, their insistence on making the most of the 'historic opportunity' in Czechoslovakia led them to the pursuit of the impracticable and unattainable. Journalists, writers and commentators, driven by great ideals and with the best of intentions, became politically active. They did not, however, know one of the basic rules of politics, the art of arriving at a compromise. Like real idealists, they were zealots, who asked for everything and wanted it all at the same time. It made many of them popular and famous in the country. But none of them ever asked themselves what was actually possible under the given circumstances in Czechoslovakia. And that was not much.

It certainly did not include direct or indirect criticism of the leaders or political systems in the brother countries. To give one example, on 13 June, the day that Dubček arrived in Budapest with a party and government delegation to conclude an important treaty, *Literární Listy* published a commemorative article about the execution of Imre Nagy, stating that János Kádár had unlawfully executed this Hungarian hero of 1956 in order to rid himself of a troublesome idealistic opponent. In addition, the author drew a parallel between the Hungarian reforms of Nagy and the Czechoslovak experiment.[31]

It goes without saying that these and other examples of freedom of the press seriously harmed the leadership of Alexander Dubček. It was grist to the mill of the opponents of the reform process at home and in the neighbouring socialist countries. Dubček and the politicians surrounding him indeed tried to temper the mass media, but to no avail. Freedom of opinion, the most tangible achievement of the Prague Spring, had become too precious to – even temporarily or partially – dispense with. Moreover, in a political system in which the old power structures had basically remained standing (which was still true of Czechoslovakia), freedom of the press was considered by many to be the best guarantee of the continuation of the reform process.

Not only the mass media, but the entire population breathed a different atmosphere. Problems were openly discussed on the street, and Prague had several Hyde Park Corners, where heated debates were conducted. Some of these meetings were not free of emotion, especially when members of the public got up to speak about their experiences as political prisoners of the communist system. It was completely understandable that at such moments the Communist Party and the communist state were bitterly blamed. As the Prague Spring progressed, however, another tendency became apparent. The attitude of individuals towards the state underwent an important change. The barrier of distrust which had held out for twenty years, was breaking down. The Czechs and Slovaks felt proud citizens again, not ashamed of their Czechoslovakia. They began to feel responsible for their state. Several spontaneous actions were evidence of this change. A 'Fund of the Republic' was established to which citizens could donate money or gold. Between February and August 1968 the equivalent of almost 200 kilograms of gold had been paid into the account of this fund.[32]

Important to this new course was the increasing dedication - after initial hesitation - of the workers. The trade unions welcomed the reforms at the national conference of the Czechoslovak Trades Unions in June 1968 in Prague, and pronounced themselves in favour of an independent, progressive policy for the sake of the employees. In some factories experiments were taking place with democratic forms of self-management, and workers' councils (Rady pracujících) were being set up.[33]

The strong involvement in political events manifested itself in the establishment of new groupings wishing to take part in the political life of the country. Among the most active ones were the KAN, *Klub angažovaných nestraniků* (The Club of Non-Party Activists); the *K 231* (The Club of Former Political Prisoners), which owed its name to the notorious article 231 of the Czechoslovak criminal code, under which many had been convicted; *Přípravný výbor Sociálně-democratické strany* (The Preparatory Committee of the Social Democratic Party) and *Společnost pro lidská práva* (Society for Human Rights). There was also an increased activity in the small parties of the National Front, which up till then had been parties merely in name, especially in the People's Party and the Socialist Party.

For Dubček and his followers the demand to re-establish the Social Democratic Party, which had been forced to merge with the CPCz in 1948, was a difficult problem. The communist leader did not much like the idea of a second workers' party. After prolonged negotiations with the ex-Social-Democrat officials they managed to put off discussion of this problem until after the XIVth Congress.[34]

In this respect it is interesting to know what the people thought of an opposition party. In a representative opinion poll conducted among the Czech population in July 1968, 77 per cent of the Czechs turned out to be in favour of an opposition party in one form or another, while 21 per cent indicated they were against such a party. Characteristic of the atmosphere at that time was what the Czechs thought of the programme of an opposition party; 48 per cent thought this party should have a socialist programme 'in agreement with the Communists but with a different concept for its realization'.[35] Moreover, as many as 74 per cent thought the opposition party should govern in a coalition with the CPCz.[36]

On the basis of this information and these figures one could easily be led to assume that the people's faith in the CPCz must have been immense. Yet the situation was more complex than it seemed at first sight. It was not the Communist Party, which was also the party of Bilak and Indra, which enjoyed the confidence and popularity amongst the population, but the progressive (or thought to be progressive) leaders Dubček, Smrkovský, Svoboda, Černík and others, in their personal capacity. Public opinion in the country sided with them on a massive scale, not only because of the new popular policies (the introduction of the five day working week and the reduction of working hours, for instance), but especially because these politicians were prepared to brave pressure from the Soviet Union and other socialist neighbours. As the outside pressure increased in the summer of 1968, the enthusiasm for them in Czechoslovakia only grew.

Such popularity was unprecedented in the history of any communist state. Dubček and others in the progressive group discovered the taste of power when it is not begrudged, and what it means being a well-loved politician in one's own country. They were optimistic and full of confidence that the reform experiment would end well.

Intoxicated with freedom, Czechoslovak society as a whole shone with optimism and a certain carelessness. Some communist reformists - politicians, scientists, managers, journalists - developed a truly messianic zeal after years of frustration. With 'kettledrums and trumpets'[37] they sang the praises of 'socialism with a human face' as something very special to the world.

But was there anything special going on in Czechoslovakia? Not really. An authoritarian regime had been toppled. It was indeed special that it concerned a communist dictatorship in eastern Europe. Furthermore, the new strong men behaved in a way decent leaders should behave, and in the way that the majority of every people would want them to behave after a period of suppression: they restored several democratic ground rules, devised a programme of reforms to overcome the crisis of the old system, vowing that there would not be a repeat of the past, and that in future everything would be greatly improved. In exchange for this, the population trusted them 'to finish the job'. There are ample examples of countries where internal developments followed a more or less similar pattern. And yet there was an essential difference between Czechoslovakia after the fall of Novotný and, for example, Greece after the expulsion of the colonels or Spain after the death of Franco. Greece and Spain were not within the sphere of influence of the Soviet Union.

PRESSURE FROM OUTSIDE

Brezhnev's concern about the policies of Dubček manifested itself quite early on, during the festivities in Prague of 22 to 24 February 1968 on the occasion of the twentieth anniversary of the communist take-over. Insiders claim that Brezhnev threatened to leave the country early, if his host, Dubček, did not change his proposed address to the celebratory meeting of the Central Committee.[38] 'We had to re-write the complete paper', Vasil Bilak declared later.[39] Apparently this was not to Brezhnev's entire satisfaction, as can be seen from his reproaches to Dubček in the Kremlin during the eventful days of August, recorded by Zdeněk Mlynář: 'As early as February I told you of my objections to your paper, I pointed out to you that some formulations were incorrect. And yet you did not change them.'[40] Brezhnev's confidence in Alexander Dubček, who, until then was considered the man of the Kremlin, received its first serious blow in Prague.

Yet Brezhnev and the leaders of other countries present in Prague, that were to take part in the military intervention in Czechoslovakia in August, maintained a rather reserved attitude.[41] A month later the situation had changed completely. At the summit meeting, hastily summoned in Dresden the day after president Novotný's fall (23 March), Leonid Brezhnev and especially the Pole Wladyslaw Gomulka and the East German leader Walter Ulbricht, voiced a series of reproaches and warnings against the Czechoslovak delegation.[42]

In Dresden, the systematic pressure on the Prague reform course and its protagonists began. A few days later the press of the allies started a smear campaign against Czechoslovakia, which, apart from a few days in early August, did not cease. The East German press started with a personal attack on Josef Smrkovský, written by the Politburo member of the SED, Kurt Hager.[43] Czechoslovakia's response was a diplomatic protest to the GDR; a response which had never been exchanged before between socialist allies.

The biased reporting in the GDR about developments in the ČSSR knew no bounds. A few East German newspapers reported for instance that American tanks with members of special American forces had arrived in Prague, while soldiers of special American units, disguised as tourists in buses, were on their way from West Germany to Czechoslovakia.[44] But the press of the Soviet Union, Poland and Bulgaria, too, campaigned in a way strongly reminiscent of the treatment of Yugoslavia in the early 1950s. In comparison, only the Hungarian mass media showed a remarkable restraint.

From May 1968 onwards relations between the reformists leaders and the Kremlin grew noticeably worse. During the 'consultations' in Moscow on 4 May, where Dubček, Smrkovský, Černík and Bilak took part on the Czechoslovak side, it was obvious once more that the opinions of the two parties on the situation in Czechoslovakia were diametrically opposed. A statement by Smrkovský, moreover, tells us something about the atmosphere in which the talks took place. Participant Smrkovský:

> Essentially, we spent the day listening to a long list of everything the Soviet Union or its representatives did not like about the events and developments in our country. [. . .] We, on the other hand, especially Dubček and the others, came with facts and information, which were incomparably more relevant than their ragbag of so-called information. [. . .] We were heartily fed up with these negotiations, because we saw that the facts and the entire situation in our country did not interest them, but that they were looking for pretexts for them to justify their attitude towards us. It even damaged our position, that Bilak argued against us from their point of view; in fact he was not so much the fourth man in our delegation, as the fifth man in theirs.[45]

The political pressure increased. On 8 May the leaders of the five member countries of the Warsaw Pact had an emergency meeting, to which Czechoslovakia had not been invited. On 17 May two parties of visitors from the Soviet Union arrived simultaneously: prime minister Alexei Kosygin called at Karlovy Vary, and a sizeable military delegation headed by the minister of Defence Andrei Grechko arrived in Prague. Both in Prague and during the visits of various delegations from the ČSSR to Moscow the Czechoslovaks were told again and again of the Soviet's view of the unacceptability of the reform process.

Even downright blackmail was used. As early as 10 May - two days after the meeting of the Five - Poland, the GDR and the Soviet Union began to move their troops in the direction of the Czechoslovak border. From then on the ostentatious display of military power in the immediate vicinity of Czechoslovakia became a regular sight. To prove their loyalty to the alliance with the Soviet Union, Dubček and Černík took the initiative of holding Soviet staff exercises on Czechoslovak territory at the end of June. It was to their surprise, however, that the Soviets changed their original plan of these manoeuvres without first informing Prague. Not only did they move into the country much earlier (at the end of May), but they also increased their military force gradually to a strength of about 30,000 men.[46] After the completion of the exercises, the Soviet military authorities kept postponing the withdrawal so that the last contingents did not leave the republic until early August.

The threatening presence of the troops encouraged the opposition of the dogmatic politicians, who by then were convinced that the Extraordinary XIVth Party Congress would end their careers. There was great turmoil amongst the people. Sharp reactions from the ranks of the radical-progressive supporters of the reform movement, and from the side of mass media were inevitable.

Under these circumstances the author Ludvík Vaculík published his much-discussed call to defend the reformist course. This so-called *2000 Words Manifesto*[47] and other similar actions convinced Brezhnev's party leadership that Czechoslovakia was 'slipping slowly into capitalism'.[48] In their eyes a counter-revolutionary situation analogous to the one of Hungary in 1956 was developing in the country, the only difference being that this time the same symptoms of crisis were spreading slowly and without any upheavals. In this respect they thought the 'creeping counter-revolution' in Czechoslovakia even more dangerous - that is, more difficult to expose and to fight - than the 'open counter-revolution' in Hungary.[49]

Of course Dubček and others could not accept this logic. They thought that the Soviet comrades did not properly understand the reform policies. They reasoned that misunderstandings arose because the leadership of the CPSU had not been well informed about the Czechoslovak developments.[50] Dubček and his sympathizers argued, and came with the evidence to prove, that, on the contrary, socialism in the ČSSR had been strengthened, that the people welcomed the new policies of the CPCz and its leading role in society enthusiastically, and that the few manifestations of 'extremism' were only of a temporary nature. In short, everything was under control and the Soviet comrades need not worry.

In order to refute the criticism of its allies, Prague pursued a cautious, reticent foreign policy. The government emphasized through Jiří Hájek, its minister of Foreign Affairs, to whoever wanted to listen, that the reform process was an internal Czechoslovak affair. It was careful not to turn the events into an international issue, nor to canvass potential allies, nor to search for support for the reform policies in any other active way. In this way the Czechoslovaks hoped to take away any grounds for interference by the other eastern bloc countries. The Soviet Union was not interested in an internationalization of the Czechoslovak problem. It, too, thought 'the less fuss, the better'. But contrary to Prague it did not consider the developments in the socialist neighbour a purely Czechoslovak affair, but something affecting the Soviet Union and the whole eastern bloc.

Without the Prague government realizing it, Hájek's foreign policy served the tactics of the Soviet Union more than they served to back up the reform process in Czechoslovakia. It contributed to Czechoslovakia's isolation, which worked only to the advantage of the Kremlin. At the time of the Prague Spring, foreign policy did not cover the reform process. While the reform process was gaining momentum, foreign policy did not react to this. The cautious and reticent approach did not go well together with the 'kettledrums and trumpets' of the noisy prophets of 'socialism with a human face'.

Of course it was not due to the traditional pro-Soviet foreign policy that tanks finally drove into Czechoslovakia, but to the phenomenon of 'socialism with a human face' itself. Being good communists, Dubček, Černík and the other leaders strove for good relations with Moscow, but at the same time they wanted to stick to the reformist course, which had been received with such enthusiasm by the Czechs and Slovaks, and to which they owed their popularity. However, the one absolutely excluded the other. During the Prague Spring they were repeatedly faced with this dilemma. When they finally had to choose they chose for the process of reform and for the people in the hope that they would somehow succeed in neutralizing the negative effects of this choice, i.e. increasing dismay in the Kremlin, and further deteriorating relations.

To the great relief of the Czechoslovak citizens, a majority of the leadership declined the invitation to a 'consultative meeting' with the five sister parties at Warsaw. Nevertheless Czechoslovakia was condemned in the Polish capital on 14 and 15 July. the CPCz Party Presidium answered the letter from Warsaw (which included an ultimatum) with its own letter in which it explained its position once more 'objectively and without emotions',[51] refuted the accusations, and proposed bilateral negotiations. Of all the countries involved, only Czechoslovakia published both letters.[52]

The meeting between the Czechoslovak Party Presidium and almost the entire Soviet Politburo in the east Slovak border village of Čierna nad Tisou, from 29 July to 1 August, formed a new low point in relations between the two states. The Czechoslovaks had hardly prepared themselves for this meeting. They had not outlined a strategy in advance, they had not worked out concrete proposals and alternatives, they had not even thought about possible concessions.[53] In view of the fact that a lot depended on these negotiations and that they were the weaker party, this was an unforgiveable omission.

The negotiating position of Dubček and his followers was weakened in Čierna because the Bilak group turned against the rest of the leadership and took the side of the Soviets. The Czechoslovak delegation had a hard time of it: they were met with reproaches, imputations and gross insults. It even came to such a pass that the Czechoslovaks stood up and left the conference room during the fire-and-brimstone sermon of the Ukrainian party leader, Pyotr Shelest. Dubček, Smrkovský and the others told the Russians that they did not want to take any further part in 'such humiliating and offensive negotiations'.[54]

The conference was resumed, and the Czechoslovaks finally

agreed to take some restrictive measures.[55] But the political pressure from the Soviets did not achieve much more than that. Straight after Čierna, on 3 August, the summit of the Five of Warsaw and the ČSSR took place in Bratislava. Behind the usual façade of ceremonies and manifestations of brotherly unity, the points of view regarding the Czechoslovak reform process remained unchanged.

After Čierna and Bratislava there was a cheerful mood in Czechoslovakia, which was stirred up even more by the mass media. The reformist leaders, too, supposed that the worst was over. They still considered the situation to be a serious one, but they ruled out the possibility of a military intervention, especially since they were taking the promised restrictive measures. They much sooner expected the Soviets to turn to an economic blockade or for their conservative opponents in the Presidium and the Central Committee to undertake some kind of internal action.[56]

This analysis proved to be wrong. During the same period the Soviet leaders had come to a different conclusion. If they wanted to make Czechoslovakia tow the line, they had to act forcefully and quickly. At the time their Czechoslovak sympathizers were still in important positions, but after 26 August (the beginning of the Extraordinary Congress of the Slovak CP in Bratislava) and after 9 September (the start of the Extraordinary Congress of the CPCz in Prague) they would no longer be.

The discussions with Dubček were over. The patience of the Soviets had run out. Time was pressing, as were Ulbricht, Gomulka and the marshals. A military operation under the code name 'Danube' was given the go-ahead.

Chapter Five

MILITARY INTERVENTION AND THE NEW REALITY

'Mein lieber Bohumil' ... Henrich said softly in Cafe Jáma, 'now that I have seen them there, those Soviet soldiers ... even if all of us at the "Ostfront" had fought as bravely as the "Löwendivision aus Pommern", the bravest Pommeranian division "der langen Beinen" ... even then we would have lost, for the providence that Hitler relied on ... "der böhmische Feldwebel", as Hindenburg called Hitler jokingly or in studipidy ... that providence chose the Soviet army as conqueror ... mein lieber Bohumil. ... Only yesterday was I a guest of the Czechoslovak Union of Writers, there on the first floor ... and today a cannon is aimed at the building ... this is history, mein lieber Bohumil.... Only now do I realize this, here in Prague and at this moment.'

Recollections of Bohumil Hrabal of his talk with Heinrich Böll (21 August 1968)

THE REACTION TO THE INVASION

In the night of 20 to 21 August 1968 military units of the Soviet Union, the GDR, Poland, Hungary and Bulgaria invaded Czechoslovakia overnight and to the surprise of the whole world. In this intervention twenty-seven divisions at full strength, with about half a million soldiers took part, making it the biggest armed action in Europe since the end of the Second World War. The amount of equipment was impressive: 800 planes, over 6,300 tanks, about 2,000 artillery pieces and even, among other things, special missile units.[1] Some highly-placed Czechoslovak military men were initially mystified as to the main aim of the Russian plans, and seriously wondered whether this action was not the beginning of a large-scale Soviet attack on western Europe.[2]

Around 3 a.m. in the morning, the first column of Russian tanks arrived from Ruzyně Airport in Prague, where Russian transport planes were landing. According to a statement of the official Soviet press agency TASS this happened at the request of 'the Party and government leaders of the Czechoslovak Socialist Republic', who 'had asked to render the fraternal Czechoslovak people urgent assistance, including assistance with armed forces'.[3] In the early hours of the morning, Dubček, Smrkovský, Černík, Kriegel, Špaček and Šimon, the legal representatives of the sovereign state of Czechoslovakia and of the Communist Party, were arrested and taken away at gunpoint.

The scenario of the operation which was to force the developments in Czechoslovakia back under control, was drawn up in co-operation with a few Czechoslovak officials trusted by the Kremlin.[4] The Russian ambassador in Prague, S. V. Chervonenko, also played an active part.

The plan foresaw a request for help from a group of leading Czechoslovak officials from the Party, government and parliament. This request would provide the fraternal countries with a pretext for military intervention. In co-operation with the pro-Soviet politicians in the high party and state bodies a new revolutionary government would be formed, headed by Alois Indra, who would sanction the international assistance. At the same time, the proponents of right-wing opportunism and revisionism (the Dubček group) would be arrested and taken outside Czechoslovak territory with the help of members of the STB, the Czechoslovak security police.[5] Furthermore, the nests of counter-revolution, such as radio, television, newspaper offices and various important institutions would be occupied and taken over by the faithful and sound workers of the Czechoslovak Communist Party, who – it was apparently imagined – could be easily mobilized thanks to the internationalist assistance.

The armed forces of the five member states of the Warsaw Pact would behave like true allies towards the civilian population, in the spirit of internationalism, and were to avoid any unnecessary confrontation. This correct behaviour and intensive propaganda were to convince the Czechoslovaks that the actions of the allied forces were carried out to their own advantage and that the soldiers had come to defend the socialist achievements in Czechoslovakia against the counter-revolution.

Right from the start the operation met with an unexpected setback. The request for help, to be broadcast via the Czechoslovak radio and ČTK (The Czechoslovak Press Agency), failed to appear. The personnel of these two institutions thwarted attempts to do so. Later, when the anonymous request of 'a group of Czechoslovak members of the CC of the CPCz, of the government and parliament' was published in the press of the fraternal countries,[6] there was not a single political leader to be found in Czechoslovakia, including the dogmatists, who was willing to own up to this request for help. On the night of the occupation of the country, and even before tanks could reach the building, the Presidium of the CPCz Central Committee strongly condemned the aggression.[7] At the same time it urgently appealed to the population not to offer any armed resistance to the aggressors, and to keep calm. Condemnation by the Czechoslovak authorities (government, parliament and National Front) followed.

For Bilak's group, the condemnation of the invasion by the Party Presidium meant a nasty blow, which they and their protectors had not allowed for. Bilak had been convinced he would have a majority against Dubček in the newly created situation, one which would vote down any anti-Soviet statement. In the end only Bilak, Kolder, Rigo and Švestka voted against the declaration, while Barbírek and Piller, together with the Dubček group (Dubček, Smrkovský, Kriegel, Špaček and Černík), voted in favour, so that the vote was four against seven.[8] If Bilak and his followers had succeeded in getting a 'friendly' resolution passed by the Czechoslovak Party Presidium, the initial position of the aggressor would have been considerably more favourable.

Another development to upset Soviet calculations concerned the formation of a collaboration government. The discussions about this took place in the Soviet embassy under the watchful eye of Chervonenko. It soon became apparent that the composition of the government would be no easy task, as there were far more ministerial posts to be given away than there were candidates. Some politicians from the Bilak-Indra camp hesitated, a few others who had remained faithful to Dubček (Mlynář, Sádovský), strongly protested against a possible appointment, and even managed to unsettle everything again. After the negotiations had been moved to the Prague castle, and president Svoboda confronted with the plan, the old general – who, according to the constitution, should install the government – dealt the final blow. He refused to talk with the candidate ministers about another government and pithily summarized his point of view: 'What you are proposing, I cannot and never will approve. If I were to do so, people would chase me out of this castle like a mangy dog.'[9] And with that the 'revolutionary government of workers and farmers' was swept away.

In itself, the opposition of the president did not pose an insoluble problem, provided everything else went according to plan. But then there were the Czechoslovak people. The foreign troops met with a massive non-violent resistance never seen before in twentieth-century Europe.[10] Against the physical presence of tanks and other military hardware, the Czechs and Slovaks pitted the ingenuity of the mind. Road signs and house numbers in Prague and other big cities literally disappeared, as did the telephone books from the public telephone booths and the names on front doors; the names on the signs of villages and towns in the country were changed into 'Dubčekovo' (belonging to Dubček), or made unreadable. Signposts were moved, turned round or removed.

The population acted according to the 'Ten Commandments' which were seen as an indication of how to behave towards the invading troops and spread by the mass media: 'you don't know, you don't care, you don't tell, you don't have, you don't know how to, you don't give, you can't do, you don't sell, you don't show, you do nothing.'[11] Whenever possible, people entered into discussion with the occupying forces. The arguments against the intervention and for socialism with a human face were enforced by massive protest demonstrations at every place the troops found themselves. The streets in the big cities were full of placards and graffiti. These spoke of suport for Dubček, Svoboda, Smrkovský and Černík, and ridiculed, often in Russian, the presence of the occupying forces, demanding their immediate withdrawal.[12] This tactic of psychological warfare, born out of need, did not fail to have an effect on the occupiers. The demoralization (or, one could say: moralization) of the soldiers went so far, that the troops in Prague and a few other towns had to be replaced by other contingents only three days after the intervention.

Nor did the invasion forces succeed in silencing the mass media. Despite the fact that the editorial offices of newspapers and the newspapers' printers had been occupied, in Prague alone, fifteen newspapers and journals appeared underground, with an increased circulation. The Czechoslovak radio went into hiding and kept on broadcasting in co-operation with the provincial broadcasting stations, informing people at home and abroad of the situation and the opposition in the country, and passing on important information. The free Czechoslovak broadcasting stations were of tremendous importance to the resistance: they stimulated, called for action, calmed if necessary and strengthened the feelings of unity and solidarity among the population.

The fact that the plans of the occupying forces misfired should be ascribed especially to this non-violent national resistance. The Soviet strategists were unprepared for this spontaneous resistance of the entire population and they did not know how to handle it. Moreover, the atmosphere of total national resistance made such a deep impression on pro-Soviet elements that they were not prepared to collaborate with the occupiers. The co-operation on which the Kremlin had counted with confidence, almost completely failed to materialize, for that moment at least.[13]

As if all this was not enough, on 22 August the Extraordinary XIV Party Congress took place at a factory in the Prague workers' district Vysočany. The initiative for this had been taken by the Prague City Committee of the CPCz, which had the delegates called up by the Czechoslovak broadcasting stations. Over 1,200 delegates took part in this congress, despite the 'extraordinary' circumstances. The manner in which the delegates managed to reach the secret meeting place in the besieged city, as well as the fact that the occupying forces had not found out about the congress, were proof of the tremendous unity among the thousands of people involved, and of the excellent organization and vitality of the Czechoslovak resistance.

The Congress rejected the intervention as an illegal act and demanded an immediate withdrawal of all occupying forces and the release of all imprisoned leaders. In order to lend force to their demands and to demonstrate the unity between the Communist Party and the population, the participants called on the Czechoslovak workers to hold a 'one hour long general strike'.

This was promptly carried out the next day. The XIVth Congress called on all communist parties in the world to support the CPCz in its defence of 'socialism with a human face'.[14] The delegates then went on to elect a Central Committee, in which the anti-reformist leaders lost their seats. Accordingly the new Party Presidium also consisted of reformist communists.[15] Alexander Dubček was unanimously chosen as first secretary. During his absence his position was filled by Věnek Šilhán, an economist and a member of the Prague Party Committee.

The unexpected turn of events in Czechoslovakia after the intervention soon forced the Kremlin to change its tactics. There was nothing the Soviet leaders could do but to bring the imprisoned 'Czechoslovak heretics', who had already been written off, to Moscow and to negotiate with them.

THE MOSCOW PROTOCOL

Despite the insistence of their closest colleagues Dubček and the others resolutely rejected the opportunity to go into hiding.[16] Arrested like criminals, they were first dragged to Poland and from there to the Ukraine. The only high Czechoslovak representative not to be arrested was president Svoboda. He decided on his own accord to go to Moscow in order to negotiate directly with the Kremlin leaders. The arrival of the Czechoslovak president gave the Soviets another chance to get out of the precarious situation caused by the fiasco of the intervention:

> In this way the political solution of the conflict, which would normally have demanded the most thorough preparations, was spontaneously initiated by one man acting on his own authority. On his own authority Svoboda gave his mission another function.[17]

Both the National Assembly and the new CC of the CPCz would have preferred Svoboda not to have left the republic. His mission was seen merely as an attempt to mediate about future negotiations. It was not the intention that Svoboda should act as leader of a negotiating team, let alone that he was authorised to come to an agreement. President Ludvík Svoboda was received with full honours in Moscow on 23 August. With him arrived a delegation, including, besides deputy prime minister Husák, M.

Dzúr, the minister of Defence, B. Kučera, the minister of Justice, and also, on the express request of the Kremlin, Bilak, Indra and Piller.

At first, the Soviets did not find Svoboda an easy opponent. He refused to start a dialogue with them unless Dubček and the other imprisoned Czechoslovak politicians were involved in the negotiations. The Soviet leaders had to give in, and Dubček, Smrkovský, Černík, Špaček, and Šimon, who had meanwhile been 'taken from the woods to the Kremlin',[18] could take part in the negotiations as from 25 August. Initially they did not know anything about the situtation in their own country nor about Svoboda's arrival, which Brezhnev and the other Soviet leaders tried to take advantage of in order to break their resistance. The attitude of the Soviets was overbearing, arrogant and humiliating to the ex-prisoners. In the Kremlin, Dubček's group was informed about events in the country and the clandestine XIVth Party Congress by Z. Mlynář, who had arrived from Prague in the company of several dogmatic Party leaders, among them M. Jakeš.

The composition of the Czechoslovak delegation finally taking part in the talks in the Kremlin was unfavourable towards the progressives and strongly set its mark on the proceedings of the negotiations. Opposite eight politicians from the Bilak-group who had lost their high positions in the party at the XIVth Party Congress in Vysočany, and officially no longer had the right to represent the CPCz, stood six progressive leaders (the five who had recently been arrested and Z. Mlynář), and also, in a sense, the four members of the Svoboda-group, of whom, however, only the president and Gustáv Husák actively participated in the negotiations.

Although the original Russian version of the protocol was at first rejected by the Czechoslovak delegation, it was eventually accepted as starting-point of the negotiations by the Czechoslovak delegation as a result of the tough and threatening attitude of the Soviets and at president Svoboda's insistence. The Soviet leaders made it clear to their 'interlocutors' that only after signing the protocol would they be allowed to leave Moscow. The words of the secretary of the CC of the CPSU, B. N. Ponomarev, addressed to the Czechoslovaks, are typical of the Soviet way of negotiating:

If you do not sign straight away, you will do so in a week's

> time. And if you do not sign in a week's time, you will do so in two weeks' time, and if not in two weeks' time, you will sign in a month's time.[19]

Fatal to the outcome of the negotiations in the Kremlin were not so much the Soviet threats, however, but the attitude of the strong man in the Czechoslovak delegation, Ludvík Svoboda. The general, who thought in military terms and did not appreciate the art of political negotiating, was prepared to accept a compromise, when the Soviets promised him that the Czechoslovak leading politicians could remain in their jobs. The striking change in the attitude of Svoboda, after he had fought for the liberty of the Czechoslovak leaders, cannot just be explained by his fear of bloodshed in his own country and by the responsibility he felt for this. It was also caused by his strong loyalty to the Soviet Union, which made a total split unthinkable to him, and drove him to come to an agreement at any cost. The Soviet leaders cleverly made use of this during the negotiations.

In his memoirs Smrkovský relates how Dubček and some others offered resistance to the protocol and the pressure of the Kremlin. This could not be said of the general.

> Svoboda acted in the sense that retorts were useless, that they had to stop and that the protocol had to be gone through item by item, word by word, meanwhile saying something along the lines of everything going to be alright and that, when the Russian soldiers were to leave our country, they would be covered with flowers.

Somewhere else he mentions: 'he shouted about responsibility, about stacks of bodies at home, about whether we fully realized all that'.[20]

The conditions of the fifteen-point protocol,[21] finally accepted and signed by the Czechoslovak delegation, in effect meant a surrender to the Soviet demands. Declaring the XIVth Party Congress invalid and agreeing to a new congress only being convened 'after the normalization of the situation in the party and in the country' (point 2), were grave concessions exacted from the progressives. The future of the reform process was up in the air.

On the other hand, Dubček, who collapsed several times and had to be put under strict medical supervision, and his allies were able to prevent the worst. They returned to their posts, contrary to the original intention of the Kremlin. Besides, they managed to prevent the inclusion, both in the secret protocol and in the official final communiqué, of an explicit statement that a counter-revolutionary situation had developed in Czechoslovakia. They were also able to obtain the promise from the Soviet leaders that their troops would not get involved in domestic affairs (point 5). Furthermore, the Kremlin had to delete a couple of passages from the first draft of the protocol, such as the passage about the Czechoslovak request for assistance, and the official recognition that the arrival of the troops was necessary fraternal aid.

The division in the Czechoslovak Party top between the Dubček group and the dogmatists played into the hands of the Kremlin, of course. But of even more importance to the Soviet leaders was the difference of opinion between the progressives and the group of 'realists': politicians like Svoboda and Husák who were prepared to give in to the Soviet pressure at the cost of the reforms, to the benefit of their own positions. Even as early as this stage, the Kremlin leaders managed to drive a wedge between 'the Czechoslovak Four', i.e. president Svoboda on the one hand, and Smrkovský, Dubček and Černík on the other. As far as Černík was concerned, his views about a solution to the crisis that had developed were closer to the president's than to those of the most uncompromising Smrkovský.

On reflection the secret protocol only contained a few concrete measures, but it was elastic enough for the Soviet authorities to postpone the end of the normalization *ad infinitum* and to push back reforms again and again. The signing of the protocol cleared the way for the Soviet 'salami tactics', which only catered for one interpretation of the term *normalization*: that of the destruction of the Czechoslovak reform movement and the removal of its proponents.

THE MESSAGE FROM THE LEADERS

Finally, on 27 August 1968, the Czechoslovak delegation returned to Prague from Moscow. Also in their midst was František Kriegel, who had not been allowed to take part in the negotiations by the Soviets and had been put in solitary confinement. Kriegel was added to the Czechoslovak delegation just before the signing of the protocol, but was the only one to refuse to sign the text of the document. President Svoboda and the others managed to take Kriegel with them to Prague only with great difficulty, as the Soviets at first refused to allow him to leave. Only when the Czechoslovaks refused to leave the Kremlin without Kriegel was he taken straight to the plane.[22]

Although the Czechoslovak population remained ignorant of the harsh conditions of the secret agreement, the text of the official communiqué,[23] co-signed by people who were traitors in the eyes of the Czechs and Slovaks, made them suspect the serious consequences of the negotiations in Moscow. People had an even worse shock hearing the addresses by the Czechoslovak leaders that followed the communiqué. The leaders did their best to present the Moscow agreement in as favourable a light as possible. On the one hand they implored the population to accept the presence of the troops as a political reality, but on the other they declared 'not to deviate a single step' from the course that had been followed since January, and to devote themselves as before to the realization of the Action Programme of the CPCz.

President Svoboda, the first speaker to go on the radio, called for discipline, caution, and calm from the population in patriotic speech. 'Neither you, nor we have had an easy time' he declared and added 'I am convinced that we have not betrayed the confidence [of the people]'.[24] In the light of the communiqué and of the rest of his address this assurance from the president did not sound at all convincing. The older generation remembered only too well the address of president Emil Hácha, made on 15 March 1939 – on the first day of the German occupation – after his return to Prague from Berlin following 'negotiations' with Hitler. The nature of the two addresses and the circumstances under which they were given, resembled one another too closely. Nor could the resemblance between the 'Dictate of Moscow' and the 'Dictate of Munich' imposed on Czechoslovakia only one month short of thirty years previously, be taken away by the speech of Svoboda or those of any of the other leaders.

Far more importance was attached to Alexander Dubček's address than to the bad tidings of Svoboda. Dubček also asked the Czechs and the Slovaks to accept the inevitability of the compromise. The Party leader, who could not control his tears during his speech, and had to interrupt his words with long pauses, indicated which direction the normalization would take: 'to take some temporary extraordinary measures, which will restrict the degree of democratization and the freedom of speech which we have achieved up to now, and which we would not have taken in normal circumstances'.[25] In this moving speech there were also encouraging words to be found which confirmed people's impression that Dubček was not prepared to capitulate, but determined to continue his present political course 'despite the extremely difficult circumstances'.

The final passage of Dubček's speech was in many ways typical of the manner in which the Party leader hoped to find an 'honourable way out' of the situation which had developed:

> A people, of which everybody is led by both reason and conscience, will not go under. I beg all of you, my dear fellow citizens, Czechs and Slovaks, communists and members of other political parties, the National Front, I beg all workers, farmers, I beg our intelligentsia, all our people – let us stay united, calm and, especially, cool-headed. Let us understand, that only in that, in our allegiance to socialism, in our honesty, in our endeavour and character the way forward can be found!

It is striking how important unity between the people and Party leaders was to all Dubček's tactics. This unity, and trust in the leaders of the Prague Spring, who vouched to take the country out of the difficult situation, were the cornerstones of his policies, which, on the one hand, were now bound to pursue a 'normalization' and, on the other, still aimed at defending the reform process and developing it further, depending on the circumstances. The speeches of Smrkovský, Černík and Husák were in the same vein. These also created the impression that the troops would leave the country within a relatively short period: 'In our negotiations relatively short term periods were mentioned. It is not a question of years', Husák said.[26]

Josef Smrkovský's speech showed great courage. The old communist, who was the only one of the leaders to speak plainly of 'the occupation', painted a gloomy picture of the atmosphere during the negotiations in the Kremlin:

> Our talks in Moscow took place in unusual circumstances. You know that we did not arrive there together and you know the

> circumstances under which some of us arrived there and had to negotiate. I do not think it is necessary to go into details, which for me and comrade Dubček and the others would be too painful and grievous. To take decisions in these conditions was, as anyone can imagine, extremely problematical.[27]

These words shed a completely different light on the negotiations in Moscow to that which the final sentence of the official communiqué indicated: 'The talks proceeded in an atmosphere of frankness, comradeship and friendship.'

The general public, which did not know the full truth of the 'Dictate of Moscow', accepted the attitude of Dubček and his followers. People showed understanding for Dubček's situation because they firmly believed in his sincere intentions and in those of the other leaders. The following table, based on a survey in September 1968, shows how great the confidence in the four living symbols of the Prague Spring was.[28]

confidence in %	Svoboda	Dubček	Černík	Smrkovský
complete confidence	97.8	97.2	90.4	90.1
confidence with reservations	1.4	1.8	6.0	6.6
no confidence	0.3	0.2	1.2	1.3
no opinion	0.5	0.8	2.4	2.0
	100.0	100.0	100.0	100.0

Opinion polls held in the first weeks after the intervention also showed what expectations the Czechoslovaks entertained regarding their new future. Out of all those questioned 94.6 per cent declared themselves in favour of the Action Programme;[29] in addition, 73.6 per cent thought that the post-January policies could be carried out completely or, possibly, with small changes. A mere 7.5 per cent ruled out such a development altogether.[30]

Interesting in this respect is an opinion poll in Slovakia. An absolute majority of the Slovaks (92.4 per cent) rejected any return to the situation, as it was under Novotný (0.5 per cent preferred this), and over half (52.9 per cent) were of the opinion that no attempts should be made to restore the old situation. Their reasoning was simple: 'it could not happen, it would not get the support of the people'.[31] The influence of eight months of Prague Spring in this assessment was unmistakable. But what did the people's support for the reform policies mean when none of the progressive leaders asked for it?

SEEKING A WAY OUT

Dubček and many of his sympathizers in the Party leadership assumed that it would be possible to overcome the crisis and yet keep the essence of the reform process intact. The Party leader hoped he could reach a compromise with the Soviet leaders if he succeeded in dispelling their distrust. He saw the whole tragedy of 21 August mainly in the fact that the leadership of the CPCz, and he himself personally, had not succeeded in convincing the Soviet Union and the other allies, who had invaded the country with their forces, of Czechoslovakia's good intentions and loyalty. Dubček did not realize sufficiently that the Czechoslovak reform process was first of all an attack on the conservative policies of the Brezhnev regime and the other east European regimes. From Brezhnev's point of view Soviet policies - which had been made the measure of everything - should not be harmed or undermined by the separate interests of a satellite country, in this case by a Dubček in Prague.

Gustáv Husák was quick to understand what the Kremlin leaders were really concerned about. It soon became clear to this ambitious Slovak politician that the Kremlin was waiting for concrete results, which were to drastically limit the Czechoslovak experiment, and that in the light of this new reality it would be Moscow, and no longer Prague, who would determine what was and what was not permitted in the reform process. During the negotiations after the invasion, Husák belonged to those who, on the Czechoslovak side, had actively collaborated in the realization of the protocol. Even when he was still in Moscow, he had attempted, though without success, to take steps in accordance with the Soviet demands in the protocol. Via the telephone, Husák got in touch with party officials in Bratislava, for instance, who were preoccupied with the holding of the congress of the Slovak

Communist Party (CPS), which had a special status within the Czechoslovak Communist Party.

Husák urged postponement of the Slovak congress, which was to start on 26 August (as was originally planned).[32] Neither he, nor Dubček himself, could stop the congress from taking place. And thus what Husák had wanted to prevent, happened: straight after the opening of the congress of the CPS it affirmed the legality of the Extraordinary XIVth Congress of the CPCz in Vysočany and declared its agreement with all decisions taken there. Only when Husák himself later appeared at the congress and informed those present of the negotiations in Moscow, did the whole event take a different course. Husák, chosen as first secretary of the CPS at the congress (in which function he succeeded Bilak), induced the Slovak party congress to distance itself from the Vysočany congress in the final communiqué.

The arguments used by the new Slovak Party leader were a sensitive point for the delegates since they were taking advantage of the Slovak national sovereignty. Gustáv Husák, who proclaimed the federalization of the Czechoslovak state to be an important aim of his policies, used at the same time the future constitution of the republic to reject the Vysočany congress:

> What should interest us here in Slovakia most of all is the Slovak contribution [to the Fourteenth Congress in Vysočany]. We are talking about federalization, [...] about the sovereign right of this nation [...], the Slovak representation [...]. Not even ten per cent of the Slovak delegates were present. [...] This is not the right way to install the Central Committee. [...] One cannot expect a sovereign nation and party to be politically represented by a group of people whom nobody ordered to do so. This is a question of principle.[33]

This 'matter of principle' would later be cunningly used once more against the chairman of parliament Smrkovský.

Husák also managed to play on Dubček's readiness to accept compromises, chiefly by making use of the fact that Dubček and his sympathizers had no clear conception of how to master the new situation. Husák would invariably stress to his audience at the congress that he was resolutely on Dubček's side:

> I completely agree with Dubček and the others, that the

> solution to the present situation lies in working towards a normalization on the basis of the agreement of Moscow [. . .] I back Dubček's concept entirely. I was there when it was formulated, and I will support him completely, I shall stand or fall with him. [. . .] Long live the CPCz under the leadership of Dubček.[34]

In this way Husák, who had also distanced himself in no uncertain terms from the Bilak group in the Party leadership, could start his 'realistic way-out', which in reality followed the tactics of the Kremlin, using Dubček's name as no more than a false label.

Some followers of Dubček, amongst them the secretary of the CC of the CPCz, Z. Mlynář, shared Husák's opinion that there was very little room left for the continuation of the reform process after 21 August. They were also insistent that the conditions of the agreement with Moscow would be accepted as there was no room 'to play tricks' with the agreement. Contrary to Husák, who might have presented himself as a champion of the post-January policies, but offered no opinion as to which of those policies could actually be retained, was Mlynář's highest priority which stated that the important positions in the Party and the state should not fall into the hands of dogmatic pro-Moscow communists. He hoped it would be possible for the progressive cadres to 'hibernate' in their functions, in order to be able to continue democratization when a suitable occasion arose in the future.[35]

In itself this was an interesting solution, but, having been superseded by the course of the negotiations in Moscow, it was no longer realistic. The plan would only have had a chance of succeeding if all reformist politicians had consistently presented a common front. But the unity, so widely proclaimed, no longer existed in reality. Moreover, Mlynář had failed to notice what Husák had sensed straightaway and had been prepared to accept, that the Soviet leaders felt that the prerequisite for a successful normalization lay precisely in an extensive and radical change of the top cadres, at the cost of the reformists. In order to fight the Czechoslovak heresy effectively, the heretics themselves first had to be removed.

Chapter Six

THE PROCESS OF NORMALIZATION

> People remembered the actors and knew their roles all too well. Therefore it was with a certain eagerness that they watched how they would act in a completely new play with a completely new director. I think I can state without exaggeration that for the people here the post-1970 events certainly did not appear as an abstract process of 'strengthening the leading role of the Party, removing right-wing elements, purging Czechoslovak culture, deepening co-operation between socialist states', but rather as a historical drama with live characters. It was a play about betrayal, love and hate, about sacrifice and deception, greatness and baseness, revenge and forgiveness, cowardice and heroism, a drama of courage and cunning, decline and fall, about money, envy, and in fact everything that is splendidly human. I do not wish to conceal the fact that I myself viewed the historical events primarily in that manner, and only in that fashion did they fascinate me. It was not until later that I forced myself to view them with professional eyes and started to investigate abstract trends, lines of development, the intrinsicality of observed phenomena, historical generalization, parallels and lessons.
>
> Milan Šimečka (1977)

THE TROOPS STATIONING TREATY

At first sight the situation in occupied Czechoslovakia did not look too bad for Dubček's supporters in the first few weeks after the intervention. The direct political consequences of the surprise military attack were confined to the closing down of political clubs, a certain check on the mass media, declaring the Extraordinary XIVth Party Congress invalid, and to a number of changes in the government and the Party top. As regards the latter, these changes in the highest levels of the Party did not bring about a weakening of the progressives but, on the contrary, a strengthening, to the annoyance of the Soviets.

A few reformists had to go; Kriegel, for instance, did not return to the Presidium, Císař did not go back to the Party secretariat, Pavel, Hájek and vice-premier Šik left the government, and the director of Czechoslovak radio broadcasting, Z. Hejzlar, and of television, J. Pelikán, had to go as well. On the other hand, the dogmatic bloc in the Party Presidium, which had increased from 11 to 21 members, was severely depleted. Only Bilak, Barbírek and Piller managed to retain their positions; the first because of his relationship with the Kremlin, the other two only because of their voting behaviour on the night of the intervention. No fewer than 13 politicians, including Gustáv Husák, had also been chosen for the Party Presidium in Vysočany.[1] By means of this reshuffle the reformists tried to safeguard the results of the Vysočany congress with regard to the composition of the Party leadership.

The Soviet answer was not long in coming. The statement in the Moscow *Pravda* of 31 August 1968 that 40,000 counter-revolutionaries in Czechoslovakia had to be dealt with, and the smear campaign in the press which followed, make it clear how the Soviet idea of normalization differed from the measures taken by Alexander Dubček. The Soviet Union itself first publicly indicated what it understood by the normalization process in Czechoslovakia on 6 September - 'by chance' on the same day that the special envoy of the Kremlin, V. V. Kuznetsov, arrived in Prague to hasten the implementation of the Moscow agreements:

> The process of normalization means, first of all, the complete exposure and stamping out of the subversive activities of the right-wing, anti-socialist forces; the elimination of their influence on a part of the population, especially youth; the resolute strengthening of the leading role of the Communist Party in the activities of the state agencies, in the ideological and public spheres, in the whole life of the country.[2]

The most important task of the Kuznetsov mission, which lasted a total of one and a half months, was to find out which

Czechoslovak politicians were prepared to accept the Soviet vision of normalization and to what extent they were useful to the Kremlin.[3] Compared with the negotiations prior to 21 August the Soviets had an easier time of it now. The presence of military troops in the ČSSR[4] was an efficacious means to give the Soviet normalization demands the necessary weight, to provide the willing Party leadership 'realists' with 'realistic arguments' that things had to be changed, to back the collaborators as much as they needed, and to put pressure on the Dubček leadership again and again in order to steer the normalization into the desired direction.

How little the reformists surrounding Dubček were really allowed to say became evident during the visit of the Czechoslovak delegation (composed of Dubček, Černík and Husák) to Moscow at the beginning of October. Not only did Dubček have to promise 'to reinforce party and state bodies with people who stand firmly on positions of Marxism-Leninism',[5] in other words with people who were regarded as traitors in their country, but the Party leader was also forced to accept an agreement about the stationing of Soviet troops on Czechoslovak territory. With it, the hope that the entire occupying force would leave Czechoslovakia shortly, as soon as the situation in the country had normalized, evaporated. With this hope the Czechoslovak leaders had sustained the population and themselves.

'The Treaty on the Conditions for the Temporary Stationing of Soviet Troops on ČSSR territory', as the document was called, was signed by the prime ministers A. Kosygin and O. Černík in Prague on 16 October 1968. A more detailed definition of the term 'temporary' was nowhere to be found in the treaty, nor was there any mention the numbers of troops to be stationed, and even a cancellation clause was missing. According to article 15 the treaty could only be changed 'with the agreement of both partners' and would 'be in effect for the duration of temporary stationing of Soviet troops on the territory of the Czechoslovak Socialist Republic'.[6] Due to this curious formulation a *temporary* stay of the Russian military units was equated with a *permanent* stay; since then the Soviet troops - an estimated 60,000 to 70,000 strong - have not left Czechoslovakia.

The ratification of the Treaty by the Czechoslovak parliament followed a few days later. With 228 votes in favour, and only four votes against - those of F. Vodsloň, general V. Prchlík, F. Kriegel and Mrs G. Sekaninová-Čakrtová - and 10 abstentions, the presence of the Soviet troops in Czechoslovakia received a formal, legal basis after all. The process of the political capitulation of Dubček and his supporters in the Party leadership, which had started in Moscow with the kidnapping, was now nearing completion in Prague. What made this affair so tragic was that Dubček and the others did not comprehend what they were doing: they were actively killing off what they had called into life themselves and what such a short time ago they had called 'democratic socialism'.

THE PRAGUE SPRING WASHED OUT

Dubček's group found itself caught between two fires. The Soviet Union, Bilak and his followers, and the 'realists' demanded concessions, whereas the Czechs and Slovaks expected a firm attitude - the same attitude they had admired so much in 'their heroes' before the intervention. Instead they had to suffer the reversal of the priorities of Dubček and the other leaders of the Prague Spring. Time after time, making concessions to the Kremlin dominated the political behaviour in Prague, in spite of all the sentiments and desires of the overwhelming majority of the population.

The Czechs and Slovaks did not fail to notice that in most of the Party leaders' speeches, references to fundamental points in the Action Programme were becoming rarer and rarer. At the same time, politicians with a progressive past began to use a completely different language from that which people were accustomed to hear. Their greatest worry was no longer the preservation of the reforms and the continuation of the post-January policies, but the activities of the 'anti-socialist, liberal and anarchistic powers' in the country and the restoration of peace and order.[7]

The total reversal of political values had begun. While those within the Party and among the population who resisted the break-down of the reforms, were painted as troublemakers and hooligans, the real troublemakers had free play because they enjoyed the protection and support of the Soviet troops (and of the dogmatists in the Central Committee). Among those, for instance, was a militant group of ex-Stalinists - around the old-guard hardliner J. Jodas, the painter E. Famíra, and V. Nový, a member of the CC of the CPCz - which was later to grow into a movement of several thousand members, the *Levá Fronta* (Left Front); or the radio station *Vltava* (Moldau) which broadcast from the GDR in Czech; or the paper *Zprávy* (Messages) edited by an anonymous 'Board of Editors connected with the Soviet Troops', printed in the GDR and distributed in Czechoslovakia by the Soviet units and local helpers.

In the same way as they used to do under Gottwald, the 'ultras' launched a smear campaign against Dubček, Smrkovský, and the other progressive leaders, and against everything that was brought forth by the process of democratization. So as not to give the Soviets a reason for criticism, Dubček did not dare make an end to these excesses. This was to his own detriment, for in the eyes of the people nothing proved his impotence more clearly than his allowing these activities to take place unchallenged.

The influence that the supporters of Dubček within the Party leadership had on the happenings of the CPCz was definitely curbed at the plenary session of the Central Committee in November 1968 by two organizational measures with far-reaching consequences. A so-called 'Executive Committee of the Party Presidium' consisting of eight members, was created. On this committee, a kind of presidium within the Presidium, only Dubček and Smrkovský could be counted as true defenders of the reforms. The others belonged either to the 'realists' (i.e. politicians who owed their positions to the Prague Spring, and who, before the intervention, represented the progressive wing, but now clearly followed an anti-reformist course) or to that category of politicians who had formerly always managed to survive every change of the regime without any effort, and now diligently joined in the normalization *à la russe*.[8]

The second measure regarded the establishment of the 'Bureau of the CC of the CPCz for the Direction of Party Work in the Czech Lands'.[9] This new Party body, which all Czech party organizations came under, was chaired by Lubomír Štrougal and was granted powers similar to those of the Central Committee of the Slovak Communist Party. The position of Štrougal in Bohemia and Moravia was now matched by that of Husák in Slovakia, which meant an undermining of the function of Dubček as Party leader, and a considerable reduction of his power.

From November onwards the power of the reformists was going downhill. Smrkovský and Dubček were at the mercy of the 'realists' in the Executive Committee and, in addition, Dubček had to rely on the co-operation of Husák and Štrougal who were anything but his political friends. In this situation a 'continuation of the reforms without extremes', an interpretation which Dubček, both stubbornly and desperately, attempted to give to the normalization,[10] was a completely unattainable goal. Continuation of the reforms was out of the question; the elimination of the 'extreme' aspects of the Czechoslovak reform process was not. And exactly what was and was not extreme was now decided by the 'realists'. Dubček's aspiration was thus reduced to futile attempts to save what could be saved of the reforms in the Action Programme, without anybody being at all sure of what *should* and *should not* be saved.

What was once seen as a progressive bloc, became divided. Some thought that Dubček had gone too far in his willingness to accept compromises, and became alienated from him; others followed the first secretary with the hope of safeguarding a minimum package of reforms; yet others - and there were quite a few of them - showed a surprising flexibility. With the same ease with which they used to plead for the reforms, they now adapted to the changed set-up and moved over to the 'realistic' camp of Husák. Nobody had a monopoly on wisdom, however.

THE FALL OF SMRKOVSKÝ AND DUBČEK

Alexander Dubček tried to combat the polarization by taking a middle position. He even sacrificed Josef Smrkovský for the sake of the 'realists' (and Moscow, of course), which caused a serious crisis.

The conflict concerning Smrkovský arose in December 1968, when Husák demanded in the name of the Central Committee of the CPS that the chairman of parliament be a Slovak, so that the four highest functions in the federalized ČSSR were held by an equal number of Czechs and Slovaks. At that moment, the ratio was three Czechs (president Svoboda, prime minister Černík, and chairman of parliament, Smrkovský) against one Slovak, Party leader Dubček. Although Husák swore by all that was holy that it had nothing to do with the person in question but merely with a fair sharing of the offices, worthy of the Slovaks, it was clear to everybody what he had in mind with his manoeuvre - to push Smrkovský out.

Husák's advance was as transparent as it was cunning. It sowed discord between the reformist Czechs and Slovaks and isolated the latter group. Even though the progressive Slovak politicians were not at all happy with Husák's move, they did not dare oppose this administrative logic of the Slovak-Czech *Ausgleich*. Slovakia remained generally quiet, not in the least because the normalization had made more headway there than in Bohemia and Moravia (for instance, regarding control of the mass media).

The Czech countries, on the other hand, were in turmoil. Such a storm of protests and massive willingness to campaign for the defence of the values of the post-January policies had not been seen since the intervention. Not even during the big anti-Soviet demonstrations of 28 October, the day of the fiftieth anniversary of the Czechoslovak state, or during the sit-in strikes of students and various actions by secondary school pupils in the second half of November, meant as a protest against the compromises and to support the reform policies. The struggle to keep the people's tribune Smrkovský in the position he had held during the Prague Spring caught the imagination of large sections of the population. According to official estimates some four million citizens aligned themselves behind Smrkovský.[11]

It was a struggle where the winner and the loser were known beforehand: despite a stream of delegations to Prague demanding that Smrkovský stayed on, and despite innumerable resolutions, petitions and efforts of the media. Even warnings by the Czech Union of Metalworkers (900,000 members) and a few other unions, saying that they would strike 'if comrade Smrkovský or anybody else of the prominent political leaders were to be recalled from their functions',[12] were of no avail. Husák was determined to cut the knot. He and his Slovak fellow Party member Sádovský declared they would leave the Executive Committee if the Slovak demand was not met and also threatened with a counter campaign in Slovakia if the campaigning for Smrkovský in the Czech countries did not stop.[13]

An ultimatum had been placed on the table. The Kremlin provided Husák with the necessary support and during the most critical days sent an important delegation to Prague (arriving 27

December, leaving 10 January), headed by Party secretary K. F. Katushev, while Kuznetsov was also present. In the Executive Committee, Smrkovský came under enormous pressure from, amongst others, Černík and especially Svoboda, to resign from his post, while Dubček wanted to prevent an escalation of the conflict and did nothing to save his political ally. Even before Husák had started his manoeuvre, the Party leader had more or less written off Smrkovský.[14] There was nothing left for the latter but to give in. He promised to withdraw his own candidacy 'for the good of the Slovak nation' and in order to calm the population and the militant trade unions in particular, which he did indeed do in a speech broadcast on radio and television on 5 January 1969.[15]

The population witnessed how the *Big Four* fell apart. In the eyes of many Czechoslovaks they personified the last tangible guarantee of a continuation of the Prague Spring, with the result that the psychological effect of Smrkovský's removal was great, also because he, more than anyone else, had become the symbol of resistance to the inflated demands of the normalization. One only has to read through a few copies of the Czechoslovak newspapers dating from just after Smrkovský's resignation to experience the disappointment and sense of powerlessness then prevalent.

This was the background to the drama which took place on Prague's historic Wenceslas Square on 16 January 1969, the same day that the Central Committee of the CPCz met: the self-immolation by fire of the 21 year-old student Jan Palach. His self-sacrifice was a desperate attempt to force the Czechoslovak leaders to stop the demolition of the reforms. The act occurred in a political atmosphere in which people's ordinary means to make their wishes known to the rulers had no longer any effect. Palach's short farewell letter reminded the Czechoslovaks of their resistance in August and asked support for two concrete demands: the banning of the distribution of the paper *Zprávy* and an abolition of censorship.[16] In various university towns and other places this immediately resulted in mass demonstrations.

The 25th of January, the day of the funeral of the Prague student, turned into an impressive day of national mourning in Czechoslovakia. Czech history, which knows remarkably few armed revolts, acquired another martyr. The Soviet press, the circles around Bilak and Indra and the ultras, however, gained more proof of a 'comprehensive imperialist conspiracy' against socialism in Czechoslovakia.[17] Dubček's position had not improved after the death of Jan Palach, which was followed a month later by another self-immolation tautology of the student Jan Zajíc. The Party leader, who seriously thought that he had gained Brezhnev's trust, desired peace in the country to prove to the Kremlin that he was still 'in complete control of the situation'.[18] Even then he did not want to see that the Soviets were only waiting for the right moment to send him packing.

In the Smrkovský affair, Dubček did not make use of his last chance to show friend and foe alike, that there were limits to his policy of compromises in matters of principle. (Dubček's authority was such that he could have parried Husák's demands both as a Slovak and as a prominent politician of the Prague Spring.) Instead he confirmed the impression that he lacked the personal courage for a firm stance, and that he was not at all able to say 'no' to his opponents. He preferred to seek respite in cabinet policies and dubious arrangements with Brezhnev rather than in support from his own people.

Politically, Dubček did not survive the next wave of unrest. This time the explosion of pent-up frustrations and emotions was directly due to the two games of world championship ice hockey held between the two arch rivals in this field, the Soviet Union and the ČSSR on 21 and 28 March 1969, in Stockholm. The Czechoslovak team, understandably not short of motivation, gained a hard-won victory in both games. For a moment sport took over the role of politics, where politics failed.

The population was now at least handed an 'Ersatzsieg über die Besatzungsmacht' ('surrogate victory on the occupying force', HR)[19] and it acted accordingly. An enthusiastic flush of victory spread in a large number of towns in the country, which then quickly transformed itself into anti-Soviet demonstrations. The symbols of the hated occupiers paid for it. In various places the buildings of the Soviet military command were damaged, some Soviet vehicles were destroyed, Soviet flats were burned, and numerous cartoons with the same content as those of the August days, appeared on the walls. In Prague the office of the Soviet airline company Aeroflot on Wenceslas Square was destroyed and set on fire, while a crowd of some 200,000 people chanted slogans addressed to the Soviet Union, which, of course, expressed sentiments other than gratitude for the international fraternal help and promises of eternal friendship.

This time the Kremlin struck hard. Forty-eight hours after the riots the Soviet minister of Defence, marshal A. A. Grechko, paid a surprise visit to the headquarters of the Soviet troops in the ČSSR. 'These Soviet generals come and go as if we were a Soviet province', president Svoboda is alleged to have said at this occasion.[20] The deputy minister of Foreign Affairs, V. S. Semyonov, arrived in Prague at the same time. The Soviets let it be known that they thought the situation 'more serious than in August 1968' and threatened in an ultimatum to put things right in Czechoslovakia.[21] These and other instances of blackmail, confidential talks of the Soviets with Husák and Štrougal and the scheming of these two with Svoboda and a number of other politicans who had come round, brought about, in April 1969, what a half million strong army of intervention had not succeeded in doing in August 1968: the fall of Alexander Dubček.

His departure was the result of a Soviet-Czechoslovak co-production, carried out directly by Dubček's former political supporters or fellow-travellers; they were people like Svoboda, Husák, Černík or Štrougal, and not by Bilak, Indra and other conspirators of the never installed 'Revolutionary Government', who at this stage of the normalization played only second fiddle.[22]

In the Executive Committee meeting Alexander Dubček did not resist his dismissal as first secretary. He pleaded for Černík as his successor, but acquiesced when Svoboda and the others supported Husák. In a secret ballot on 17 April Gustáv Husák was elected by the Central Committee into the highest Party office on the proposal of the Presidium. None of those present openly turned against Husák's candidacy. The Czechs and Slovaks accepted the change of power with resignation.

CAPITULATION

Husák had never been popular with the people close to him. He did, however, command the necessary respect. After the intervention he established the image of a skilful tactician who not only knew what he wanted, but who also - and not infrequently going against the current - managed to have his own way. His background helped. Husák, a prominent victim of Stalinism, became widely known to people because of his revelations about the terror of the 1950s and his attacks on Novotný at a time when public criticism was not yet commonly accepted in Czechoslovakia.

Gustáv Husák was therefore automatically considered a reformist in the Prague Spring, despite the fact that hardly anyone really knew the depth of his reformist convictions. After all, following his arrest in 1951 he had disappeared from political life, and after his release in 1960 (and rehabilitation in 1963) he had not held any posts within either Party or government until the fall of Novotný. This was in contrast to, for example, Josef Smrkovský and other persecuted and jailed communists. In reality Gustáv Husák's political viewpoints had hardly changed over the years. He remained what he had always been: a rather orthodox communist leader, keen on power, with strong authoritarian traits; a Slovak variant of the Pole Wladyslaw Gomulka rather than of the Hungarian János Kádár.

More than ever, there was despair and a feeling of helplessness in the camp of the reformists. Some, however, greeted the fall of Dubček with a certain relief. They had had to experience from close by how Dubček had not been able to stand up against the aggressive interventions from the Kremlin and they nourished some hope that Husák would succeed where his predecessor had failed and would save something of the reforms that Dubček had seemed likely to lose. Husák himself made promises in this direction in secret negotiations with various reformists to ensure himself of their support.[23]

These were the main reasons why there was no significant opposition from the progressive bloc (or rather from what was left of it); not even against the new composition of the Party Presidium in which the reformists had to vacate all but one of the seats. Only Alexander Dubček, now chairman of parliament, was allowed to stay on in this power base, reduced to eleven members.[24]

The hope of a miraculous rescue of reforms by Husák was like the hope of a drowning person clutching at straws. It can safely be said that with the removal of Dubček as Party leader the political capitulation of the reformist politicians was complete. They put the fate of the reforms as well as their own fate in the hands of a Party leader and a Party leadership with only one aim in mind: a voluntary and unconditional fulfilment of the Soviet demands, despite all former promises of Husák.

First, all reformists, including Alexander Dubček, were removed from the Central Committee and important Party and public offices. This process took place in a few stages between May 1969 and January 1970. At the same time the reforms suffered an increasingly rapid reversal and the broom of normalization was making a clean sweep of the mass media. Within a period of two to three months press, radio and television had been gagged.

Dubček, as a member of the Presidium (until September 1969) and chairman of parliament (until October 1969) was personally jointly responsible for all these developments. He was a member of the Party leadership at the time when Ota Šik was thrown out of the Central Committee and František Kriegel's Party membership was taken away from him; he railed angrily against the intellectual radical supporters of the reforms and against the members of the Central Committee, because under Husák they were not prepared to recant their opinions and points of view of 1968 and because they refused to revoke their signatures under the *Two Thousand Words Manifesto*,[25] and – probably his most controversial action – as chairman of the National Assembly he, together with Svoboda and Černík, signed the emergency laws of 22 August 1969, which were proclaimed after the anti-Soviet demonstrations on the occasion of the first anniversary of the military intervention, and which formed a 'legal' basis for mass dismissals and persecutions in the country in the following months and years.[26]

It is unclear what motives drove the symbol of the Prague Spring, Alexander Dubček, to stay on in the Presidium after his dismissal as Party leader. A number of ex-reformists and political friends clearly find his behaviour in those days hard to stomach. Did Dubček think he would be able to prevent the worst? Did he originally trust Husák to such a degree that he expected a symbiosis between his (weakened) post-January policies and the normalization practices of his successor? Did he speculate (like other Prague Spring officials) that he could maintain himself in a high position by an accommodating attitude? Or did he submit to the collective decisions of the Presidium as a good Party member and did he obediently carry out the orders to serve the Party? One can only hope that Dubček, after the example of Smrkovský and Mlynář, will one day feel the need to write his memoirs in which he explains his attitudes after April 1969.

However it may be, it is certain that Alexander Dubček did not master the art of getting out in time: an art, by the way, which is still very rare in the world of communist politics. On the other hand, Dubček has always refused categorically to submit to the ritual of self-criticism, which his opponents in the Central Committee repeatedly demanded him to do.

What followed was a fiasco. Dubček was appointed ambassador to Turkey in December 1969, then a month later he was expelled from the Central Committee; at the end of May 1970 he was withdrawn from his political post, and in June was expelled from the Party. Compared to many of his political friends he did not do badly from then on. The idol of 1968 got the job of a lowly official with the State Forestry administration in Bratislava. His personal fortunes illustrate the drama that took place all over the country in the second half of 1969 and especially during 1970, and which went down in history as the greatest purge ever held in the Communist Party of Czechoslovakia.

THE PURGES

In January 1970, after the expulsion of the 'realists' Černík and Sádovský (Černík was succeeded as prime minister by L. Štrougal),[27] Husák's modified team decided to introduce new Party membership cards. Vasil Bilak was put in charge of this large-scale operation, the aim of which was to purge the Party drastically of all reformist elements. Miloš Jakeš, as head of the Control and Auditing Commission of the Central Committee, became his right hand. For this 'purgation' 70,217 Screening Commissions (prověrkové komise) were formed, with a total of 235,270 members. They belonged to what was called 'the sound core of the CPCz', in other words the fervent opponents of reforms during the Prague Spring. But on these commissions there were also various officials who were seeking an alibi, and who managed to secure their own positions by denouncing their colleagues. For seven months the commissions interviewed some 1½ million Party members. Questions about their activities during the Prague Spring and their attitude in the August days and in the period up to the dismissal of Dubček took a central place in the interviews.

A considerable number of members of the CPCz did not wait for this humiliating interview but resigned from the Party in protest. The first wave of resignations started in August 1968. Most people, however, left the Party after the fall of Dubček and in the beginning of 1970. All in all some 150,000 communists left the CPCz of their own accord, over half of them workers.[28] According to official figures, 326,817 people were refused the new Party cards, with the Party losing a total of 473,731 members, 28 per cent of its membership (on 1 January 1968).[29] Over 21,000 communists (in the words of M. Jakeš 'predominantly members holding important state offices, economic and other leading positions') lodged an appeal against their exclusion.[30] It was to no avail. Apart from a mere 100 cases all decisions were upheld. Amongst those purged away were as many as 260,000 communists who had entered the Party before 1948 – they could be called the most active pioneers of communism in Czechoslovakia – so that at one stroke the number of pre-February members in the CPCz was halved.[31]

Dismissal from the Party was often followed by loss of one's job or the other way around. Active non-Party members were not safe either. At schools, in firms and institutions, employees were forced to carefully fill in questionnaires in which they had to describe their behaviour during the events of 1968 and 1969. The norms of human decency and traditional human values were severely taxed by the passion to purge of the communist dogmaticians, the insecurity about what was going to happen and the free hand given to careerists showing no mercy to anyone or anything.

The staff of the mass media were dealt with in a particularly severe manner, which led to 1,500 dismissals at the Prague broadcasting station alone. A number of papers were closed, starting in May 1969 with *Reportér* and *Listy*.[32] Other journals or papers got partially or completely new editorial staff. At the Party organ *Rudé Právo* for instance, 45 of the 80 editors were dismissed, and in the country as a whole, some 2,000 journalists, or every second member of the Union of Czechoslovak Journalists, were turned out onto the streets.[33]

The universities, schools and scientific institutions offered a similar picture, while it should be noted that the purges in the Czech countries, headed by Prague, took place in a far more drastic fashion than in Slovakia. This was due to the Czech minister of Education and one of the leaders of *Levá Fronta*, Jaromír Hrbek, who conducted a veritable reign of terror. In the academic year 1969/1970 lecturers and professors at the universities were summoned not only to explain their own activities during the past period, but also to report the names of colleagues and students who had been engaged in activities in favour of the reforms and against normalization.

In the entire ČSSR 900 professors (out of about 3,500) were dismissed, including those who refused to fill in the forms. The Czechoslovak Academy of Sciences fared no better: 1,200 scholars were sent away, and five departments were closed.[34] In the Academy it is particularly the name of Dr Radovan Richta that had become notorious. This philosopher and sociologist belonged to the theoretical pioneers of the reforms in 1968 and participated in the drafting of the Action Programme. The slogan 'socialism with a human face' emanated from him.[35] Under Husák, Richta revealed himself as a ruthless inquisitor, who, in return for a high position in the normalized world of science, started a witch-hunt against his former colleagues and political friends.

The brand new minister of Cultural Affairs in the Czech countries, Miloslav Brůžek, and his colleague in Slovakia, Miroslav Válek, dealt with all Art Unions and Cultural Unions, and wreaked particular havoc among the writers, the most influential group of reformist intellectuals. Here again, it was true that the repression in the western part of the republic was more relentless, but the opposition was fiercer, too. The new cultural policy used the old principle from the 1950s: there was only place for purveyors of culture who approved and supported the political line of the Party unequivocally. The consequences were drastic. In the Czech countries a total of 25 literary and cultural journals were wound up, so that by May 1970, there was no literary journal left. At least 117 members of the Czech section of the Union of Writers – among whom the best and most famous authors in the country – lost the licence to have their work published due to the 1970 measures: this was a considerable figure, in view of the fact that this department numbered 299 writers.[36]

It is impossible to present a complete picture of the havoc caused by the cultural normalization policies in the fields of film, theatre, music, visual arts and literature, musea, etc. Data from the provinces are lacking, especially from districts where the purges did not erupt in full force until 1971 and the two following years. A few figures by way of illustration: at the 17 provincial theatres in Bohemia and Moravia 344 members of the artistic personnel were dismissed, which amounted to 40 per cent; in the 12 publishing houses more than 80 per cent of the editors and the executives disappeared; at 17 provincial museums 196 researchers (89 per cent) were sent away, as were 70 per cent of the graduate staff at the galleries.[37] 'It was a veritable cultural cemetery' - as Heinrich Böll described the situation in Czechoslovakia on accepting the Nobel prize for literature in 1972.

All these 'proponents of revisionist and rightwing opportunist forces' were not offered any suitable position. They were forced to accept almost any job, which usually meant either a badly-paid one, or heavy physical labour, with always the same result: a painful step down the social ladder.[38]

The total number of dismissals in Czechoslovakia - in the fields of politics, science, and culture, economically and socially - can only be estimated roughly, as the figures are far from common knowledge. We know, for instance, that 30 per cent of the full-time officials of the Czechoslovak Revolutionary Trade Union had to leave,[39] 40 per cent of the economic managers had to step down, as did 30 per cent of the commanding officers in the army and police forces.[40] It is also known that around 14,000 Party officials and other paid employees were dismissed from the Party ranks.[41]

Estimates are also hampered by the fact that many tens of thousands of employees had first 'voluntarily' resigned from their jobs and left Czechoslovakia after the intervention, and were then officially dismissed. From August 1968 to the end of 1970 the number of Czechoslovak emigrants came to about 130,000 to 140,000.[42] All in all, including the emigrants there were somewhere between 250,000 and 300,000 direct victims of the dismissals. As it concerned the most active and most capable people, the consequences for Czechoslovakia were simply disastrous. The almost complete stagnation and even regression of social life in the 1970s and early 1980s are for an important part due to the purges. The inflexible policies of Husák's Party leadership and apathy under the population did the rest. Even the greatest pessimists and sceptics among the reformists had not foreseen in April 1969 that events would take such a turn.

Chapter Seven

CZECHOSLOVAKIA IN THE LATE BREZHNEV ERA

> I remember the first half of the 1970s in Czechoslovakia as a time when 'history stopped'. Public matters seemed to lose their structure, thrust, direction, tension, rhythm, and mystery; I do not know what happened sooner and what happened later, how one year differed from another, what was in fact going on; and it seems to me that on the whole all this makes no difference. As unpredictability has petered out so has the feeling that things make sense.
>
> History has been replaced by pseudohistory, with its calendar of regularly returning official anniversaries, party congresses, festivities and mass sport meetings. [. . .]
>
> Totalitarian power has brought 'order' in the organic 'disorder' of history, thereby numbing it as history. The government, as it were, nationalized time. Hence, time meets with the sad fate of so many other nationalized things: it has begun to wither away.
>
> Václav Havel (1987)

THE CZECHOSLOVAK DUUMVIRATE

In December 1970 the plenum of the Central Committee of the CPCz issued a document which Moscow had long been waiting for. It was called *The Lesson Drawn from the Crisis Development in the Party and Society after the XIIIth Congress of the CPCz*, and was praised by L. Brezhnev as an 'in-depth Marxist-Leninist analysis' of the events in Czechoslovakia since 1966. The distribution of *The Lesson* with a print-run of several millions took place both inside and outside Czechoslovakia.[1] *The Lesson* adopted the Soviet version of the developments in 1968 down to the smallest details, called the Action Programme 'revisionist' and the situation in the country 'counter-revolutionary', while Dubček, Černík, Smrkovský and others were accused of committing treason, and Svoboda, Husák and Bilak (in this order) were praised for their attitude during the days of August.

The document included a passage about the Czechoslovak appeal for assistance, which in accordance with the original Soviet statement of 21 August ran as follows:

> Thousands of Communists, individual citizens and entire collectives of working people, representatives of all strata of the population and various organizations, including members of the Central Committee of the Communist Party of Czechoslovakia and the Central Committee of the Communist Party of Slovakia, as well as members of the Government of the ČSSR and deputies of the National Assembly and of the Slovak National Council, aware of their class, national and international responsibility for the fate of socialism in Czechoslovakia, were persistently seeking a way out of the difficult, critical situation. In view of the fact that the rightist part of the Party leadership did not want to adopt any measures which would have led to thwarting the counter-revolutionary coup and to averting civil war, they began to turn to the leadership of the fraternal Parties and to the governments of our allies with the request that at this historically important moment they should grant international assistance to the Czechoslovak people in the defence of socialism. They did so in the deep conviction that their class brethren would not leave Czechoslovakia at the mercy of counter-revolution which threatened bloodshed, and that they would prevent our country from being torn out of the socialist community.

The matter of the request for assistance initially caused great problems for Gustáv Husák and the surviving 'realists'. In December 1970, in the normalized Central Committee where people 'faithful to Marxist-Leninist and proletarian internationalism' had been co-opted into the vacant positions, the dogmatists began to stir. Encouraged by the course of the purges but dissatisfied with the fact that these did not, according to their standards, go far enough, Bilak, Indra and other hard line advocates considered the time ripe for a move against Husák. After all, in their eyes Husák, Colotka and Štrougal did not belong to the 'sound core' of the Party, but to a group of clever opportunists who were not really entitled to their high functions. Bilak and his sympathizers wanted to use the request for assistance to undermine the position of the Party chief and, at a later stage, push him out.

They circulated a copy of a letter from August 1968 among members of the CC of the CPCz, in which some forty politicians asked for international assistance. In actual fact, it was an 'adapted reconstruction' of a document that had never existed in such a form.[2] The list included among others the names of Bilak, Indra, Kapek, Hoffmann, Auersperg and Bohuslav Chňoupek, then ambassador in Moscow (and from 1971 minister of Foreign Affairs), but not those of Husák, Svoboda or Štrougal.[3]

In the discussion Bilak and others demanded the publication of the appeal and of the names of the signatories, so that 'everybody would know who had been concerned for the rescue of socialism in the most difficult time'.[4] Husák, in his turn, felt he could not permit another round of divisions of the normalizers into loyal and less loyal sons of the Party. He succeeded in getting the majority of the Central Committee on his side and in hushing up the letter affair, but not without the indispensable support of the Kremlin.[5] For that matter, it was not the first time that Husák, feeling threatened, appealed to Moscow. In September of that same year he had dealt with the conspiring ring leaders of the *Levá Fronta,* among whom had been minister Hrbek. They were removed from their posts and put into more modest positions, thus ending the existence of *Levá Fronta* as an independent organization.

In view of the dependence of the Husák group on Moscow (which was true of the entire Czechoslovak Party leadership) these measures could never have been taken without the approval of the Soviet Union. But now that the progressive wing of the CPCz had been liquidated, *Levá Fronta* was no longer important to the Soviets. Moreover, even the Kremlin politicians balked at their out-and-out Stalinist opinions. In short, *Levá Fronta* – the Czech version of the Gang of Four and its sympathizers – was no alternative for eastern Europe in the Brezhnev era. On the other hand, the spectre of the 1968 Czechoslovak reforms haunted both

Prague and Moscow. For this reason the Soviet leadership played it safe regarding the recently normalized ally: 'Brezhnev's choice was a duumvirate after all, with honours and eulogies going to Husák and the duty to sharpen his policies to Bilak'.[6]

It can also be put differently. Husák had proved to be very useful to Moscow, but a 100 per cent guarantee that Czechoslovakia would from now on follow the same course as the Soviet Union of Leonid Brezhnev was provided by the person of Vasil Bilak. This led to the strange situation that in no other country in the eastern bloc of the 1970s and 1980s was the position of the second man so unassailable, and his influence on politics so palpable over such a long period as in normalized Czechoslovakia. It would therefore be more correct to speak of the 'Husák-Bilak' period.

The start of this period can be considered to be the XIVth Party Congress, held at the end of May 1971 in Prague, with Brezhnev and the highest representatives of the four other intervening countries, Gierek (Poland), Honecker (GDR), Kádár (Hungary), and Zhivkov (Bulgaria) as guests of honour. The 1,183 delegates naturally gave their approval to the (by then concluded) purges and accepted *The Lesson* as an 'obligatory guideline for the work of the entire Party'.[7] A remarkable detail was that none of the 1,219 delegates who had been present at the Vysočany Congress in August 1968 were present at this Congress, and that of the 144 members of the Central Committee chosen in Vysočany only 10 members could be found back among the 115 members of the CC of the CPCz in 1971.[8]

Leonid Brezhnev called this party meeting 'the Congress of victory over the enemies of socialism'.[9] In any case, it was a complete victory - albeit rather delayed - of Kremlin policies. But it also was a personal victory of Gustáv Husák, as he managed to maintain himself in the highest position. The eleven members of his Presidium consisted of two groups of normalizers; they were groups which had formed after the fall of Dubček and which balanced each other out. The one group included officials with a reformist background or politicians who had more or less adapted themselves to the reformist course during the Prague Spring. Their opinions were moderate compared to those of the Stalinist Presidium members Antonín Kapek and Karel Hoffmann. To the other, dogmatic group belonged politicians who, if the developments in Czechoslovakia had taken their course, would not have stood a chance. The 'internationalist aid' was their salvation.[10]

Although the individual members of the two groups differed in their political attitude in 1968, and also in their degree of dogmatism and political opportunism, there was a strong binding element which turned out to be of overriding importance, namely their activities during the normalization. Without exception, they eradicated the reforms and eliminated, both politically and socially, their carriers. And it was exactly on the grounds of these 'merits' that they seized a place in the Presidium, took other high positions . . . and managed to keep them for years on end.

To the Czechoslovaks it did not make much difference who belonged to what group in the leadership. Of course, they realized that Bilak as Party leader would be even worse than Husák, but that did not alter the fact that they regarded all members of the Party leadership in the first place as the same gravediggers of the freedoms of the Prague Spring and the same proponents of Soviet policies in their country.

According to the standards of August 1968, all these politicians sooner or later became plain collaborators. The people's greatest disappointment was probably president Ludvík Svoboda. With Dubček he had been the most celebrated hero of the Prague Spring, with Husák he was the highest representative of a normalized ČSSR, the 'Czechoslovak Socialist Soviet Republic', as it was popularly called.

THE ATTITUDE OF THE PEOPLE

Normalization and capitulation, coupled with resignation or collaboration; the communist rulers of 1968 landed the Czechs and Slovaks with this reality. The leaders of the Prague Spring were found wanting twice over. Politically, because they had been unable to save any of the reforms. This defeat was painful, but even more painful was the way in which they had lost. To a population who initially trusted them implicitly, they had also failed morally, by their mostly shameful behaviour.

There were only a few politicians who behaved with dignity and whose attitude could serve as an example to the people, for example leaders such as František Kriegel or Josef Smrkovský. A few prominent politicians left for the west so as to actively oppose the Prague regime from there. They included Ota Šik, Jiří Pelikán, Zdeněk Hejzlar, Eduard Goldstücker and Eugen Löbl. They and others showing brave political and personal commitment, could not, however, take away the negative impression ultimately left with the Czechoslovaks by the reformist leaders.

People felt manipulated and deceived, disappointed and disillusioned. 'Czech society has morally deteriorated to an extent unknown since its inception (that is, since the time of the national revival)', an author from Prague stated in 1978.[11] Older people compared the dreary atmosphere of the middle of the 1970s to that of the Czechoslovak rump state after the Munich conference and the subsequent Protektorat Böhmen und Mähren during the six months preceding the outbreak of the Second World War. But 'even then there was a ray of hope' one of Beneš's followers remembered thirty-five years later. 'President Beneš, and almost the complete political leadership of the First Republic were abroad, and we knew that all of them would continue to dedicate themselves to freedom and national sovereignty'.[12]

Enthusiasm, optimism and social involvement - so characteristic of the Prague Spring - gave way to passivity, political apathy and an unprecedented mental marasmus, rooted in the realization that the situation was completely hopeless. A massive withdrawal by the people into their private occupations followed.

The Husák regime encouraged the de-politicization of society in two ways. On the one hand by harsh repression of every opposition voice, numerous arrests and political trials.[13] These and other deterrent measures revived fears of a return of the Stalinist terror in the early 1970s, all the more so because the reign of terror of the 1950s was still fresh in people's minds due to the disclosures of the Prague Spring.

On the other hand, the leaders decided to greatly increase the standard of living. Such a policy had considerable advantages. It was an excellent way to prevent any possible unrest among the population, and to show the Czechoslovak citizen the results achieved under the recentralized economic system. In addition, the government badly needed a tangible success on the home front after a long series of unpopular measures. As a result, during the years 1970–8 private consumption rose by 36.5 per cent.[14] It was self-evident that official propaganda did not fail to sing the praises of the new Marxist-Leninist Party leadership because of this, and to picture the period after the XIVth Party Congress as 'one of the most successful chapters in the history of socialist progress'.[15]

The Husák-Bilak team's approach combined harsh political persecution with an improvement of material circumstances, in order to maintain calm and order in Czechoslovakia. An escape into private life, a negative attitude towards anything symbolizing the communist state and having double moral standards - one towards the outside world and one for one's inner circle[16] - became the answer for the great majority of the population. It was essentially the same attitude as in the years before 1968 and in the 1950s; the difference being that this time the Czechoslovaks were eager to make use of the possibilities which the poorly functioning east European consumer society had on offer. Durable consumer goods and important status symbols such as cars and weekend cottages, especially, were much coveted. If in 1969 there was one car for every 21 people, in 1971, 1975 and 1981 the number of people per car decreased to respectively 15, 10, and 7.[17] In the same period the number of weekend cottages in the Czech countries alone rose from 120,000 to 225,000 in 1981.[18]

The Czechoslovaks have adapted themselves to a system which they would never have chosen for themselves, but in which they were doomed to live. They have gained another negative experience in their history, and for this reason they are possibly even more cynical and suspicious than before. 'Central Europe is an extremely unpromising setting for national heroics' a prominent dissident from Bratislava wrote in the second half of the 1970s.[19] In any case, some may hope, while others may not even care, that the Czechoslovak people have always had a great sense of reality in times of political adversity.

THE PARTY AND ITS MEMBERS

First a CPCz with Antonín Novotný in charge, then with Alexander Dubček and finally with Gustáv Husák. An unwritten communist code of behaviour says that 'it is safer to be wrong *with* the Party than to be right *against* it'.[20]

The upheavals and changes in the CPCz which the Czechoslovak communist - provided he had remained a member - experienced within the period between the XIIIth and XIVth Party

Congresses (1966–71), were indeed enormous: the erosion of the old system; the transition from Novotný to Dubček; the internal democratization and free discussions during the Prague Spring; the military intervention which soon after turned out to be internationalist fraternal assistance, and the normalization policies with purges.

Four times in a row (if we consider Dubček's post-August policy of concessions to be something separate), the Party member was presented with different political courses said to be the only correct ones, and each time he was asked to actively support and promote the Party line. After all these metamorphoses it is small wonder that the Party had finally lost all its attraction for its members as an idealistic social organization (let alone as a source of inspiration for the advancement of socialism and communism). What remained was the great advantages offered by a Party membership. The attitude of the average members regarding the events in the Party became one of lack of interest and passivity, and in this the communists did not differ from their fellow citizens, the non-Party members.

According to a confidential report to the Party Presidium from the beginning of 1972, not a single Party activity had been undertaken by some 400,000 members (a third of all members at that time) in the preceding year, and some 4,000 branches (or about 10 per cent) had not even convened a general meeting for months on end,[21] despite the fact that they were obliged by statute to hold a meeting at least ten times a year. It was remarkable that this situation existed in a year in which Party activities were especially encouraged by the authorities, with a view to the Party Congress and the elections.

In particular, the basic Party branches at firms that were dominated by worker communists were conspicuous by their lack of activities and interest:

> The majority of the real working class members of the CPCz are 'dead souls'. They are good for embellishing the statistics [. . .] The workers' organizations are exceptionally passive. Members who do not pay any dues for months on end and only come to a meeting once in a blue moon, when they are sick of the eternal admonitions or want to get even with someone, or when they need a reference for their child's admission to a

> college, or need permission for a trip abroad, are not the exception, but rather the rule,

a well-informed source reported from Czechoslovakia in 1973.[22]

Both in the internal political life of the CPCz and in the functioning of society, the fact that the cadre members who had risen as a result of the purges were often unequal to their tasks, was beginning to show. In 1975 the percentage of leading officials without the required qualifications was estimated at 40 per cent. At the same time over 75 per cent of the expelled reformist communists did unskilled labour.[23] This situation was reminiscent of the 1950s when many capable and talented people (members of the defeated 'bourgeoisie') were also forced to do manual work, and their places were taken by communist officials who, although thought to be politically reliable, did not possess the necessary qualifications and abilities.

It is not surprising that under the given circumstance these new officials of the 1970s put their trust in the instruments of power with which the Party controlled society. These people did not much like changes, partly because of their incompetence or lack of interest, and partly because of the conviction that they were right, but also out of fear that any change would affect the stability of the system and with it their recently acquired positions. Therefore, they welcomed the fact that order had been restored in the Party after all the stormy and uncertain years, not in the least because of the prospect of security and stability in their lives.

Apart from the years 1969–71, the Party could not complain of any lack of interest in membership. In the period 1971–6 as many as 334,000 Czechoslovaks joined their ranks, and between 1976 and 1981 another 321,000.[24] At the XVth Party Congress in April 1976, Husák even created the possibility for expelled Party members 'who did not belong to the active supporters of rightwing opportunism' to rejoin the CPCz.[25] In practice it turned out, however, that the Party authorities' principal interest was to gain ex-communist workers in order to strengthen the CPCz's workers' ranks. But the response of this group was poor.

According to official figures the CPCz numbered 1,538,000 members and candidate members, or 10 per cent of the total population, at the time of the XVIth Congress in 1981.[26] 'One in seven of the adult citizens, one in five men, and one in fourteen women in Czechoslovakia carries a Party membership card', Alois Indra boasted of the numerical strength of the CPCz.[27] It is interesting to mention that over 40 per cent of these communists had become a member after 1971, i.e. after the normalization in the Party had been completed. Also remarkable is the high number of younger people. The age of more than 90 per cent of the newcomers was under 35, about half of them were even younger than 25.[28]

How can this interest in Party membership be reconciled with the passivity and dislike of political commitment displayed by the average communist? The answer should be sought in the power monopoly of the CPCz in every sector of society. In the beginning of the 1980s some 550,000 of the higher offices and responsible positions were under direct Party control,[29] which meant that these posts could only be filled with the agreement of the Party. For most of these jobs Party membership was a prerequisite. In this way a favourable career development was linked to CPCz membership.

Ambitious young people were sooner or later faced with the dilemma of having to choose to be a member of the CPCz or not. In addition, to the less capable of them, who in normal circumstances would not have stood a chance of a responsible position, Party membership compensated for the lack of necessary qualifications.

This was nothing new. After all, this situation had existed in Czechoslovakia from the moment the communists seized power. Yet, an important shift in Party mentality as a whole could be perceived. The 'communist prophet' type, still prevalent within the CPCz in the 1960s (the enthusiastic Party member who had kept on believing in the communist ideals of his youth, and tried to change the existing system, which did not answer to his expectations), had disappeared from the Party. His place had been taken by a different kind of Party member: the 'communist profiteer' of the 1970s and 1980s. He joined the CPCz under completely different circumstances and with motives different from many of his predecessors who grew up before or during the war.

THE PARTY LEADER

At the top of the pyramid of power, Husák managed to strengthen his authority and keep the dogmatists at bay. Presidium member Alois Indra, for instance, had to give up his position as Party secretary as early as 1971, and was shifted to the representative but not very influential post of chairman of the National Assembly. In 1975 the Party leader also managed to succeed the 80-year-old, demented Ludvík Svoboda as head of state, while, of course, retaining his other posts. Husák has never become 'boss in his own country', however. The majority of the members in the Presidium and Party secretariat under his leadership were not politicians of his own choice, people he would have brought into these bodies himself, and who would therefore have been very dependent on him in person.

In this respect the start of János Kádár as Party leader at the time of Khrushchev had been a lot easier. With the knowledge and the help of Khrushchev the Hungarian managed to get a grip on the Party leadership relatively soon after 1956, by way of not only throwing the supporters of Imre Nagy, but also Stalinists such as Rákosi and Gerö, out of the Party. Consequently there was nothing in the way of his pragmatic 'middle course', at least for the time being, and five years after the suppression of the Revolution he was able to embark on the reformist course. In the 1980s, Wojciech Jaruzelski went about it in a similar way in Poland.

Contrary to Kádár or Jaruzelski, Husák has never battled with the dogmatic elements in the Party leadership. Nothing illustrates the relations in the CPCz under Husák better than the difference between the way in which the Prague Spring communists ended up, and what happened to the sympathizers of Novotný and other supporters of the old regime. The latter group had no need to fear for their future, after they had lost their high positions in 1968 and later. They were given compensation by means of lucrative jobs in the diplomatic service, foreign trade, and cultural organizations, and were honoured with important state decorations, state prizes, etc.

The old Antonín Novotný, leader of the CPCz at the time that Gustáv Husák had been sentenced to lifelong imprisonment, received his Party membership back, after his suspension in 1968; Vasil Bilak, once a fierce opponent of Husák's political rehabilitation, now became his closest colleague; Milan Hübl, once a personal friend of Husák, a reformist and someone who had tried his hardest to get him out of prison and back into public life, was given a six-and-a-half-year prison sentence under his regime.

One might wonder whether this course of events was Husák's intention. Probably not. It is true that he was an authoritarian leader for whom only power counted, and a politician without scruples, jointly responsible for the reprisals and abuses during normalization in Czechoslovakia. But it should not be forgotten that, after the completion of normalization, the Kremlin did not leave him much room for developing his own policies, starting with the elimination of supporters of the hard line in the Presidium and the Party secretariat. Not only was Husák, of all eastern European leaders, the most dependent on Leonid Brezhnev, he was also politically tied down to the Party dogmatists in his country - a development that spared both Kádár under Khrushchev, and Jaruzelski, in Leonid Brezhnev's latter days, as well as after his death in 1982

This does not lessen the degree to which Husák was responsible for the suffocating atmosphere in the 1970s and the beginning of the 1980s, and for everything that took place in Czechoslovakia then and later. But anyone searching for a sufficient explanation for the fact that it was in this country, of all places, that a 'spirit of immobilism' developed, 'rarely to be found anywhere else in contemporary Europe',[30] cannot avoid this point.

THE COUNTRY OF 'REAL SOCIALISM'

In the east European political jargon of the 1970s a new term came into fashion, the so-called 'real socialism' (Czech: *reálný socialismus*). It was said to be 'a socialism based on the scientific foundations of Marxism-Leninism in a number of countries where it has already become reality',[31] that is, in the Soviet Union and the other countries of the socialist community. According to the theoreticians of Marxism-Leninism of the late Brezhnev-era, 'really existing socialism' was the only true socialism 'in contrast to all other kinds of socialism propagated by bourgeois-ideologists, right-wing opportunists and revisionists', as the definition puts it.

The communist ideologists also pointed out that this concept referred to a concrete situation, namely 'the practice of the construction of the developed socialist society'.[32] They characterized this practice as follows:

> Despite the fact that is has to overcome certain problems and difficulties in its development, real socialism guarantees [. . .] a

> sustained growth of the standard of living of working people, social security, real government by the people, and flowering of culture. It is real socialism which protects peace and social progress all over the world.'[33]

The Czechoslovak chief ideologist Vasil Bilak once pithily summarized it thus: 'Real socialism is what we have got here!'[34]

Compared to some of the other eastern European countries Czechoslovakia was doing reasonably well in economic terms.[35] This did not take away the fact that the problems of the country were gigantic and, what is worse, without any prospect of solution. The unfavourable development of the Czechoslovak economy lead to an economic crisis in 1980 and 1981. The growth rate of national income decreased sharply and fell to -0.1 per cent and 0.2 per cent respectively.[36]

Not only the model of the command economy, which the economists of Dubček had been so keen to get rid of, was restored, with the result that, economically too, Czechoslovakia could be counted as one of the most dogmatic countries in eastern Europe, but also the economic structure, with its one-sided orientation on heavy industry - a legacy of the Stalinist concept of the 1950s, much criticized by the reformists - was not to be tampered with.

This structure was not suited to Czechoslovakia's own potential and needs. Nevertheless, the country, poor in raw materials, kept on producing steel, heavy machinery, equipment and other energy and raw material consuming capital goods, in accordance with the task of the ČSSR within the Comecon, and completely in line with the Soviet efforts towards integration within this organization. On top of that, Czechoslovak industry was severely outdated and in urgent need of high-quality modern western machinery. But there was not sufficient hard currency available for such investment, all the more so because the Husák regime did not much fancy the idea of applying for credit on the western money market.[37]

Apart from these two important internal factors - central planning and the imbalanced structure of the economy - external factors had a negative influence on the Czechoslovak economy. The price increases of raw materials, for instance, and especially those of crude oil on the international market, got the ČSSR into great difficulties. The Soviet Union, the main supplier of raw materials (93 to 98 per cent of crude oil came from that country), passed the price increases on to its trading partner and doubled the price of crude oil in 1975. The raw materials became considerably more expensive in relation to the finished products, which had enormous consequences for Czechoslovak foreign trade: the terms of trade deteriorated by some 20 per cent.[38] Czechoslovakia was no longer able to cover the more expensive import of raw materials with its export of machinery.

At the same time the demand for some traditional industrial export articles decreased, especially to the west. This was not solely due to the recession at that time. The low technical standard of the Czechoslovak manufacturers did not meet the high requirements of potential western users, service was inadequate, and the entire organization of foreign trade too complex and cumbersome. Between 1970 and 1980, the ČSSR, so strongly dependent on export, lost 33 per cent of its share of the market in the western countries. In the same period the Czechoslovak share in the world machinery and equipment trade decreased from 2.1 to 1.47 per cent.[39]

Apart from being one of the biggest producers of steel and the world's number one user of steel per head of population, Czechoslovakia also acquired the dubious honour of possessing one of the most energy-intensive economies in the world. Given the increasing energy demands of industry, the supply of fuels and energy posed an extremely difficult problem for the planners every year. They tried (and are still trying) to overcome the situation by an increased exploitation of brown coal supplies. Under the given circumstances, this source of energy with low calorific content is indispensable in Czechoslovakia, where approximately 85 per cent of the total quantity of electricity is generated by thermal power plants. By way of illustration: in 1975, 71.7 per cent of the electricity from thermal power plants was generated by brown coal, ten years later this figure was 78.3 per cent.[40] The increased extraction and burning of brown coal also made heavy demands on the environment. In addition, the authorities had seriously neglected environmental problems and treated them as taboo for years.

The vulnerability of Czechoslovakian power supplies was exposed in the severe winter of 1979. With brown coal production affected by the weather, and transport in disorder, the authorities could only solve the ensuing serious energy shortage by partially stopping industrial production – including the most vital sectors.

The standard of living, still one of the highest in eastern Europe, declined at the end of the 1970s and the beginning of the 1980s. Two big price increases for a number of food products, industrial products and fuels in 1977 and 1982 especially hit financially less well-off citizens, and families with many children. Corruption, abuse of power, black marketeering, theft of state property and other similar practices, which reached a record level for Czechoslovakia, sharpened the social differences even more. They also contributed to a hardening of human relations, something which strikes every visitor to this country straight away.

Whole systems of graft developed in almost every area of daily life. Corruption was and is most harrowing in health care, which is officially supposed to be free, and in public housing, in the retail trade and in some repair services.

According to usually reliable reports from Charter 77, socialist Czechoslovakia of the 1980s has some tens of thousands of millionaires, both communists and non-Party members. Ironically, this is significantly more than it had before the communist take-over.[41] The luxury and the unlimited opportunities of the 'new socialist plutocrats' in state service and the communist elite contrast sharply with the drab lives of the average worker who has to make do with about 2,800 crowns a month, with all those who are far below this level, or with the living conditions of 10 per cent of families, who have no home of their own.[42]

Yet, to a part of the nation, the economic perils, the chronic shortages of various industrial products and foods, the poor functioning of services, or other daily inconveniences were not felt to be the greatest shortcoming. However strange it may sound, people had grown used to such things, in many respects they were better off now, and again, according to eastern European standards, they had nothing to complain about. The citizen also learned to live with ideological propaganda, and to treat it as if it hardly existed.[43]

This was not the case with the cultural and intellectual climate in the country. The repressive attitude of the Party and the pervasive censorship of cultural activities knew no bounds. In this respect the Czechs and Slovaks were given a very raw deal indeed, especially when compared with the relatively great intellectual freedom enjoyed in Poland or Hungary. Morever, the difference compared with their own 'golden Sixties' was alarmingly great. In intellectual circles, and to anyone for whom a glaring shortage of good contemporary literature, films, drama, visual arts or music weighed more heavily than a shortage of tropical fruit, beef, car parts or toiletries, this curtailment was found to be both very painful and frustrating.

Cultural historians will have to take stock of the damage done to the Czech and Slovak national cultural heritage. It is certain that the ČSSR, a country with a flourishing cultural life in the 1960s, became the mirror image of the Soviet Union of Leonid Brezhnev in the following decade.

Chapter Eight

OPPOSITION UNDER THE RULE OF GUSTÁV HUSÁK

> If anybody had told me twenty years ago that Jan Patočka and Jiří Hájek would be united in a common, basically political battle, that the - forgive me - fanatical communist Zdeněk Mlynář would openly defend and fight for underground music, that Václav Havel and Mrs Gertruda Sekaninová-Čakrtová would go together to the Ministry of Justice to protest against abuses, I would immediately have advised him to visit a psychiatrist.
>
> Pavel Tigrid (1978)

UNDER THE SPELL OF THE PRAGUE SPRING AND AUGUST

In itself, the presence of once influential ex-communists amongst present-day east European dissidents is no strange phenomenon. We find them both in Hungary and Poland and to a lesser degree in the Soviet Union. Yet Pavel Tigrid, a Czech who fled to the west after 1948, highlights in the above quotation something that is unique to Czechoslovakia. In no other country within the Soviet sphere of influence does the opposition number so many expelled Party members with, among them, so many formerly prominent communists. What is more, nowhere but in Czechoslovakia do we find such close co-operation between ex-communists and other activists.

This co-operation did not come about all at once. It has a history called the 'Prague Spring'. This short-lived Czechoslovak process of liberalization, with its almost unlimited freedom of speech, brought the reformist communists and the active non-

Party members together in a dialogue which resulted in better understanding of each other's point of view. Personal meetings on various occasions also helped.[1] This did not mean that the political ideas of the two groupings came any closer together. After all, the communist partners belonged to the power elite of the country, and ultimately determined the state of affairs.

During the Prague Spring the Party leadership under Alexander Dubček did not like the idea of actually sharing political power with those who thought otherwise. It is true it tolerated the activities of some new organizations such as the KAN (Club of Committed Non-Party People) and the K-231 (Club of Former Political Prisoners), but on the other hand it resolutely turned against the attempts to re-found the Czechoslovak Social Democratic Party. In other words: when the power, resulting from the monopoly position of the Party, was at issue, Dubček remained in the first place a faithful promoter of the Communist Party's traditional leading role in society. In April 1968 this leading role was emphasized once again in the Action Programme of the CPCz. It goes without saying that the opinions of the reformist communists and the others differed on the concrete interpretation of the term 'democracy' in the 'democratic socialism' proclaimed during the Prague Spring.

The question whether this unyielding communist attitude was, by tradition, inherent to the CPCz leadership's way of thinking in terms of power politics, or whether it was a temporary emergency measure dictated by the increasing pressure from socialist fellow countries, will be left aside. I am strongly inclined to believe the first explanation, but the developments of August 1968 have made it difficult to answer this question.

The military intervention by the Soviet Union and the other four Warsaw Pact countries came as such a shock to Czechoslovak society that it forgot all about political differences of opinion. It was followed by spontaneous non-violent resistance with which almost the complete Czechoslovak population identified, if it did not take part. For the first time in the post-war history of the country the difference between the communists and the non-Party members, this contrast which had always felt as *them* and *us*, had now gone. Many Czechs and Slovaks experienced the unity – brought about by solidarity and the realization of having the moral right on their side – as something permanent. The joint resistance and the immense faith in the leaders of the Prague Spring only served to strengthen these feelings. In the eyes of many they were the main guarantees that the reforms would be continued without abatement, despite the presence of tanks and occupying forces: *ubi concordia, ibi victoria.*

Just one example serves to illustrate the atmosphere in those first days after the intervention. A special edition of *Literárni Listy* of 22 August 1968 published an 'Appeal to all citizens', which included the following passage:

> We appeal to you all! Do not accept this situation, do not lend it any semblance of normality and legality. This is our last chance to influence our common future. In our minds we are all free. [. . .] Be united - without paying attention to political belief, age and profession. Create a wall of united will, of human pride and dignity.[2]

As is well-known this wall did not last very long. After Dubček's replacement by Husák in April 1969, the reforms were demolished. A series of courageous protests by individuals and groups could not turn the tide.[3] Two large-scale protest actions at the beginning of the Husák period, both concerning the marking of the first anniversary of the Soviet invasion, should be mentioned. The first concerned an appeal signed by 'workers and students' which had circulated in numerous pamphlets in Czechoslovakia since June 1969. It contained guidelines on how the Czechs and Slovaks should behave on the 'day of disgrace' and was overwhelmingly followed by the population on the day in question.[4] The other protest was the so-called *Ten Points Manifesto,* a petition drawn up by ten prominent intellectuals and directed to the Czechoslovak parliament, government and other state and party organs. In ten points it strongly denounced Husák's normalization policy.[5]

THE ORGANIZED OPPOSITION IN THE YEARS 1969–72

Groups were formed which, in one way or another, protested against the authorities over a longer period of time. The most extraordinary of these was probably the so-called *Revoluční socialistická strana* (Revolutionary Socialist Party), a conspiratorial Marxist-Trotskyist organization. This name was really the pseudonym of the already existing *Hnutí revoluční mládeže,* the

HRM, (Movement of Revolutionary Youth), which had been founded on 2 December 1968 out of dissatisfaction with the policy of Party leader Dubček.

The HRM originally consisted of radical students, mostly children from communist families, with the workers forming only a small minority, but these proportions gradually changed. After barely a year the organization had a core of about a hundred members, half of whom were workers. With a few exceptions they were young, no older than 30. They were organized in a number of independently operating cells with a maximum of ten activists.[6]

The 'revolutionary programme' of the HRM was naive, and dubious in many respects, as could only be expected of a Marxist-Trotskyist initiative in those days. Moreover, the programme was clearly inspired by the radical left wing groups in the west.[7] HRM members had particularly close contact with like-minded groups of *neuen Linken* ('new leftists') in the Federal Republic of Germany.

It was child's play for the security service to infiltrate a 'real' revolutionary worker in the HRM. This happened at a very early stage. A metal worker from Kladno founded his own cell and afterwards another two. He managed to gain the confidence of the younger people, not in the least because of the genuine callouses on his hands, his proven organizational skill and his radical tone.[8] He was co-opted in the co-ordination group of the organization, and that was the end. In December 1969 the secret police struck and arrested twenty leaders of this 'Trotskyist conspiracy with international branches'. Well over a year later the leaders were brought before the courts and found guilty.[9]

The same happened to the *Socialistické Hnutí československých občanů* (The Socialist Movement of Czechoslovak citizens), an opposition group of mainly reformist ex-communists. This group, which included amongst others the former members of the Central Committee of the CPCz, Milan Hübl and Jaroslav Šabata, as well as the historian Jan Tesař and the student leader Jiří Müller, was first heard of in its foundation declaration, the so-called *Manifesto of 28 October 1970*.

The date, the anniversary of the foundation of the First Czechoslovak Republic in 1918, had not, of course, been chosen by accident, but had a symbolic meaning. In the declaration the initiators rejected the 'bureaucratic dictatorship' of Husák and pledged themselves to 'a political struggle for a socialist, democratic, independent and free Czechoslovakia'.[10] Unlike the HRM, which hoped for a revolution, they aimed exclusively for the restoration of the values of the Prague Spring.

The group's approach to the Czechoslovak reality was rather inconsistent. On the one hand the founders recognized that the situation in the country was precarious, and that Czechoslovakia was 'more than ever before' in the midst of 'a political, economic, intellectual and moral crisis'.[11] On the other hand they excelled in optimism about the way in which this situation could be overcome. They seemed to think they were still in the heyday of the Prague Spring. One only needs to read their *Short Action Programme* from the beginning of 1971 to discover how they overestimated their capabilities and how wrongly they assessed the then situation in what they themselves called 'realistic political considerations'.

The founders of the Socialist Movement assumed that the communists within the socialist opposition would outnumber the others, and at the same time be the most homogeneous group. They put their hopes in the mass of hundreds of thousands of reformist Party members whom Husák had expelled. In their opinion the purges in fact meant a split of the CPCz into two antagonistic parties: the official, normalized party of Husák and Bilak and the 'party of the excluded'. They now considered it their task to form a 'new, political vanguard of socialism' out of the latter, consisting of some tens of thousands of ex-Party functionaries who had strongly engaged themselves during the Prague Spring.

This vanguard was to lead the hundreds of thousands of people, for, in the eyes of the founders, this was a broad opposition movement. In order to achieve this it was first of all necessary to mobilize a new set of leaders. The authors of the *Short Action Programme* spoke in this relation of an 'elite', or an 'avant-garde of the avant-garde'.[12] From an international viewpoint, they hoped that the Socialist Movement would be supported and recognized as an official 'left wing' opposition by the left in western Europe and especially by the west European communist parties.

The first and also last big action undertaken by the Socialist Movement, was their appeal to boycott the general elections of November 1971. They campaigned under the slogan 'January, not

August', and had some success in the big cities. There was no question of a mass boycott by the Czechoslovak voters, however, not even by the hundreds of thousands of expelled communists. The secret police, who had been keeping a close eye on the leaders of the movement, struck after the elections. More than 200 people – not all members of the Socialist Movement, but also many other more or less well-known opponents – were run in and arrested. In the summer of 1972 several dozens of them were sentenced to (frequently long) terms of imprisonment.[13]

Although the activities of the Socialist Movement should not be trivialized, it has to be pointed out that its supposed roots in society were not very deep, and that its influence and importance in Czechoslovakia were far more modest than some left-wing sympathizers from the array of Czechoslovak émigrés would have liked us to believe at that time. Jiří Pelikán, for instance, spoke of the 'historic battle of the Czechoslovak socialist opposition' which justified the hope of 'the entire Czechoslovak people' for a 'real, fair and free socialist society'. Even after the trials he was certain that 'the Czechoslovak people and the socialist opposition would continue their fierce struggle', because 'the socialist opposition was broad-based, and had become too solidly rooted to be destroyed by a police action'.[14]

The reality was different. The protagonists of the Czechoslovak socialist opposition in the west should have known – and perhaps they knew – that this movement did not have, nor could it have, a mass character. In fact it only involved a small group of brave people, of 'generals without divisions'. For at the time there was no longer a bond between the reformist communists and (to use Pelikán's words) the Czechoslovak people. The experience with Dubček's policies after August 1968 had been too negative for that.

Should the Czechs and Slovaks as late as 1972 have risked their future and have fought for a castle in the air that was called 'socialism with a human face'? Should they have tied their fate once again to the communist leaders, who had abandoned them at the crucial moment? Should they have trusted reformist politicans, some of whom openly collaborated with Husák, some of whom had fled abroad, others who behaved like frightened hares, and most of whom remained silent, whereas few had the grit to bear the terrible ordeal at home? Or should they have opposed Husák's policy, while they were confronted every day with the attitude of numerous expelled local party functionaries, an attitude which was not remarkable for its courage?[15] And should they under such circumstances have fought a 'fierce struggle' for socialism? That was obviously asking too much.

Nothing happened. There was not even any protest worth speaking of when the trials took place. Husák's normalization policy did not fail to have an effect, which caused V. V. Kusín to remark the following:

> The effect of normalization [...] was so strong that it held people back from direct pursuit of something that had increasingly begun to be felt as a lost cause. [...] The population continued to retreat into private preoccupations and political passivity.[16]

THE EX-COMMUNISTS AND THE NON-COMMUNISTS

There followed some years of relative quiet round the opposition: 'the period of general atomization and disintegration' as Havel called it.[17] The opposition seemed to have resigned after the blows inflicted by the regime. There were no more spectacular plans and programmes. The years 1972–5 were years of mainly individual actions and individual protests. It came mostly from members of the 'overthrown dynasty', usually ex-communist reformers from 1968, who tried in open letters to bring the dismal situation in which they and others found themselves, to the notice of the authorities, and to point out violations of human rights to them.[18]

The ex-communists also presented themselves together to the outside world. For instance, they sent a message of congratulation to the Spanish communist Dolores Ibarruri, the legendary La Pasionaria from the Spanish Civil War, on the occasion of her 80th birthday in 1975. The letter they sent to her Russian home was signed by 75 people and contained hidden criticism of the Prague regime.[19]

It is not difficult to find an explanation for the fact that the initiative in those days was being taken by the ex-communists. By their forced descent down the social ladder they had been hit in their existence much more directly and painfully than the non-communists. For the first time since the communist revolution of 1948 the peculiar situation arose in Czechoslovakia whereby the communist regime was actually more tolerant of the non-communists than of those who still felt communists, but who meanwhile had become non-Party citizens. 'Non-Party' meant being powerless and without rights. The non-communists had long been used to this situation, but the ex-communists found it very hard to reconcile themselves to their new position of second-rank citizens.

In addition, the fact that they could count on a certain degree of solidarity from western left-wing (not only communist) parties, and especially on that of left-wing intellectuals, was of great importance to the ex-communist opposition. On top of that, some of the ex-communist reformers were well known in the west due to their social and political activities in 1968, which meant that a possible prosecution would not be without risks for the Prague regime.

The situation for the non-communist dissidents, both the democratic and religious, was far more difficult. Apart from a few exceptions (people like Václav Havel) they were then unknown abroad. They could not count on much support from the west. In those last years of the Vietnam War public opinion in the west was concerned about other things. Anyway, it did not serve very well as a sounding board for their protests. In this respect things only changed at the end of the 1970s and at the beginning of the 1980s.

Contacts, let alone co-operation, between the group of ex-communists and other dissidents were the exception rather than the rule in the years 1972–5. This could be blamed on both groupings. As regards the ex-reformists, it took some time for them to wake up to the facts, and realize that the situation of the Prague Spring and 1969 absolutely belonged to the past. This process of sobering up went slowly and with great difficulty and often hand in hand with the loss of the communist belief.[20] Actually, only in 1976, after the Conference of European Communist Parties in East Berlin, did the ex-reformist communists give away. They had placed all their hopes on this repeatedly postponed conference and finally had to accept that there was to be no political solution for Czechoslovakia in general and for their position in particular from the side of the international communist movement.[21]

The non-communist dissidents, too, initially found it difficult to try to make overtures to the opposition group of ex-communists. A certain 'exclusiveness' of the latter and their orientation towards the western communist parties instead of the opposition streams in their own country, necessarily caused distrust. Apart from that there was the unsavoury, fanatically Bolshevist past of some of the opposition reformist ex-communists which played a role. It took some time for the non-communists – in the past often the victims of the communist regime – to cross this threshold.

It can be stated that the dissidents from non-communist opposition circles adopted an attitude towards their future ex-communist partners that was both open and tolerant, if slightly cautious, but certainly not dismissive. They were, moreover, inclined towards co-operation sooner than the reformist ex-communists. Co-operation was only possible, however, after the ex-communists had given up their claim to 'the leading role in society' and had accepted the principles of equality and political pluralism as the starting points for activities in the opposition movement.

There was one opposition group where the Party past no longer played an important role as early as the beginning of the 1970s. It was the cultural opposition with the dissident writers in front: as a rule these were people who had been among the most famous Czechoslovak authors during the 1960s, and who under Husák had been hit by a ban on publication. In them, solidarity and a sense of national culture rapidly overcame any political convictions. The core of this group, which later signed the foundation document of Charter 77 *en masse,* included the ex-communists Pavel Kohout, Ivan Klíma, Jan Trefulka and Ludvík Vaculík; former members of the *Kruh nezávislých spisovatelů* (Circle of Independent Authors) founded in 1968, the non-communists Václav Havel (who also was the main link between the ex-communist and the non-communist authors), Alexander Kliment, Jan Vladislav, Josef Vohryzek, Ladislav Dvořák and Petr Kopta; furthermore the famous literary historian Václav Černý, the poet and famous artist Jiří Kolář, authors of the younger generation such as Josef Topol, Milan Uhde, Jiří Gruša, Petr Kabeš, Karol Sidon, and others.[22]

One of the most remarkable activities of the dissident writers was the publication of their own work as *samizdat* literature. The initiative for this was taken by Ludvík Vaculík by establishing *Edice Petlice* (Edition Padlock) in 1973. Václav Havel followed in 1975 with his *Edice Expedice* (Edition Expedition).

The Czechoslovak authors were also the first since the political trials in the summer of 1972 to concern themselves about the fate of the political prisoners in their country. In a petition of December 1972 addressed to the Czechoslovak president they asked for amnesty for them. This petition, signed by thirty-five people, was unique in the sense that it bore the signatures of both forbidden authors and a number of officially allowed writers, of Party members and non-Party members. The reaction of the authorities to this request was so furious that some signatories withdrew their names.[23]

Yet this Christmas appeal was put very mildly. A couple of years later an *Open letter from Václav Havel* was completely different in tone. In April 1975 he gave expression to the most powerful political protest for years:

> I will take the liberty to state that despite all apparently positive outward appearances our society not only is not consolidated, but on the contrary is going through a deepening crisis which in some respects is more dangerous than all crises we have known in our modern history.[24]

With these words he addressed Gustáv Husák personally. In his long letter Havel not only provided a sharp analysis of the then situation, but he also warned the Party leader of the catastrophic and long-term consequences of his policy, and reminded him and the other representatives of the regime of their personal responsibility towards history. The letter was a perfectly stylized essay and a model of the use of the Czech language by a man of letters. For this reason alone it rose high above the stereotyped Party jargon used in the speeches of the communist leaders, and daily fed into the papers and other mass media.

The letter had the effect of a successful chain letter. Its text was copied by innumerable people and spread through the whole of Czechoslovakia. By now it has become an important historical document, an incomparable testimony of the moral responsibility of a Czech writer-intellectual to the state of affairs in society. A writer, moreover, who showed the mighty secretary-general of the CPCz that he was his superior in a moral respect by confronting him with the plain truth.

In addition to the writers, there was another group which found its way to an 'ideological ecumenism' in the early 1970s. The Husák regime itself created this group: the political prisoners.

After their release many of them kept in touch. In the summer of 1974 twenty-eight ex-prisoners published the so-called *Letter of Czechoslavak Political Prisoners.* The immediate cause was a sympathy action organized by the Prague regime on behalf of the political prisoners in Chile under General Pinochet.

The Czechoslovak ex-prisoners felt that the publication in the national press of a protest resolution against violations of human rights in this South American country was the last straw. It so happened that the resolution originated from the official 'Association of Czechoslovak Lawyers' and those who submitted it demanded access to the trial against the Chilean communist leader Luis Corvalán and his comrades in order to give them legal assistance.[25]

The political prisoners reproached the lawyers of the Husák regime for their hypocrisy, and pointed out to them what had happened at the trials in the summer of 1972. They asked the editor of the Party paper *Rudé Právo,* albeit without success, to publish this letter, which they concluded as follows:

> We are convinced that the just struggle of our Chilean comrades, friends and brothers against fascism and terror, a struggle for democracy, freedom and socialism will triumph. We would like them to know that they have many true supporters in Czechoslovakia.
> Signed: Political prisoners detained in Czechoslovakia during the years 1969–1974.[26]

THE ROAD TO CHARTER

During 1976 an important shift in the attitude and actions of the Czechoslovak opposition took place. The various dissident circles – sometimes inward-looking, as in the case of the Roman Catholics, for instance – made contact with each other and became aware of each other's presence. The same was true of a number of more or less prominent dissident *Einzelgänger,* people who did not feel connected to any one opposition group. Co-operation and a feeling of solidarity developed, something which no-one in these circles would have deemed possible one or two years earlier.

The immediate cause was an action by the authorities, which on the face of it was hardly alarming. In March 1976 twenty-two young people, musicians and sympathizers of the rock groups

Plastic People of the Universe and *DG 307* were arrested. Most of them belonged to the Czech musical underground and led a withdrawn life in a few (weekend) communities in the country. In these *komunity* they organized their life according to their own ideas and ideals.[27] Some striking personalities in this headstrong environment at that time were the singer of self-composed spirituals, the Protestant clergyman (obviously without official permission) Svatopluk Karásek, the forest worker and singer Karel (Charlie) Soukup and the art theoretician, Roman Catholic and leader of the Plastics, Ivan Jirous, alias Magor, the intellectual instigator of the underground.

Jirous was also the person who introduced the term 'second culture' in Czechoslovakia, in reference to non-official activities in the field of music. Later he gave the term a more general meaning. In his essay of 1975 'The Message about the Third Czech Musical Renaissance' he wrote:

> The aim of our underground is to create a second culture. A culture, which will be independent of the official channels of communication, and independent of the official systems of social values and hierarchies, which are controlled by the establishment.[28]

The concept of a second culture soon took hold among the dissidents and was used to indicate non-official utterances in the fields of art and literature, humanities, and in publishing.

In March 1976 hardly anybody had heard of Jirous and his followers. This included the dissident circles. The long hair of the pop-musicians, their behaviour, their lingo and the wild rumours that circulated, whether or not spread or stirred up by the secret police, did not help. Everything pointed to the fact that when confronted by authority these young people would not stand a chance, especially as the authorities pictured them as a bunch of drug users, alcoholics and ordinary criminals. For this reason they had especially severe punishments hanging over their heads.

The first steps towards action in aid of the non-conformist musicians were taken by Václav Havel, who knew Jirous personally and respected his work, and Jiří Němec, a Roman Catholic psychologist who had close contact with the underground. They set themselves the task of stripping the whole affair of its front of criminality and to mobilize as many voices as possible to support the pop musicians. Havel later explained why he had made such a strong stance for the underground. He thought the confrontation between the regime and the young underground people essentially more serious and more dangerous than the political trials of the early 1970s:

> The long sentences of the political prisoners then were an act of political revenge. The regime regarded them - and not unjustly - as opposition. It realized that they had not given up their resistance, and for this reason it got even with them, as with people who had been beaten, but who refused to behave in that way.[29]

According to Havel the situation now was completely different:

> It no longer was a question of settling accounts with political opponents, people who to a certain degree take the risks into account. It had absolutely nothing to do with a struggle between two alternative political sections. It was worse: it was an attack by the totalitarian system on life itself, on the essential human freedom, on integrity. The objects of their attack were not the veterans of the former political arena. They were not people with a political past, they were not even people with pronounced political views. It concerned people who wanted to live according to their own views, who wanted to play the music they loved, who wanted to sing what they liked, [...] who wanted to speak the truth.[30]

The Plastics could not have wished for a better advocate than Havel. His arguments caught on. Apparently the fact that Havel and the others did not see this matter as a political, but as a general human and moral affair played an important role. In wide dissident circles many became convinced that they should not remain silent in this specific case. The solidarity with the young prisoners awaiting their trial was therefore surprisingly high.

The impression that the affair with the pop-musicians made on some Czechoslovak citizens and how this influenced their decision to leave anonymity behind and become actively involved, is shown clearly in the following statement by the Roman Catholic Václav Benda, one of the later spokesmen of Charter 77.

> Maybe I have been too patient on the borderline of the acceptable. Silently I took note of the fact that with one stroke of the

> pen practically [. . .] the complete literary world was eliminated. Consequently I devoted myself to philosophy. Silently I took note of the fact that membership of the Communist Party is a necessary condition for the practising of the profession of philosopher. Consequently I retrained to be a mathematician. Silently I took note of the fact that as a believer I cannot become an editor in the field of mathematics nor work as a scientist or acquire a science degree [. . .] and I devoted myself diligently to programming. My conscience was only shaken awake by the perfidy of a totalitarian power which, despite the fact that it can do absolutely anything, did not direct its hatred of culture towards the renowned and respected bearers of this culture. It chose as victims a small peace-loving group of defenceless young musicans.[31]

The protests started with a *Letter by Jaroslav Seifert* and a few other prominent Czech intellectuals to Heinrich Böll with the request to speak up internationally for the young people who, because they were unknown, 'were in danger of being convicted as criminals without the world of culture noticing anything'.[32] A *Declaration of Solidarity with the Persecuted Young Musicians by 70 Czechoslovak Citizens* followed. Those who take a closer look at the names under this declaration can see how wide the range of dissidents had become by then. On the list we naturally find the names of members and sympathizers of the underground, most of them workers, but also of a number of former political prisoners, some ex-communists, members of the group of Petr Uhl, intellectuals and artists.[33] A series of declarations of sympathy was the result.

Even before the main trial at the end of September 1976 in Prague, the Plastics got support from an unexpected quarter; Zdeněk Mlynář, one of the most authoritative reformist leaders during the Prague Spring, wrote an unprecedented strong protest, which he sent to, among others, the government, the parliament and the Central Committee of the Party. Mlynář, originally a lawyer, accused the government and highest authorities of abuse of the criminal law and demanded an immediate stop to the prosecution. In addition, the circles of the reformist communists (both 'at home' and in exile) in particular took care that the case of the Plastics got plenty of attention in the international left-wing press, especially in the Italian communist press. It is difficult to decide which harmed the Husák regime more, the international criticism or the blunt and direct rebuttals in the mass media at home.[34]

The internal resistance and the unwelcome publicity abroad did not fail to have an effect on the proceedings against Jirous and his followers. In the end only four musicians were tried (apart from three organizers of pop concerts who had been convicted earlier in a trial in Pilsen), and given relatively light sentences.[35] That was not the end of the matter, however. The sentences were publicly challenged in a letter addressed to the Czechoslovak president, the prime minister, the chairman of the Czechoslovak parliament and the judicial authorities, written by ten prominent Czechoslovak lawyers. They were all former Party members who had held important positions under Alexander Dubček.[36]

In this atmosphere of joint effort towards a common goal, in which new friendships grew straight through old barriers, various groups of dissidents came to the conclusion that ad hoc actions, however broadly based were not sufficient. People realized that it would be worth the effort to strive for a more permanent co-operation.

Meanwhile, the same ambition was also noticeable in other east bloc countries. Poland saw the foundation of the KOR (Committee for the Defence of the Workers) after the industrial unrest in June 1976, whereas the Soviet Union had had its first Helsinki group, founded in Moscow, since May of that year. The Helsinki group made it their aim to inform the governments which had taken part in the Helsinki Conference on Security and Co-operation in Europe about the Soviet Union's violations of human rights listed in the final act. In November of that year the Ukraine Helsinki group was set up in Kiev. Other groups were to follow.

On 10 December 1976 a historic meeting took place in a private house in Prague, which was attended by, amongst others, Václav Havel, Jiří Němec, Pavel Kohout and Zdeněk Mlynář. After this two other meetings were convened, at which, besides the above-mentioned people, Petr Uhl, Jiří Hájek and Ludvík Vaculík were present.[37] The *Citizens' Initiative Charter 77* was born. The declaration of foundation bore the date 1 January 1977. The main author of the text was Václav Havel, assisted by Zdeněk Mlynář and Pavel Kohout, who had thought of the name Charter 77.[38]

By mutual agreement it was decided to appoint three spokesmen who had a lot of authority and who, in addition, were known to be able to propagate the complete range of ideas of the movement. They were Professor Jan Patočka, a well-known 70-year-old philosopher and humanist, the author Václav Havel and finally one of the protagonists of the Prague Spring, the ex-communist Professor Jiří Hájek. Neither they nor any of the others could then have expected Charter 77 to be granted the longest life of all human rights movements in eastern Europe.

The final question that remains is how the ex-communists found their way to Charter. They represented over half of the first 240 signatories, whereas nowadays they form almost a third of the *c.* 1,200 Charter members. These people have undergone a truly Copernican turn-about. After their experiences since the suppression of the Prague Spring they have come to the conclusion that defending human rights and pleading for civil liberties was the only conceivable means of political action against the communist system, and also the only practical one - against the same communist system, by the way, that they themselves had introduced in Czechoslovakia after the Second World War.

Now almost thirty years later, trodden on, humiliated and made destitute by this self-same system, they returned to the traditional democratic values, or more exactly, they discovered those values, which the others, the non-communists, had fought for before 1948, then with little chance of success. This must have been a strange experience, not only for the earlier mentioned Pavel Tigrid, but for many other Czechoslovak *émigré* democrats from 1948, and of course for all those who stayed in their country. Whether they really rejoice in the radically changed attitude of a few hundred ex-communists, remains to be seen. One's own memories are difficult to erase. And why should they be erased?

CHARTER 77: UNITY AND DIVERSITY

In its declaration of foundation[39] Charter 77 describes itself as: 'a free, informal, open community of people of different convictions, different faiths and different professions, united by the will to strive, individually and collectively, for the respect of civil and human rights'. The same manifesto also clearly states what Charter was not:

> Charter 77 is not an organisation; it has no rules, permanent bodies or formal membership. It embraces everyone who agrees with its ideas, participates in its work, and supports it. It does not form the basis for any political opposition of any kind. Like many similar citizen initiatives in various countries, west and east, it seeks to act in the interest of the general public. It does not aim, then, to set out its own programmes of political or social reforms or changes.

Finally regarding its objectives:

> within its own sphere of activity it wishes to conduct a constructive dialogue with the political and state authorities, particularly by drawing attention to various individual cases where human and civil rights are violated, by preparing documents and suggesting solutions, by submitting other proposals of a more general character aimed at reinforcing such rights and their guarantees, and by acting as a mediator in various conflict situations which may lead to injustice and so forth.

From the beginning Charter presented itself as a movement that emphasized moral principles and an ethical approach to social problems. Against the docile survival of the citizen in the communist society they set the higher ethical postulate of 'living in truth'. Instead of uncritically remaining silent and watching they advocated the principle of 'resisting the lie', within legal limits. It was Professor Patočka who set Charter 77 on this course. His ideas proved to be a strong inspiration for Charter and were set out in two essays: 'What Charter is and what it is not' and 'What can we expect of Charter 77?' Others, amongst whom were Václav Havel in his treatise 'The Power of the Powerless' followed the way shown by Patočka, this 'pure, clean man'.[40]

Throughout the years Charter has stood by its moral principles. They have become the main binding element wherever cracks threatened to appear in the movement, either because of disputes about the strategy to be followed, because of a difference of opinion about the organizational form, because of differences of opinion about its ideological nature or because of other matters.

There were plenty of fierce polemics within Charter, certainly regarding the practical side of its activities, as the founders (Havel,

Hájek and the others) initially had no idea how Charter would function in reality.[41] Quite often these polemics were aimed at a particular person. Jan Tesař, for instance, attacked the then Charter spokesman Jiří Hájek in an open letter (February 1978). Two views on the activities of Charter 77 collided with one another: Tesař's radical view and Hájek's pragmatic one.

The historian Tesař, who had served a long prison sentence and had completely broken with his communist past, went so far as to suspect Hájek and other ex-communist leading figures of attempting to seek a reconciliation with the authorities in return for high positions in party and state.[42] This insinuation was painful for Hájek and obviously undeserved, and Tesař was brought into line by others (Hejdánek, Mlynář, Luboš Kohout, Uhl).

Peter Uhl and the ex-communist Milan Hübl had fundamental differences of opinion, again, amongst other things, about organizational matters. Moreover, Uhl was annoyed by the, in his eyes, not very co-operative attitude and the pedantic tone of some of his fellow-chartists from the ranks of the ex-communists. He was not alone in finding it hard to swallow that some ex-communists regarded Charter as the brainchild of the Prague Spring. Zdeněk Mlynář, too, pointed out that everything was not alright in the circle of ex-communist Charter members. Mlynář attributed the insensitivity, the thinking in stereotypes, and the clichéd actions of the former comrades to the fact that 'they had all their lives only been active in their own communist environment'.[43]

Possibly even more excitement was caused by the two critical articles 'Remarks on Courage' by Ludvík Vaculík and 'On the Shoulders of Some' by Petr Pithart, both written at the end of 1978.[44] A deluge of critical contributions and retorts from various chartists, from people surrounding Charter and also from the Czechoslovak opposition in exile followed. The tenor of the criticism remained the same throughout the years: warnings against the danger of isolation and against the forming of a 'Charta-ghetto', consisting of a host of heroic, introverted activists, beyond reach of the ordinary citizen.

In hindsight, this criticism, however sharp, turned out to be quite useful. It kept the discussion going within Charter about its position and its role in society, forced Charter and its members not to lose sight of reality, and, last but not least, functioned as a remedy against any kind of mythologization round Charter 77, both internally but especially externally, that is, towards society and the west.

In this respect an extremely unorthodox way of demythologizing Charter should be mentioned, namely a remarkable book by Ludvík Vaculík, a very colourful figure in Czechoslovak cultural life. It was his diary in novel form *The Czech Book of Dreams*,[45] originally published in the *samizdat* edition Padlock.

In it, Vaculík describes a year in the life of the Chartist milieu in Prague, as he himself had experienced it. Not a world of heroes and heroines, but of ordinary people with their own ordinary daily worries and conversations, with their relationships, weak moments and strong sides, their problems with totalitarian power, their broken marriages, bitten nails and extra-marital children. Vaculík immortalized the members of his own family, his friends and acquaintances, mentioning them by name, no doubt to their displeasure and dismay. He did not spare anyone, least of all himself. In this way he not only created a masterly novel (in my opinion one of the greatest in post-war Czechoslovak literature), but also an interesting and rare period document.

It was not only discussions about the organizational form or the activities that have regularly occupied Charter 77 in its whole existence. There were also exchanges of ideas about subjects of a completely different nature. One of the most tempestuous discussions, both within the circles of Charter 77 and outside it, including the Czechoslovak opposition in the west, concerned a historical subject. It was a strongly emotionally loaded subject: the transfer of the Sudeten Germans from Czechoslovakia to Germany after the Second World War.

It all started in 1978 with the essay 'Theses about the expulsion of the Czechoslovak Germans' which appeared in the exile journal *Svědectví* under the pen name Danubius.[46] Later the well-known Slovak historian and signatory of Charter 77 Jan Mlynárik was found to hide behind this pen name. Mlynárik aroused a lot of hostility but also support (and not only from the German side) with his damning criticism of the way in which the Czechoslovak authorities had treated the Sudeten Germans. The attitude and actions of the political parties and the population regarding this matter were not spared in his criticism either. The discussion lasted until 1986 and to all appearances the last word about this subject has not yet been written.

Mlynárik wrote the much-discussed article as an individual, but there were other Charter documents, signed by spokesmen and therefore official, which gave cause to friction. For instance, two analyses from the end of 1978, namely the *Safety of Nuclear Power Stations in Czechoslovakia* and *The Status of Gypsies-Romanies in Czechoslovakia*.[47] Although they were meant as social subjects of debate, their contents were not seen as current and socially relevant problems and they were therefore not welcomed with open arms by everybody within the Charter movement. Anyhow, in retrospect, with the Chernobyl disaster of 1986 fresh in our minds, those who doubted the relevance of the first document proved to be wrong, for in that analysis the inadequate safety system was exposed, and undisclosed accidents revealed.

Admittedly, these and other documents by Charter 77 only found their way to society on a limited scale; a weakness often pointed out by critics, also within the Charter itself. Yet this was not so much caused by the nature of the articles in question, or by the degree of their relevance to the general public, but was due to the difficult circumstances in which Charter 77 operated and is still operating in Czechoslovakia.

At least one other Charter document should be mentioned here because of the great deal of controversy it caused in certain dissident circles. It is the analysis *The Right to History* of May 1985.[48] This time the commotion did not concern the question of relevance, but the contents of the document itself. *The Right to History* stood up for the right of Roman Catholic historiography, which did not go down very well with the ex-communist Marxist historians from the ranks of the Charter signatories, giving, as result, a lively discussion about the interpretation of Czech history.

It is not my intention, however, to present Charter 77 as a quarrelling debating club. This is not what Charter 77 has turned out to be. It is a lively organism where different opinions and ideas can be freely expressed. In the end what united the signatories of Charter 77 proved to be stronger than what separated them; first of all, their willingness to do their best for the realization of human rights in their country, and second, their acceptance of the most important rule of the game which puts moral standards above political beliefs.

Besides these two, there were other important factors that promoted unity. For example, Charter 77 had a pool of personalities at its disposal for the function of spokesmen; men and women who were not only greatly respected by the others, but who - and that was just as important - also displayed a great measure of tolerance, mutual trust and solidarity. And the less prominent signatories should not be forgotten either, chartists like Petr Uhl, who kept the spirit of the Charter up and put in a lot of work year after year.

Finally, the Husák regime itself - completely contrary to its intentions - paved the way to unity.

THE REACTION OF THE REGIME

On 6 January 1977 Charter 77 first stepped into the limelight and first clashed with the authorities. This confrontation gave a taste of the way in which the Czechoslovak authorities were to treat the new movement.

On the morning of the same day, a few cars of the Czechoslovak secret service forced a car to stop in the middle of the Prague traffic. The occupants (the intellectuals Havel, Vaculík and the actor Pavel Landovský) were on their way to the post office to send off the foundation declaration of Charter 77 to the Czechoslovak government, the parliament, the Czechoslovak press agency and all signatories. Instead of the post office, they ended up at the police station, where they were interrogated for the rest of the day and night. During the interrogations they were photographed and filmed by television cameras with the stack of letters as if they were a group of dangerous terrorists. Arrests of some other signatories, hour-long interrogations and house searches followed. Some days later the foundation declaration appeared in the western media.

The Czechoslovak authorities started a smear campaign against Charter 77, the form of which reminded the older people straight away of the hysteria of the early 1950s. Only demands of the death penalty or long prison sentences from the 'indignant working classes' were missing. This campaign of slander started with the by now infamous editorial in *Rudé Právo* called 'The Has-beens and the Self-chosen'.[49] Day after day, for two months running, Charter 77 was sharply attacked in the mass media, which did not fail to include especially coarse personal allegations about some prominent chartists.

The articles, radio and TV programmes of that time speak for themselves. They were an example of journalism of the lowest kind. But that was not the worst. The authors of these articles, journalists who were faithful supporters of the regime, had no scruples in their attacks and were guilty of violation of the most elementary standards of journalistic ethics and human behaviour. If there were ever to be a judgement upon the personal responsibility for the outrages of the Husák regime, it will be these Czechoslovak Goebbels figures in particular, alongside the leading politicians and the corrupt judges, who, alongside the members of the security forces and the ruthless administrators, will have to account for their activities.[50]

Just as in the 1950s, hundreds of mass meetings were organized in factories, offices, ministries, cultural institutions and at schools. Without having read the text of Charter, the participants in these meetings were supposed to declare themselves openly against Charter in letters, statements and resolutions and to call its signatories traitors.

A precarious climax to the campaign was a pledge of loyalty to the regime under the heading 'For New Creative Deeds in the Name of Socialism and Peace'. This document was given to thousands of intellectuals to sign, usually in person by their superiors, behind closed doors at their place of work. Besides some general, insignificant passages it contained one paragraph in which Charter 77 was sharply condemned, although the movement was not called by name.[51] It was very difficult to refuse to sign this 'Anti-Charter', as the document was soon popularly called. A refusal to sign was regarded as support for Charter and was therefore equal to existential suicide.

Great pressure was exerted on people to sign the Anti-Charter by bosses who in their turn were held personally responsible for the success of the signature action in their work area, and who resorted as often as not to blackmail, with corresponding results. No fewer than 7,500 writers, artists, academics and other intellectuals from both the capital and the provinces signed the statement, whether voluntarily or not. Their names were published daily in long columns in *Rudé Právo*.

Only a few people were brave enough to refuse to sign the Anti-Charter. For some the smear campaign against Charter was even a reason to join it. In this way the number of signatories of Charter increased to over 750 in the first half year.[52]

After initial uncertainty about the effect of Charter on society the authorities could rest easy. The tried and tested method of intimidating people had worked. Potential supporters of Charter had been scared off, 7,500 intellectuals - including friends and acquaintances of the chartists - had been humiliated and discouraged, and Charter as a whole had been banished to the periphery of society. Moreover, it had been manoeuvred into an isolated position by the authorities, who had bared their teeth, with the help of the 7,500 signatures of those who had let themselves be intimidated at the decisive moment. From then onwards matters were as of old under control again. From summer 1977 the regime returned to its well tested tactics and pretended to ignore Charter, as if it no longer existed.

Yet this campaign also had a drawback for the authorities. It resulted in the name Charter becoming known and turning into a household word in the furthest corners of Czechoslovakia. The sympathies of the population unanimously went out to this maligned, persecuted and defenceless small group of people.

The chartists were never left alone. The first arrests took place as early as January 1977. Very early on, for instance, the journalist Jiří Lederer had been run in, and after ten months of being remanded in custody was sentenced to three years in prison for 'undermining the republic'. This was Lederer's third prison sentence within ten years. A lot of commotion and a wave of protests in the west were caused by the stage-managed trial against some signatories of Charter who were also the founders of VONS, the 'Committee for the Defence of the Unjustly Persecuted', founded from the ranks of Charter in April 1978.

In this Kafka-like trial, held in Prague in October 1979, Petr Uhl was sentenced to 5 years in prison, Václav Havel to 4½ years, the then spokesman of Charter, the Roman Catholic Václav Benda and the journalist-ex-communist Jiří Dienstbier to 4 and 3 years respectively, and the journalist Otta Bednářová to a 3 year sentence. Only the child psychologist Dana Němcová was given a suspended sentence of 2 years.[53]

The years 1979–81 were difficult ones for Charter. The number of signatories, for example, that ended up in prison in 1979 and 1980 was significantly higher than that in the first two years of the Charter's existence. Between 1977 and the summer of 1980 a total of 61 chartists were sentenced to imprisonment. At least 108 other signatories of the document were run in for a shorter or longer period of time.[54] In addition there were innumerable other harassments and persecutions, affecting not only the signatories but also their close family including their children, friends and acquaintances.

The range of intimidations seemed well nigh inexhaustible: disconnecting the telephone, confiscating driving licences, bugging, constant watching, dismissal from (often unskilled) jobs, were among the least form of suffering that could befall the Charter signatories. There were also stacks of threatening letters, anonymous threats of child abduction, frequent house searches, forced moves and even a macabre delivery of a coffin. A harrassment often used by the security forces was to pick up somebody in the evening – preferably in winter – who had been to visit a chartist friend, for instance, and to drop him or her dozens of miles outside the town in a deserted area or deep in the forest, without any money and often without sufficient clothing. And worse things than that happened. Several chartists, both men and women, were attacked by 'unidentified persons' on the street or even in their own homes and severly beaten up; others were put in psychiatric clinics.

Charter 77, however, managed to withstand this pressure, as well as all later actions by the authorities against it. It could even be said that this joint experience of persecutions, arrests, prison sentences and so on, had a salutary influence on the Charter. A strong, mutual feeling of solidarity grew up in the chartists, which welded together a close group of both ex-communists and non-communists, believers and atheists, underground youth and former policital heavyweights. This was very noticeable at least in Prague, which had seen the formation of the active core of the Charter movement.

The Czechoslovak authorities became very nervous indeed during the activities of the Polish trade union *Solidarity* in 1980–1, especially in the second year, although mass trials as in the earlier days did not take place. Several chartists were taken into custody, however, amongst them the journalist Jiří Ruml, the Slovak historian Jan Mlynárik and the essayist Milan Šimečka, especially well-known for his brilliant treatise 'Restoration of order, a contribution to the typology of real socialism'.[55] They all spent over a year in prison under suspicion of 'subversive activities'.

In the same year, 1981, the sociologist Rudolf Battěk received a

7½ years' prison sentence, which was later changed to 'only' 5½ years' imprisonment. Of the many other cases, the trial against the worker Jiří Gruntorád should be mentioned. In July 1981 he was sentenced to 4 years' imprisonment along with an additional 3 years of so-called *ochranný dohled* (protective surveillance), for spreading unofficial literature and music. It was the first time this measure, which strongly restricted the freedom of movement of a person was used in a 'political case'. Since then the authorities have repeatedly imposed *ochranný dohled* on dissidents.

The psychological pressure on signatories of Charter 77 to leave the country was also increased. The possibility to emigrate in itself was not a new phenomenon. Ever since the summer of 1977 the Husák regime allowed chartists to leave for the west. The purpose behind this was obvious. They wanted to weaken the movement and at the same time rid themselves of troublesome critics. The most active chartists were often given a choice which did not leave them any alternatives: either prison or packing a suitcase.

The secret police carried out more and more brutal actions during house searches and interrogations of Charter signatories. They have even been known to knock at the door at night presenting themselves as 'a pressure group in favour of emigration', before raiding the house of the dissident in question.[56] On these occasions, but also during interrogations at the security forces Prague headquarters in the notorious Bartolomějská Street, chartists (especially the less well-known among them) were often mistreated.

Between 1977 and 1987 the total number of chartists obliged to leave the country, or - what also happened - thrown out of the country, was about 300. It was a wide range of people and personalities, of different convictions and backgrounds, as wide as Charter 77 itself. Some stayed in Vienna, close to home, others ended up in Paris or London, others in Rotterdam, Zürich or Bonn. These emigrants included, for instance, the ex-Party secretary Zdeněk Mlynář as well as the former member of HRM Jaroslav Suk, the ex-communist writer Pavel Kohout, the non-communist authors Jan Vladislav and Jiří Gruša, the historians Jan Tesař and Jan Mlynárik, the folk singer Jaroslav Hutka, the prominent ex-communist journalists Karel Kyncl and Jiří Lederer and their non-communist colleague, publicist Vladimír Škutina (all three of them with long prison sentences behind them). And then there were the striking personalities from the Czech underground, Svatopluk Karásek and Charlie Soukup and the ex-spokeswoman of Charter 77, Zdena Tomínová.

Without any doubt the enforced departure of these and all other chartists was a heavy drain on the activities of Charter 77 at home. But what has been mentioned before applies here again: this measure hardly brought the regime any advantage. The emigration left the Charter stronger rather than weaker. The chartists now kept on working from the west for the cause of human rights in their homeland and for Charter 77, with the result that, internationally, this human rights movement attracted even more attention.

By their willingness to co-operate with different movements, their tolerance, and particularly their great dedication, the expelled chartists played, and still play, an important role in the circles of Czechoslovak political emigrants. To a great extent decency and respect for each other's different opinions had always been observed among Czech political emigrants, but there was no more to it than that.

With the arrival of the chartists and other dissidents the Czechoslovak political emigrants as a whole have gained a lot. Not only have the ties with the opposition at home been strengthened, but, just as important, the various political opinions and the different waves of emigrants have proved to be able to work together to a degree unknown to emigrant communities from other east European countries. It goes without saying, that this is a constant source of worry for the Prague regime.

From the middle of the 1980s onwards, the Czechoslovak security forces seem to have partly shifted their attention from Charter 77 to other groups, such as religious activists and the non-conformist youth. There is only sporadic mention by the VONS of methods of direct terror against the chartists as occurred in the early 1980s. The telephones of a few chartists were even re-connected and the sentries in front of the house of Jiří Hájek were removed in March 1987 (on the eve of the address of Husák to the Central Committee, in which he pronounced himself in favour of Gorbachev's plans for reform).

However, we cannot yet speak of an essential change in the attitude of the Czech authorities towards the dissidents. The case of the Protestant theologian Jan Dus, which received a lot of international publicity in the years 1986 and 1987, is only one case out of many that is proof of this. In May 1986 Dus ended up in prison, charged with committing subversive activities.

> with the intention of hampering the functioning of the state organizations of the Republic more difficult and discrediting them. He committed these activities on a large scale and during a long time, in collaboration with representatives of the illegal organizations Charter 77 and VONS, and with foreign agents.[57]

In reality the only crime of the Old Testament scholar was to have consistently pointed out for years the unlawful practices of the state security forces and to have demanded the identification of those involved. Arbitrary rule in Czechoslovakia continued. At the most we can say that the authorities have put on softer gloves.

THE SIGNIFICANCE OF CHARTER 77

In the first ten years of its existence Charter published more than 350 letters, communiqués, analyses, declarations and other documents about the most widely divergent subjects. During the same time VONS published 600 reports about unlawful practices and sentences of Czechoslovak citizens.[58] It is the great merit of Charter that, despite reprisals from the side of the authorities, it continued to speak out openly against political arbitrariness, against specific cases of unjustice and more generally against the shortcomings and excesses of the communist system in Czechoslovakia.

This expression of criticism was done on the basis of a series of special analyses, prepared by experts from within Charter 77 but also by outside specialists. In this manner interesting documents were prepared covering economic problems, ecology, education, religion, health care, problems of the younger generation and other subjects. The Czechoslovak citizens were usually informed about these subjects via radio broadcasts from the west, for them the safest way of gathering information.

It can even be said that in a country like Czechoslovakia, where public opinion polls cannot be held, Charter 77 became the voice of public opinion to a certain extent. It said and says openly what the Czechoslovak citizen would say, if he or she could speak freely. Furthermore, Charter 77 has succeeded in doing what other opposition movements in Czechoslovakia before 1977 never managed to achieve: it has become part of the Czechoslovak political scene, however modest that part may be. It has also stimulated the waning interest for Czechoslovakian problems in the west like nobody else.

Typical of the spirit of Charter, and also unique in Czechoslovakian relations is the exemplary way in which it achieved equality for women within its ranks. This is especially true of the difficult function of the Charter spokesperson which was carried out by 10 women and 19 men in the first decade of Charter's existence.

Another achievement of Charter is its contribution to the formation of so-called parallel structures in Czechoslovakia. These are structures which are independent of (or parallel to) the official structures. Theoretically they can function in various areas: from culture, education and information, to trade unions, religion and foreign relations. What parallel structures have in common is that they are all outside the power system. They could be said to ignore it.

Especially in Charter's early years, particularly under the influence of events in Poland, hopes regarding the formation and the functioning of the parallel structures within Charter were running high. Some even thought it possible to realize a complete *parallel polis*; a term introduced by Václav Benda in 1978.[59] However, it was not as simple a matter as was initially expected. Yet, the parallel structure functioned and is still functioning very well in Czechoslovakia in at least one field: culture.

Even before the arrival of Charter 77 there had been a reasonably varied 'second' culture. But the stimulating influence and support from Charter proved to be of immense importance to the further development of literature, music, visual arts, drama and some disciplines of humanities, such as history, philosophy and sociology. It is mainly due to Charter 77 that Czechoslovakia is no longer 'a perfect cultural cemetery' (Heinrich Böll) or a 'Biafra of the spirit' (Louis Aragon). There is a lot to be said for the proposition that the dissident activities in Czechoslovakia - in contrast to, for instance, Poland - are of a predominantly cultural nature,[60] and bear a clearly intellectual stamp, Charter 77 being an overwhelmingly intellectual movement.

It is therefore highly doubtful whether the reproaches directed at Charter, of not having succeeded in winning over the working masses like *Solidarność* has in Poland, are justified. The Czech tradition of resistance against political repression, in which Charter 77 fits entirely, is different from the Polish tradition. The historical circumstances which determined the developments in each country in the past, are different too. The same is true of the 1980s. The material situation of the Czech workers, for instance, is a lot better than that of their colleagues in Poland.

A Czech left-wing intellectual was right when, at the height of the power of *Solidarność*, he pointed out that compared to the Polish workers, the workers in Czechoslovakia had quite a lot to lose, giving as an example:

> While the most coveted article for the Polish Christmas was a bar of Christmas butter, the top hit of our Christmas was a folding bike. Nobody has yet proved that the working class will revolt because of a shortage of folding bikes.[61]

Especially the Czech working class, one would like to add. An important reason for the reluctance of the Czechoslovak workers to join the dissident movement must be sought in their relative material prosperity. Another reason was the repressive measures of the regime, for the price of opposition activities is high. Yet this does not sufficiently explain why the ideas - or better the ideals - of Charter 77 did not catch on, and why the number of signatories has remained so low. From 1977 until the end of 1980 about 1100 people signed the Charter statement. It is striking that the greatest increase occurred in the period in which Charter was fiercely persecuted. Afterwards the number of signatories did not grow. At the beginning of 1988, Charter had about 1,300 signatories.

No doubt this was partly due to Charter itself, not in the least because it opted for 'living in truth', which provided the chartists - rightly or wrongly - with the moral superiority of a small minority and even the aura of martyrdom, although there were also people who rather regarded them as Don Quixotes.

In this way the emphasis on the ethical aspect not only proved to be Charter's strongest, but at the same time its weakest spot. For Charter appealed to the moral conscience of the individual and to his or her personal responsibility to society. It did not have a message that the masses, only interested in tangible results, had been waiting for. The example of free behaviour within an unfree and immoral system did not get a following. In the Czechoslovak situation, with the mechanisms of suppression of the regime going at full speed, this example had a deterrent, rather than a stimulating effect.

All this does not alter the fact that the historic significance of Charter 77 in Czechoslovakia has been great. Some people - including myself - see the foundation of Charter as the most spectacular and hopeful event in Czechoslovakia since the Prague Spring. And its importance will become more and more apparent the further we move away from the 1970s and the 1980s.

Chapter Nine

FROM HUSÁK TO JAKEŠ

> Black flags were blowing. I cannot say whether I saw grieving people. There were Poles working in our factory. When they heard the news, they were besides themselves with joy and shouted at the top of their voices at every passer-by: 'Brezhnev kaput, Brezhnev kaput!', and their joy was sincere [...] And so I got the feeling that everywhere outside the black flags of joy were blowing. One of my friends said it thus: 'I do not know why, but to me life looks different. There is movement again. Who knows, it might be getting worse, or it might be getting better, but something is going to happen, and that is good.'
>
> O. K. (November 1982)

> If Mikhail Gorbachev had put forward only one of his present ideas about the need for reforms and democratization in Czechoslovakia in 1970, he would have been expelled from the CPCz and now be working as a stoker or day labourer, despite his communist convictions and university education.
>
> Zdeněk Mlynář (April 1987)

GUARDIAN OF BLOC DISCIPLINE

In 1982, the year in which Leonid Brezhnev died, Husák's Party leadership had been in power in an unchanged composition for twelve years. During this period only the sick Ludvík Svoboda had retired. Another vacancy in the Presidium was filled five years later, in 1981, by Miloš Jakeš, a dogmatic Czech politician who used to hold the positions of Party secretary and candidate-member of the Presidium. This course of affairs shows how cautiously Husák and his followers dealt with the staffing of the highest Party body, for the sake of maintaining political stability and continuity of power.

There was no sign of any differences of opinion in the Prague leadership, and relations with the Kremlin were excellent, there being complete agreement between Prague and Moscow on all issues. Several Czechoslovak leaders also had good relations with the members of Brezhnev's old guard (dating from the period of normalization or even from 1968), and some kept up personal contacts with Brezhnev.

The secretary-general of the CPSU, this 'great friend of the Czechoslovak people, twice hero of the ČSSR, champion of the cause of socialism, communism and peace in the world, and extraordinary member of the international communist and labour movement'[1] also greatly valued the friendship and unconditional loyalty of the Prague comrades, judging by the fact that, amongst other things, he personally attended all Party congresses in this country. Brezhnev, never short of vanity, thought of the solution of the Czechoslovak crisis as one of his great political successes. He considered - not without reason - post-1968 Czechoslovakia as his own creation and liked to be reminded of this service.

Although the arrival of Yuriy Andropov in the Kremlin and his more pragmatic course did not pose a serious threat to the Husák leadership, it did cause an increasing nervousness in the highest Party circles. For a short while the power holding elite was faced with the spectre of a second Khrushchev. The fifteen months of Andropov, however, were of too short a duration to leave any clear traces in the Soviet Union, let alone in Czechoslovakia. The Prague comrades did not find it very difficult to conform to the Andropov line. Copying Andropov, for instance, they started an anti-corruption campaign in February 1983, making sure that the few cases brought to light did not pose any threat to the power elite itself,[2] and for the rest they awaited developments in the Soviet Union.

After the election of the 72 year-old Konstantin Chernenko as secretary-general of the CPSU - who succeeded Andropov after his death in February 1984 - matters seemed to have resumed their old course. Chernenko, whose opinions and policies agreed entirely with those of the late Brezhnev, was the Prague dogmatists' ideal figure, especially when compared to his predecessor Andropov.

They had nothing to fear from him, as he was *the* guarantee of the continuity of the Brezhnev policies both in the Soviet Union and in the eastern bloc. Regarding the latter, the Czechoslovak comrades were always eager to help their kindred spirits in Moscow. In close co-operation with the Soviet Union, Czechoslovakia played the role of guardian of bloc discipline within the Warsaw Pact organization. The international department of the CC of the CPCz formed an important link with chief ideologist Vasil Bilak pulling the wires, mainly directed at Hungary.

For years this country had been considered a loyal ally of the Soviet Union in the field of foreign policy. As a result of closer economical ties with the west and the advancing process of liberalization a shift of emphasis took place in the 1980s. Hungary became a member of the International Monetary Fund (1982) and a warm advocate of continuing east-west dialogue and *détente*, and of an active role in this for the small European countries, such as Hungary itself.

This pioneering role was not appreciated by the Prague dogmatists. They saw in such attempts the danger of destabilization of the entire eastern bloc and, closer to home, they feared the undesirable influences from their neighbour on the large Hungarian minority within their own borders.[3] In a remarkable article in *Rudé Právo* of 30 March 1984 two of Bilak's ideologists lashed out at Hungary.[4] As is normal with such actions, they did not name the country and the politicians in question.

Besides the usual attacks against 'imperialist reaction' which had not yet given up its 'plans for a worldwide counter-revolution', the class conscious critics also warned against any weakening of the common international strategy of the Warsaw Pact by wrongful behaviour by the member states themselves. The authors condemned those who strove for 'one-sided advantages of the capitalist world and its financial and other institutions' and thus 'harmed the prestige of socialism in the eyes of world opinion'. Only 'a joint action by all socialist countries' could in their opinion strengthen the position of each separate country and 'conquer the imperialist policies of boycott and blockade'. The article was full of strong expressions such as 'nationalism', 'egoism', 'particularism', 'separatism', 'opportunism' and 'disorientation'.

The Hungarians talked back to Prague. A controversy arose,

with the GDR – because of its special relationship with the federal republic – also feeling involved, and siding with Hungary, while, as was to be expected, the Soviet Union took sides with Czechoslovakia. The difference of opinions about what did and did not serve national interests, and what attitude the individual socialist countries should adopt towards the west, became obvious to everybody.[5]

There was more going on in Czechoslovakia internally, however, than the orthodox foreign policy made apparent. Even under Andropov the first signs of a divergence of opinions within the Czechoslovak Party leadership manifested itself, when prime minister Štrougal openly pleaded for changes in the bogged-down economy.[6] His ideas went a lot further than the 'Set of Measures of Perfecting the Economic Planning and Management System' in use at that time and still entirely conceived along Brezhnevian lines in 1980.

THE XVIIth PARTY CONGRESS

Konstantin Chernenko had barely been in power for thirteen months in the Soviet Union when he died at the beginning of 1985. No doubt the Czechoslovak leadership was aware of the complications in the new round of the battle of succession in the Kremlin, and knew the ideas of the two most serious pretenders to the throne, Grigori Romanov and Mikhail Gorbachev. It takes little imagination to work out which Soviet politician was preferred by most of them: not the latter. Little could they then suspect, however, (nor could the Czechoslovak people) what was in store for them under Gorbachev. Events were to prove the leader of the 'pragmatists', Lubomír Štrougal, right, who predicted in an address barely a month after Gorbachev's election 'a review of some of our present views and concepts' which would be 'so far-reaching that we ourselves do not quite know how deeply it will all go'.[7]

A clean-up of Brezhnev supporters in the Party leadership, the government of the Soviet Union, and in the various Soviet republics, confirmed that Gorbachev seriously meant to end the period of stagnation, 'the policy of one funeral after another' as Mlynář had described the Soviet policy.[8] The Prague dogmatists were taken by surprise. They were losing their powerful political friends in the Soviet leadership and now had to watch how Gorbachev's new men showed a keen interest in the Hungarian reforms, praised János Kádár's policies, without giving any thought to the Czechoslovak Marxist-Leninist ideological purity.

Gorbachev's radical reversal of policy had irrevocable consequences for the ties between the Kremlin and Prague. Whereas under Brezhnev the interests of the Czechoslovak strong men ran parallel with those of the Soviet Union, and what was approved in Moscow, was automatically approved in Prague, this changed as soon as Gorbachev's team began to carry out reforms and to make *perestroika* (reconstruction) and *glasnost* (openness) the cornerstones of the new course. The unconditional loyalty towards the Kremlin policies disappeared and was replaced by the weighing up of their own interests with the maintenance of their own positions of power as highest priority.

Gustáv Husák's Party Presidium initially reacted in a rather reserved way to the fresh political air from Moscow. There were no indications to be found in the members' speeches (except in Štrougal's), that the CPCz intended to follow Gorbachev's course. The Czechoslovak 'normalizers' bided their time. In February 1986, a month before the beginning of the XVIIth Party Congress, Husák assured the rank and file: 'We closely follow the measures taken in the Soviet Union and other socialist countries, and look for solutions most suitable to our own circumstances and needs'.[9]

As was to be expected, the Czechoslovak Party leadership was able to meet its 'own needs' at the XVIIth Congress (24–8 March 1986), as none of the comrades had to leave the Presidium and the secretariat of the CPCz. Compared to the remarkably fresh notes struck at the XXVIIth Congress of the CPSU just concluded in Moscow, the Prague Party event mainly distinguished itself by its lassitude and its caution. So far everything stayed the way it was. On the other hand, it could be felt that Gorbachev's policies did not leave the leading cadre members of the CPCz unaffected. They could not allow themselves to simply ignore the developments in the First country of communism, however much they would have liked to. Their solidarity with, and commitment to, Moscow were too great for that. After all, the Czechoslovakia of Husák was not the Romania of Ceaușescu.

Without any doubt Lubomír Štrougal's address at the Congress with its main theme of the need for a different economic policy, was a boost for all those who – sometimes openly but mostly veiled – were exposing the shortcomings of the Czechoslovak communist system and exploring concrete possibilities for change. Although Štrougal did not as yet use the word 'economic reforms', there was no mistaking his intentions. Explicitly referring to the 'experiences in the fraternal countries, and particularly in the Soviet Union', the prime minister pleaded for decentralizing measures in the economic leadership in favour of 'socialist entrepreneurship', and actually for more autonomy for individual businesses regarding investment policies, production, and, not least, price and wage control.[10]

The other 'critical' representatives at the Congress did not go as far. On the whole they restricted themselves to lamenting the abuses in their immediate environment, with only one or two people daring to utter, even for a short moment, more fundamental criticism.[11] The main address by Party leader Husák was also notable, certainly when compared to his addresses held at the three previous 'Brezhnevian' congresses. This time it contained remarkably few ideological references and statements.[12] Such a 'de-ideologization' could definitely not be coincidence; it could be a first indication that Husák was re-orientating his opinions by keeping a certain distance from the dogmatists in the Presidium.

POLARIZATION

After his visit to Moscow in November 1986, where he had had a personal interview with Gorbachev, and impressed by the course of affairs at the long delayed session of the CC of the CPSU at the end of January 1987, Husák realized that Gorbachev's position had become unassailable. The Soviet reform policies were gaining momentum and the sly Czechoslovak Party leader realized that his country could not avoid the influences from Moscow.

At the same time, the end of January, Lubomír Štrougal reintroduced the term 'reform' which had been banned ever since the normalization, and directly linked the Czechoslovak pursuit of reconstructing the economy with the changes in the Soviet Union under Gorbachev.[13] He did this at a meeting of leading economic officials, in which he threateningly rounded on those who were trying to thwart the reforms, and who thought they could continue in the old way 'because of their former achievements'.

Interesting in this respect was the final address by Miloš Jakeš at the same meeting. Jakeš, too, sided with those in favour of reforms but in a different way from Štrougal. His speech formed a striking example of the manner in which an orthodox communist, a 'hard-liner', tries to adjust to Gorbachev's policies. The tone was conservative, the wording too general and punctuated with hollow phrases, the criticism non-committal and therefore meaningless, and the word 'reform' was absent for the time being. The same was true of any reference to democratization, whereas the necessity of discipline was explicitly emphasized by Jakeš. Contrary to Štrougal, Jakeš did not link the desired changes in the ČSSR to the pursuit of reforms in the Soviet Union, but referred to Czechoslovakia's own 'valuable experiences' from the past.[14] The other spokesmen of the dogmatic group expressed themselves in more or less the same vein.

The viewpoints within the Party Presidium about the course to be followed quickly polarized, witness for example the hardly concealed argument between Štrougal and the leader of the Marxist fundamentalists, Vasil Bilak. In an interview with *Rudé Právo*, Bilak saw in the changes in the Soviet Union little more than 'inspiring stimuli' for the work of the CPCz, and kept hammering at the validity of *The Lesson Drawn from the Crisis Development* from 1970, 'the significance of which', he put it, 'crosses all borders'. Bilak, a champion of the universal character of Soviet socialism in eastern Europe under Brezhnev, now turned into a fervent supporter of a separate route to socialism for Czechoslovakia:

> One should not copy something blindly. In accordance with our socialist practice, in accordance with our best traditions, we will purposefully learn from the rich experiences of the Soviet Union and other socialist countries. Each of us all has to learn from each of the others, because everyone contributes certain new stimuli, and certain new experiences and values in the construction of socialism.[15]

Štrougal's answer was not long in coming. At a meeting of high CPCz officials in Prague (at the beginning of March 1987), the prime minister indirectly attacked Bilak and his followers, as soon as the 'revolutionary process' came up:

> Are our internal circumstances so different, so specific, that all these matters do not concern us? Is it enough for us to just state that the decisions of the XXVIIth Congress of the CPSU, the new party programme and the decisions of the January session of the Central Committee only amount to valuable stimuli for us?[16]

His speech did not mention the validity of *The Lesson,* whereas the need for democratization was emphasized: 'We want more socialism and therefore more democracy', quoted Štrougal from a recent statement by Gorbachev, and made it clear that Czechoslovakia should follow the example of the Soviet reforms.

Until March 1987, Husák took a middle position. But at the plenary session of the Central Committee of the CPCz (18–19 March), he sided with the pragmatists of Štrougal. For the first time, the Party leader publicly declared himself as a strong supporter of Gorbachev's reforms. He was now speaking about 'reform' of the economy and, exaggeratedly, but in Gorbachevian vein, called the 'Zásady přebudování hospodářského mechanismu ČSSR' (The Principles of Restructuring the Economic Mechanism in the ČSSR) 'the most significant intervention in the economic system since the nationalization', that is since 1948.[17]

When we compare this (for Husák, 'radical') action with Miloš Jakeš's main address, conceived in the old-fashioned way, at the same plenum,[18] it is immediately understood why from then on the dogmatic faction of the Party leadership preferred the latter. Jakeš offered the dogmatists a better guarantee for the continuation of the regime as they visualized it than Husák, who in their eyes was moving too fast.

For Bilak and his followers the prospect of Husák-Štrougal tandem, with the real possibility that the prime minister would succeed the old Party leader within the foreseeable future, was not very attractive. After all, in the 'crisis years' they had both proved to possess great flexibility, when they effortlessly changed from being Dubček's supporters to Brezhnev's normalizers. Why, under the new circumstances, would Husák, Štrougal and some of the others – as Bilak and his followers must have reasoned – not try to hold their own in the Party leadership by sacrificing, of all people, the principled comrades of the healthy core?

THE MOOD CHANGES

The Czechoslovak 'normalizers' were still in firm control but their position was gradually becoming less and less comfortable. It is true that with the help of a widespread police organization they invariably kept society under control,[19] but the society they now ruled was no longer the same frightened society of the early 1970s. In the 1980s, the public mood underwent a change, at first slowly and superficially, but from the middle of the decade more clearly perceptible.

The start of this process coincided with the rise of *Solidarność* in Poland (1980/1). This trade union, with 10 million members at the pinnacle of its power, shook the Polish communist system to its foundations. The Polish events did not pass unnoticed in Czechoslovakia. The authorities became nervous, and aggressively ranted against the 'counter-revolutionary threat to socialism' in the neighbouring state, while one anti-Polish campaign after another was launched in the mass media, and tourist and other contacts were restricted for fear of the Polish virus. The Czechs and Slovaks resorted to western transmitters and TV-stations in order to find out the facts of the matter and to satisfy their hunger for reliable information. In short, the Polish developments kept all sections of Czechoslovak society occupied, even after the suppression of *Solidarność* in December 1981.

The discontent of the Czechoslovak citizen was reinforced by a feeling of resentment towards the assault on the standard of living in Czechoslovakia, and also by the fact that day after day his 'common sense' ran up against a wall of incompetence and bureaucratic rigidity of the system. Moreover, he sensed that the regime was on the retreat. This feeling was strengthened by the symptoms of decline of the regime in the Soviet Union, publicly visible in the physical deterioration of the aged members of the leadership, who, to everybody's malicious delight, waved to the world from Lenin's mausoleum with visible effort.

'The mentality of those who are not directly involved in the dissident movement, has changed', wrote a Czechoslovak activist in 1984 and he continued:

> When you visit somebody unexpectedly and he is just listening to a foreign broadcasting station, he no longer bothers to switch back to Radio Prague. On the contrary, without batting

> an eyelid he explains what is being broadcast and offers that you listen with him. [. . .] Just like during late Novotnism, it is impossible to conclude from conversations, from abuse against the state of the country, or from political jokes, who is and who is not a member of the CPCz.[20]

Certainly, this metamorphosis did not apply to everyone. It was a process full of contradictions. Just as in the past, the majority of the population remained resigned in political apathy and with an attitude of 'I don't care'; this was complained about by both the Charter 77 activists and the authorities (each from a different point of view of course). On the other hand, the references to 'late Novotnism', in other words to the atmosphere in the 1960s when the Stalinist system in Czechoslovakia visibly crumbled away, indicated that in some circles of dissidents, ex-reformist communists, and also outside, there was a revival of hope for better times. People began to wonder whether the tide would finally turn. The developments in Hungary (and in a certain sense in Poland, too), where the political climate had become a lot milder, showed that a remodelling of the communist system was a real possibility and no longer a foolish utopia.

Characteristic of this change of mood in Czechoslovakia was the growing open protest, also outside dissident circles, against the policies of the regime. The most visible, and, for the authorities, probably the most alarming, was the attitude of active religious believers,[21] especially the Roman Catholics and part of the clergy. The plainly hostile treatment of the Roman Catholic Church by the communist regime on the one hand, and the revival of religious feelings among the people on the other, were at the root of this.

The situation in which the Roman Catholic Church found itself in the middle of the 1980s was disastrous, and the state control of its activities unbearable.[22] The brave protests of the aged cardinal and archbishop of Prague, František Tomášek (born 1899), had no effect on the authorities. The Roman Catholics stood with their backs to the wall, which the result that Czechoslovak religious life partly took place in secret. A 'church of the catacombs' developed, with various small clandestine communities of radical believers managing - not without success - to escape the stranglehold of the state.

At the same time open manifestations of religious belief grew stronger and more numerous, among them pilgrimages. This culminated in the celebration of the 1100th anniversary of the death of St Methodius in the South Moravian township of Velehrad on 7 July 1985. Here 150,000 mainly young believers booed at the communist officials who were present because of their attempts to turn this religious festival into a 'peace festival'.[23]

In Slovakia in particular, where Roman Catholicism had deeper roots that in the Czech countries, the need to openly profess the Roman Catholic faith after the example of the Poles grew steadily. Despite (or more correctly thanks to) the rabid atheist propaganda of the regime and its policy of discouragement with countless measures against active believers, the Slovak places of pilgrimage Levoča, Šaštín and others drew over half a million pilgrims in 1987.[24] Again the number of younger people was remarkably high.

Not only the young Christians, but the entire Czechoslovak younger generation grown up during the Husák regime, turned out to have more fighting spirit and to be more mature than the normalized generation of parents. The young greatly disliked the system and ignored CPCz policies whenever possible.[25] The Party had to watch how, despite all its surveillance, it was losing its hold on the young. Even within the official structures some opposition from the young could be felt, which inevitably led to conflicts, as the authorities took up an uncompromising attitude. This was true of their stern action against the officials of the *Jazz Section* of the Union of Czech Musicians, a cultural organization enjoying particular popularity in the Czech countries.[26]

The change of mood in the ČSSR was not only the result of internal processes. To a large extent it was also influenced by developments outside the borders: by the new policies of Gorbachev in the Soviet Union and the remarkable results he had managed to bring about in a short period of time. Russian *glasnost* made its entry in the Czechoslovak press. The papers took over and printed various critical articles from the Soviet press, as well as important speeches and statements by the Soviet leadership. In addition, they published several critical dissertations from the hand of Czechoslovak authors, the import of which would never have passed censorship before 1985.

All this caused due commotion among the Czechs and Slovaks, both Party members and non-Party members. Just as in the days of the Prague Spring it happened again that a newspaper edition or a certain issue of a journal was sold out in record time. This was also the case, of course, with Gorbachev's address about 'perestroika and the new management policies' from January 1987,[27] which for some time was the talk of the town.

It is evident, that Czechoslovak dissidents, and particularly the ex-reformists among them, began to compare the reforms in the Soviet Union with the reform process at the time of the Prague Spring. They saw a kindred spirit in Gorbachev, somebody striving for the same goals in Moscow which they themselves had tried to realize in Prague twenty years earlier. They felt sympathy for Gorbachev's policies, which they showed him in various declarations of support, and demanded, after the Soviet example, political changes in their own country, starting with the resignation of the compromised leaders of the Brezhnev period.[28]

THE DOGMATIC SOLUTION

It goes without saying that the dogmatists in the Party leadership did not trust too close a relationship between Husák and Štrougal. They prepared themselves to block Štrougal's way to the most influential office in the Party, with a view to protecting their own positions. At the beginning of 1987 they were not doing well, but on the other hand they could still count on enough support in the Presidium and the Party secretariat, which became abundantly clear when some changes in these bodies were put through in the March session of the Central Committee. Again there were no changes in the existing balance of power.[29]

This was not surprising. Many high officials behaved like Bilak and his followers. They paid lip service to their affinity to the Soviet Union and everything that happened there. They had been used to doing so all their lives. But they now feared the consequences of the practical application of the Soviet policies in their own country, as their own future fate, both political and personal, was closely allied to this. In one respect Gorbachev's men had an easy time of it. They could distance themselves from the Brezhnev era and lay the blame for the stagnation at the door of others. The Prague leaders did not have this opportunity, or they would have had to 'distance themselves from themselves'.[30] After all, any criticism of the Czechoslovak stagnation meant criticism of their own policies. It implied a re-opening of the discussion about the reforms with a consequent rehabilitation of those who had dedicated themselves to the reform process during the Prague Spring, ultimately leading to calling those who had executed the normalization policies to account. This explained the unwillingness and fear of the comrades to actively start a new policy.

The official visit of Gorbachev to Czechoslovakia in April 1987, his first in the position of Soviet party leader, certainly did not calm the feelings of the Czechoslovak politicians. Gorbachev had had to postpone his visit a few days for a 'common, understandable and human reason, a cold' as the communiqué described it,[31] which led to a spate of rumours, both among the population in Czechoslovakia and in the west. If only for this reason his stay with Husák was followed attentively and his words scrutinized. Admittedly, Gorbachev addressed many words of praise to the Czechoslovak Party leader and president, but that was as far as it went. Anyone who had expected that, after the example of Brezhnev, he would rail at the Prague Spring and be guided by the *Lesson,* was disappointed. Rather, Gorbachev seemed to be carefully avoiding these subjects. The Czechoslovak people were disappointed too. They had high expectations of the postponed visit, seeing well-nigh a liberator in Gorbachev, and hoping for concrete changes. Nothing spectacular happened, however, Gorbachev came, left, and everything remained the same.

We do not know anything about the talks behind the scenes, however, and there is no point in speculating about them. The decisive factor for Gorbachev may well have been that the entire Czechoslovak Party leadership - as opposed to the East Germans or the Romanians - publicly pronounced themselves in favour of his political course, and being a realistic politician, he dared not hope for more at that moment. He could leave the ČSSR content.

This feeling was not shared by the Czechoslovak hardliners. They had come to realise that the time for action had come, if they wanted to prevent a split in the Party leadership. They knew from the past what should not be allowed to happen again: Antonín Novotný's Party leadership became paralyzed by internal struggles on the eve and in the beginning of the Prague Spring, with all its consequences; the lower echelons in the Party hierarchy subsequently becoming 'confused', because clear directions from the centres of power were lacking, with 'counter-revolutionaries' surfacing everywhere. This time the dogmatists decided to take control, before it was too late.

The curious behaviour of the official Czechoslovak delegation in Moscow during the celebration of the 70th anniversary of the October revolution, was a strong indication that something was brewing in Prague. Husák, Štrougal, Bilak and Indra returned home as early as 5 November 1987, subsequently attending the celebrations in their own country, and were - strangely enough - the only leaders from all Warsaw Pact countries not to be present in the grandstand in Moscow on 7 November. This was a situation unprecedented in the history of the normalized CPCz, and raised many questions.

Over a month later, on 17 December, Party leader Husák resigned completely unexpectedly at the full plenary session of the Central Committee of the CPCz. He did this 'at his own request' and proposed, also on behalf of the Presidium of the CPCz, to elect Miloš Jakeš in the function of secretary-general. As is customary in such matters the Central Committee accepted the advice unanimously.[32] Husák remained president and member of the Presidium, and his successor lavished praises on him, thanking him profusely.

The ranks were, seemingly, closed and the normalization regime continued in power.[33] Štrougal's faction had lost, Bilak and his supporters had had their way. With Jakeš in command they could leave their own mark on the speed and intensity of the Czechoslovak *perestroika*. For how long, the future will tell. The struggle for reforms in Czechoslovakia remains undecided, as long as Mikhail Gorbachev is in the Kremlin.

Interference, supervision and influence by the Soviet Union are all a leitmotif in the history of Czechoslovakia after 1945, from the post-war republic of the democratic president Beneš to the socialist state under the communist Party leader Jakeš. Not the political intentions of the Czechoslovak rulers, but the internal developments in the Soviet Union ultimately proved to be the decisive factor for the political climate and the subsequent fate of this country: a warning for the political heirs of Brezhnev, cold comfort for the defeated reformists of 1968, and a bitter experience of forty lost years for the majority of Czechs and Slovaks.

NOTES

1 THE COMMUNIST TAKE-OVER

1 *Memoirs of Dr Eduard Benes. From Munich to New War and New Victory,* London 1954.
2 *Memoirs of Benes,* p. 281 ff. Cf. also by the same author *Demokracie dnes a zítra,* Prague 1946, p. 249 ff.
3 More about the American vision on the post-war world e.g. in Louis J. Halle, *The Cold War As History,* New York 1971, p. 50 ff.
4 Cf. for instance Jorg K. Hoensch, *Geschichte der Tschechoslowakischen Republik 1918–1978,* Stuttgart 1978, p. 109 ff.
5 Tad Szulc, *Czechoslovakia Since World War II,* New York 1971, p. 25, can be numbered amongst them, as can be Eduard Táborský, then Beneš's secretary, despite all his criticism of Beneš. See 'Beneš a náš osud' in *Svědectví* (Paris) XV, 57 (1978), pp. 21 and 49--50.
6 Verbatim text of this treaty in *Memoirs of Benes.*
7 Táborský, op. cit., p. 21.
8 In March 1947 the American president H. S. Truman declared, in answer to communist activities in Greece, that every free country that was being threatened by totalitarism either from within or without, could count on the support of the United States.

The Zhdanov doctrine derived from the so-called 'two camps theory' formulated by A. A. Zhdanov, who was a close assistant of Stalin's, in September 1947. This theory, expounded at the foundation of the Cominform (Communist Information Bureau) in the Polish town of Szklarska Poreba, divided the world into two camps opposed to each other: the imperialist and anti-democratic camp, headed by the United States, and the socialist, anti-imperialist and democratic camp, headed by the Soviet Union. Thus the ideological argument for the sovietization of eastern Europe was found. In the escalation leading up to the Cold War, the 'Zhdanov offensive', with its – hitherto unknown – military aggressive language towards the United States, did not fail to have an effect.

9 M. K. Dziewanowski, *Poland in the Twentieth Century,* New York 1977, p. 154.

10 In the Czech countries the Communists got as much as 40 per cent of the votes, in Slovakia 30 per cent. There the Democratic Party became the biggest party, with 62 per cent of the voters behind it. See Sibylle Schröder-Laskowski, *Der Kampf um die Macht in der Tschechoslowakei 1945–1948*, Berlin (East), pp. 88–9.

11 In 1938 the CPCz had no more than 80,000 members, of whom only 28,485 remained after the war. Membership grew rapidly, as can be seen from the following figures:

Date	*Number of members*
July 1945	475,000
September 1945	713,000
March 1946	1,000,000
November 1947	1,410,000

At that time the CPCz had more members than all the other big Czechoslovak parties put together: the People's Socialist Party – a party closely linked with president Beneš – (562,000), the Czechoslovak People's Party – a Roman Catholic party – (550,000) and the Social Democrats (365,000). As Czechoslovakia then had a population of about 12 million inhabitants, this meant that every other adult citizen was politically organized. These figures have been taken from Jaroslav Opat, *O novou demokracii 1945–1948*, Prague 1966, pp. 68–9, and Zdeněk Hejzlar, *Reformkommunismus. Zur Geschichte der Kommunistischen Partei der Tschechoslowakei*, Cologne 1976, p. 42.

12 Jaroslav Pecháček, 'Demokraté a únor' in *Únor 1948 očima vítzů i poražených o třicet let později*, Cologne 1979, p. 72.

13 Cf. Václav Král, *Historické mezníky ve vývoji Československa*, Prague 1978, p. 121.

14 Karel Kaplan, *Der kurze Marsch. Kommunistiche Machtübernahme in der Tschechoslowakei 1945–1948*, Munich 1981, p. 45. See also H. Seton Watson, *Nations and States, An Enquiry into the Origins of Nations and the Politics of Nationalism*, London 1977. p. 156. Illuminating in this respect are the election results in the six northern districts of Bohemia, where 90 per cent of the pre-war population was German. The great mass of the new inhabitants voted for the CPCz. The Party got between 54 per cent and 65 per cent of the votes per district. Jiří Kosta, *Abriss der Sozialökonomischen Entwicklung der Tschechoslowakei 1945–1977*, Frankfurt a.M. 1978, p. 21.

15 Danubius (Bratislava), 'Tězy o vysídlení československých Nemcov', *Svědectví* XV, 57 (1978), p. 115.

16 Klement Gottwald, *Deset let. Sborník statí a projevů 1936–1946*, Prague 1949, p. 419.

17 Kaplan, *Der Kurze Marsch*, p. 124.

18 Here the reader should be reminded that the Habsburg monarchy of which Bohemia formed a part, had been a constitutional state since 1860, allowing the Czechs to take part in the political life of the empire.

19 Josef Josten, *Oh my Country*, London 1949, p. 123.
20 To give only one example: the monograph by Jaroslav César and Zdeněk Snítil, much-praised in Czechoslovakia, *Československá revoluce 1944–1948*, Prague 1979, p. 373.
21 From Gottwald's address at the meeting of the Central Committee of the CPCz, 9 April 1948. Quoted by Karel Kaplan in 'Úvahy o nevyhnutelnosti února', *Svědectví* XIV, 55 (1978), p. 362.
22 Remark by Mgr. J. Šrámek, prime minister of the London government in exile and vice-premier in the Gottwald government, quoted in Pecháček, 'Demokraté a únor', p. 73.
23 See Kaplan, *Der kurze Marsch*, p. 107 ff. Especially the report of the cabinet discussion, which was held as a result of a dispatch from Moscow, and in which the delegation urges the cabinet to immediately reconsider the Czechoslovak point of view regarding the Marshall plan.
24 This can be concluded from talks which Masaryk had with the Soviet ambassador Bodrov. See Walter Ullmann, *The United States in Prague 1945–1948*, Boulder 1978, p. 76. Also cf. Karel Kaplan, *Die Entwicklung des Rates für gegenseitige Wirtschaftshilfe (RGW) in der Zeit von 1949 bis 1957*, Stiftung Wissenschaft und Politik, Ebenhausen 1977, p. 69 ff.
25 Zdenek Krystufek, *The Soviet Regime in Czechoslovakia*, Boulder 1981, p. 48.
26 Edward Taborsky, *Communism in Czechoslovakia 1948–1960*, Princeton 1961, p. 20.
27 The Soviet embassy then (and now) has a fixed circle of Czechoslovakian informers. Among them, in the period after the war, was the influential early Bolshevik Arnošt Kolman, who openly admitted being an informer at the end of his eventful life. Arnošt Kolman, *Die verirrte Generation. So hätten wir nicht leben sollen. Eine Biographie*, Frankfurt a.M. 1979, p. 194.
28 Tad Szulc, *Czechoslovakia Since World War II*, p. 38.
29 Karel Kaplan, *Der kurze Marsch*, p. 224. At the Hungarian-Czechoslovak border the troops were on alert. Cf. by the same author 'Úvahy o nevyhnutelnosti', p. 349.
30 Walter Ullmann, *The United States in Prague*, p. 85 ff.
31 Josef Josten, *Oh my Country*, p. 145.
32 See Pavel Tigrid in *Únor 1948 očima vítězů*, Cologne 1977, p. 81 ff.
33 Z. Hejzlar, *Reformkommunismus*, p. 38.
34 Cf. the various addresses by Klement Gottwald of this period in Klement Gottwald, *Deset let*, p. 451 ff. and 457 ff.
35 Gottwald, in *Deset let*, p. 423.
36 See the excellent description of this subject in the book by Zdeněk Mlynář, *Nachtfrost. Erfahrungen auf dem Weg vom realen zum menschlichen Socialismus*, Cologne 1978, p. 7 ff.
37 Hejzlar, op. cit., p. 37.
38 Detlef Brandes, *Die Tschechen unter deutschem Protektorat. Teil I.*

Besatzungspolitik, Kollaboration und Widerstand im Protektorat Böhmen und Mähren bis Heydrichs Tod (1939–1942), Munich 1969, p. 230.

39 This statement dates from May 1942, just before the attack on Heydrich. See Brandes, op. cit., pp. 230 and 231.

40 Obviously one should be cautious in stating such sweeping conclusions. Yet it is difficult to ignore the simple observation that after the war Czechoslovak citizens with a dubious reputation and even collaborators managed to make a career for themselves in the Party. I know several examples from personal experience, but more important is that many of my contacts do so too. Czech literature in one way or the other points out this remarkably easy conversion from a cowardly, or at least passive, attitude during the occupation into one of 'revolutionary militancy' after the Soviet liberation in 1945. See, for instance, Josef Škvorecký, *Zbabělci* (Cowards) or Jiří Gruša, *Dotazník* (Questionnaire).

41 Cf. for instance Pavel Tigrid, 'Smysl Mnichova', *Svědectví* XIV, 56 (1978), pp. 553–65; Vojtech Mastny, 'Tradition, Continuity and Discontinuity in Recent Czechoslovak History', in N. Lobkowicz and F. Prinz (eds), *Die Tschechoslowakei 1945–1970*, Munich 1978, pp. 81–90; and Bruce Garver, 'The Czechoslovak tradition: an overview', in Hans Brisch and Ivan Volgyes (eds), *Czechoslovakia: The Heritage of Ages Past. Essays in Memory of Josef Korbel*, Boulder 1979, pp. 25–56.

2 BETWEEN REVOLUTION AND REVOLT

1 Jaroslav Krejčí, *Social Change and Stratification in Postwar Czechoslovakia*, London 1972, p. 145.

2 Zdenek Krystufek, *The Soviet Regime in Czechoslovakia*, Boulder 1981, p. 232.

3 See Jiří Sláma, 'Die politische und wirtschaftliche Integration Osteuropas in der Stalinära (1945–1953)', Osteuropa-Institut München January 1979, Working Paper no. 54, p. 7, and, at length, Karel Kaplan, *Die Entwicklung des Rates*, Ebenhausen 1977, p. 27 ff.

4 Zdenek Hejzlar, *Reformkommunismus*, Cologne 1976, p. 52.

5 The information is extracted from, or calculated with the help of Václav Průcha, *Hospodářské dějiny Československa v 19. a 20. století*, Prague 1974, p. 419, and Jiří Kosta, *Abriss der sozialökonomischen Entwicklung*, Frankfurt a.M. 1978, p. 78.

6 Cf. Václav Průcha, *30 let budování socialistické ekonomiky Československa*, Prague 1978, p. 20.

7 Edward Taborsky, *Communism in Czechoslovakia*, Princeton 1961, p. 564.

8 They were later to serve the Nazis as 'Grundlage für zweckgebundene Forschung'. See Jiří Doležal, 'Das Verhältnis der Nationalsozialisten zur tschechischen Kultur', in Vilém Prečan (ed.), *Acta Creationis. Independent Historiography in Czechoslovakia 1969–1980* (presented

to the XVth International Congress of Historical Sciences, Bucharest, August 1980), Hanover 1980, pp. 156–7.

9 Edward Taborsky, op. cit., pp. 565–6. Taborsky also gives precise information about the number of works translated from Russian. In a period of 4 years (1950–3) it involved 5,069 titles out of a total of 19,635. In other words, 1,267 translations per year. By comparison, in 1947, the last year before the take-over, only 90 books which had been translated from Russian were published in Czechoslovakia. Ibid., p. 481.

10 Cf. Vladimír Horský, *Prag 1968. Systemveränderung und Systemverteidigung,* Stuttgart 1975, p. 48. Other estimates are considerably higher. According to Hoensch as late as 1955 there were 240,000 prisoners in over 230 penitentiaries, 80 per cent of them for political reasons. See his *Geschichte der Tschechoslowakischen Republik 1918–1978,* Stuttgart 1978, p. 128. For more details and various estimates of the numbers the reader should consult Vilém Hejl and Karel Kaplan, *Zpráva o organizovaném násilí,* Toronto 1986, p. 231 ff. Much information is contained in K. Kaplan 'Political Persecution in Czechoslovakia 1948–1972', Research Project *Crises in Soviet-type Systems,* Study no. 3, Cologne 1983.

11 V. Hejl and K. Kaplan, op. cit., p. 235.

12 Václav Benda 'Katolicismus a politika - kořeny a perspektivy dnešní situace' in Václav Havel *et al., O svobodě a moci,* Cologne 1980, p. 114.

13 Jiří Pelikán (ed.) *Das unterdrückte Dossier. Bericht der Kommission des ZK der KPTsch über politische Prozesse und 'Rehabilitierungen' in der Tschechoslowakei 1949–1968* (the so-called Piller report), Vienna 1970, p. 316.

14 The so-called Kolman affair. The victim himself tells of the Russian role in this matter in his memoirs: Arnošt Kolman, *Die verirrte Generation,* Frankfurt a.M. 1979, p. 197 ff.

15 See Pelikán, op. cit., p. 116 ff.

16 Cf. Pelikán, ibid., p. 68, and Jan Přibram, 'Příběh s nedobrým koncem', *Svědectví,* Paris 1978, XIV, 55, p. 372.

17 V. Hejl and K. Kaplan, *Zpráva,* p. 229.

18 Cf. Jiří Lederer, *České rozhovory,* Cologne 1979, pp. 270–1.

19 Bennett Kovrig, *Communism in Hungary. From Kun to Kádár,* Stanford 1979, p. 268.

20 Cf. *Khrushchev Remembers,* New York 1977, vol. 2, The Last Testament, p. 240 ff.

21 See Khrushchev in *Khrushchev Remembers,* London 1971, vol. 1, p. 364.

22 This was in any case true for Czechoslovakia and Poland. In Hungary, the situation was more complicated; here Rákosi was no longer master of the situation. It is true that practically the whole of his group returned to the Party Presidium, but the power struggle between him and Imre Nagy and his followers was well under way. The deep divisions of opinion about the course the Hungarian party

was to take, had resulted in a coming and going within the party top since the death of Stalin. In May 1954, at the time of the congress, the position of Rákosi had become stronger again. Apart from Nagy, all other Presidium members belonged to his political school of thought. Cf. B. Kovrig, op. cit., p. 267 ff.

23 The figures are based on H. Gordon Skilling, *Czechoslovakia's Interrupted Revolution*, Princeton 1976, p. 31; *Dějiny Komunistické Strany Československa*, Prague 1961, pp. 614–52; M. K. Dziewanowski, *The Communist Party of Poland. An Outline of History*, Cambridge (Mass) 1976, pp. 238–78 and 400; and D. Nemes (ed.), *Dějiny mad'arského revolučního dělnického hnutí*, Prague 1974, pp. 623–82.

24 As a result of the currency reform real wages decreased by 12 per cent, while the cost of living rose by an average of 29 per cent. See Karel Bartošek, 'Stávkující dělník v Praze roku 1953', *Listy* (Rome), XVII, 2 (1987), p. 61.

25 In eastern Europe the term intelligentsia is interpreted in a wider sense than our designation 'intellectuals'. It is understood to refer to all those who 'do complicated, qualified, mental work, e.g. technicians, doctors, lawyers, artists, teachers and the majority of civil servants'. Cf. *Ilustrovaný encyklopedický slovník*, Prague 1980, Part I, p. 941.

26 See Hejzlar, *Reformkommunismus*, p. 60.

27 Cf. Z. Hejzlar, ibid., p. 80, and Vladimir V. Kusin, *The Intellectual Origins of the Prague Spring. The Development of Reformist Ideas in Czechoslovakia 1956–1967*, Cambridge 1971, p. 19 ff.

28 Z. Mlynář, *Nachtfrost*, Cologne 1978, p. 54.

29 *Dějiny KSČ*, p. 646.

30 See *Statistická ročenka Československé socialistické republiky 1964*, Prague 1964, p. 264, and V. Průcha, *Hospodářské dějiny Československa*, Prague 1974, p. 512. By comparison: in the same period almost 90 per cent of Polish farming land was in private hands, in the GDR and Hungary about a third. V. Průcha (ed.), *Hospodářské dějiny evropských socialistických zemí*, Prague 1977, p. 199.

31 Jaroslav Kabrhel (ed.), *Zemědělská politika KSČ*, Prague 1977, p. 16.

32 V. Průcha, *Hospodářské dějiny Československa*, p. 513.

33 At that time the GDR had (outside agriculture) some 400,000 people employed in the private sector, Hungary around 100,000 and Poland well over 400,000. V. Průcha, *Hospodářské dějiny evropských socialistických zemí*, pp. 191–3.

34 *Zápisník Agitátora 1981*. Published by the Department of Agitation and Propaganda of the CC of the CPCz, Prague 1980, pp. 87–8.

35 *Dějiny KSČ*, p. 687.

36 Cf. article 126 of the Constitution of the Soviet Union from 1936. The revision of this article in 1953 did not go so far in its definition of the leading role of the Party either. Only the Constitution of 1977 (article 6) changed it drastically. See *Sovětské ústavy*, Prague 1979, pp. 173 and 223.

37 Vladimír Flegl, *Ústavní základy Československé socialistické republiky,* Prague 1981, p. 142. The English translation can be found in 'Constitution of the Czechoslovak Socialist Republic' in William B. Simons (ed.), *The Constitutions of the Communist World,* Alphen aan de Rijn 1980, p. 139 ff.
38 Flegl, op. cit., p. 148. Cf. the phrasing of article 5, paragraph 9 and 10 of the Polish Constitution and article 18 of the Hungarian Constitution, in Simons, op. cit., pp. 290 and 199.

3 THE *ANCIEN REGIME* IN DECLINE

1 Roy A. Medvedev, *On Stalin and Stalinism,* Oxford 1979, p. 174.
2 A. P. van Goudoever, *Angst voor het verleden. Politieke rehabilitaties in de Sovjet Unie na 1953,* Utrecht 1983, p. 29.
3 This concerns the well-known Czech author Jan Procházka. See Karel Hvížd'ala, *České rozhovory ve světě,* Cologne 1981, p. 310.
4 Galia Golan, *The Czechoslovak Reform Movement. Communism in Crisis 1962–1968,* Cambridge 1971, p. 17. For interesting details read Josef Frolík, *Špion vypovídá,* Cologne 1979, p. 123 ff.
5 In 1968 Barák was discharged from prison, but not yet rehabilitated. Complete rehabilitation, including admission to the Party only followed under Husák in 1975; ironically on the same day (28 January) that Antonín Novotný died.
6 A term from A. Ostrý, *Československý problém,* Cologne 1972, p. 7.
7 Jiří Pelikán (ed.), *Das unterdrückte Dossier,* Vienna 1970, p. 241.
8 Vladimir V. Kusin, *The Intellectual Origins,* Cambridge 1971, p. 24.
9 Read, for instance, the publications of Eugen Löbl and Leopold Grünwald, *Die intellektuelle Revolution. Hintergründe und Auswirkungen des 'Prager Frühlings',* Düsseldorf 1969; Vladimir V. Kusin, *The Intellectual Origins*; and, for the official version, Jiří Hájek, *Mýtus a realita Ledna 1968,* Prague 1970.
10 For the political views and activities of some Prague Spring reformers after the revolution read the study by Peter Hrubý, *Fools and Heroes. The Changing Role of Communist Intellectuals in Czechoslovakia,* Oxford 1980.
11 M. Kundera, *The Book of Laughter and Forgetting,* Harmondsworth 1983, p. 22.
12 Though the growth figures for national income in 1961 were 6.77 per cent, and in 1962 1.40 per cent, in 1963 and 1964 they fell sharply, to - 2.17 per cent and 0.89 per cent respectively. See A. Kusák and F. P. Künzel, *Der Sozialismus mit menschlichem Gesicht. Experiment und Beispiel der sozialistischen Reformation in der Tschechoslowakei,* Munich 1969, p. 66.
13 See *Reden zum IV. Kongress der Tschechoslowakischen Schriftstellerverbandes Prag, Juni 1967,* Frankfurt a.M. 1968. For the stormy proceedings at this congress, consult A. French, *Czech Writers and Politics 1945–1969,* Boulder 1982, p. 252 ff.

14 G. Golan, *The Czechoslovak Reform Movement,* Cambridge 1971, p. 250.
15 There were even stories going the rounds that when Novotný travelled to Slovakia, food from Prague was taken along.
16 Ludvík Veselý, *Dubček Biografie,* Munich 1970, p. 173.
17 Bennett Kovrig, *Communism in Hungary,* p. 364.
18 Novotný complained about this, for instance at the session of the Party Presidium on 5 September 1967. A verbatim account of his tirade leaked out and was published in the well-known Czech historical journal *Dějiny a současnost* X, 6 (1968), pp. 44–5.
19 A. Ostrý, *Československý problém,* p. 40. For more details, see Karel Kaplan, 'Anatomie einer regierenden Kommunistischen Partei. Teil II: Das Politbüro', *Berichte des Bundesinstituts für ostwissenschaftliche und internationale Studien,* Cologne no. 26/1983, pp. 53–4.
20 *Rok šedesátý osmý v usneseních a dokumentech ÚV KSČ,* Prague 1969, p. 9.
21 For the course of events at the October session see R. A. Remington (ed.), *Winter in Prague. Documents on Czechoslovak Communism in Crisis,* Cambridge (Mass.) 1969, p. 25 ff. For the Dubček-Bilak relationship in this period see Z. Mlynář in *Nachtfrost,* Cologne 1978, pp. 118–19.
22 For this see Frank L. Kaplan, *Winter Into Spring: The Czechoslovak Press and the Reform Movement 1963–1968,* Boulder 1977, pp. 102–3.
23 Cf. Heinz Brahm, *Der Kreml und die ČSSR 1968–1969,* Stuttgart 1970, p. 14, and Zdenek Hejzlar, *Reformkommunismus,* Cologne 1976, pp. 142–3.
24 *Rudé Právo* (Prague), 10 December 1967.
25 A report in shorthand of this conversation is kept in France. This was published in abridged form in Vladimír Kadlec, *Dubček – 1968,* Cologne 1987, p. 155 ff.
26 V. Kadlec, *Dubček,* p. 156.
27 Ibid.
28 Cf. the Memoirs of Smrkovský in *Listy* (Rome) V, 2 (1975), p. 6. See also Mlynář, *Nachtfrost,* pp. 89–90.
29 Jiri Valenta, *Soviet Intervention in Czechoslovakia, 1968. Anatomy of a Decision,* Baltimore and London 1979, p. 29.
30 In this context, Z. Mlynář mentions the commander-in-chief of the Warsaw Pact forces of that time, I.I. Yakubovski, and the member of the Politburo P.J. Shelest. See Mlynář, *Nachtfrost,* p. 89.
31 Cf. J. Valenta, *Soviet Intervention,* p. 125.
32 This view is confirmed in the memoirs of General Jan Šejna, a key figure in the 'Novotný-drama'. He even mentions that Brezhnev rang Novotný on the very evening of his return to Moscow and assured him of his personal support. On the other hand, Šejna claims that Brezhnev had left instructions in the Russian embassy, in which he asked Chervonenko not to try and keep Novotný on in the function of first secretary, but in that of president. See Jan Šejna, *We will bury*

you, London 1984, pp. 172–3. The book contains a lot of information about the year 1967 and the first two months of 1968, before Šejna fled to the United States (See chapter 4). There is only one problem with the memoirs. They are just as unreliable as the author himself. It is almost impossible to determine where the *Wahrheit* ends and the *Dichtung* begins, as Šejna's main aim is to justify and explain away his own behaviour. In any case, several passages have demonstrably been made up or distorted in such a way that the greatest care should be taken in using the memoirs as a historical source.

33 R.A. Remington, *Winter in Prague*, p. 32 ff.

34 Memoirs of Smrkovský, *Listy*, (Rome) V, 2 (1975), pp. 4–5.

35 Cf. Memoirs of Smrkovský, p. 5. For the background and the course of the coup, read the memoirs of the then Czechoslovak intelligence officer Josef Frolík, *Špion vypovídá*, Cologne 1979, p. 309 ff.

36 Ibid., p. 311.

37 Zdeněk Mlynář in *Der Spiegel*, (Hamburg) 21 December 1981, p. 99.

4 THE PRAGUE SPRING

1 Cf. the biography by William Shawcross, *Dubcek*, London 1970.

2 Memoirs of Josef Smrkovský in *Listy* (Rome) V, 2 (1975), p. 6. The composition of the Presidium of the CPCz under Novotný was as follows: Antonín Novotný, Jozef Lenárt, Michael Chudík, Otokar Šimůnek, Jaromír Dolanský, Jiří Hendrych, Drahomír Kolder, Bohumil Laštovička, Oldřich Černík and Alexander Dubček. Apart from the last two politicians, they were either supporters of Novotný or politicians of a very conservative stamp.

3 The only exception was one of the conspirators, Miroslav Mamula, the mighty head of the Eighth Department of the Central Committee. The important areas of security and defence came under his responsibility. The key post of this Czechoslovak 'mini-Beria' was taken over by general Václav Prchlík, the radical supporter of reforms.

4 New full members of the Presidium were: Josef Borůvka and Josef Špaček, two champions of reform; Emil Rigo and Vasil Bilak, two outspoken dogmatists; and Jan Piller, a very conservative official, certainly no supporter of reforms.

5 Among the fiercest of critics of the Novotný regime was, right from the outset, Dr Gustáv Husák. Cf. his sharp attack in *Kultúrny Život*, 12 January 1968.

6 Dubček himself recalled this in his paper at the session of the Central Committee of the CPCz in April 1968. See *Rok šedesátý osmý*, p. 66.

7 See Jan Procházka, 'Připsáno nejen generálu Šejnovi', *Literární Listy*, 7 March 1968; and also, for instance, the article 'Proč utekl Šejna' in *Rudé Právo*, 12 June 1968.

8 Novotný's resignation was demanded in over 4,500 letters and resolutions directed to Dubček and the Central Committee of the

Party. *Rudé Právo,* 21 March 1968. The number of letters Novotný received himself was probably not less than this.

9 Jiří Pelikán, *Ein Frühling, der nie zu Ende geht. Erinnerungen eines Prager Kommunisten,* Frankfurt a.M. 1976, p. 228.

10 Jiří Pelikán (ed.), *Das unterdrückte Dossier,* Vienna 1970, p. 127. Cf. also *Khrushchev Remembers* (Vol. 1), London 1971, p. 366.

11 Cf. *Rudé Právo* of 6, 24 and 31 March 1968.

12 Besides the CPCz and the Slovak Communist Party the country also numbered a few parties whose memberships were intentionally kept small; the Czechoslovak Socialist Party (about 11,000 members in early August), the Czechoslovak People's Party (around 25,000 members) and in Slovakia, the Freedom Party and the Party of Slovak Revival (each with a few thousand members).

13 'Akční program Komunistické strany Československa' in *Rudé Právo,* 10 April 1968. Translated in R. A. Remington (ed.), *Winter in Prague,* Cambridge (Mass.) 1969, p. 88 ff.

14 Ibid., p. 93.

15 Ibid., p. 104.

16 Ibid., p. 111.

17 Ibid., p. 105.

18 Ibid., p. 115.

19 Smrkovský in *Listy* (Rome) V, 2 (1975), p. 6.

20 V. Kadlec, *Dubček - 1968,* Cologne 1987, p. 16.

21 Antonín Ostrý, *Československý problém,* Cologne 1972, p. 35.

22 Zdeněk Mlynář, *Nachtfrost,* Cologne 1978, p. 110.

23 Important representatives of the radicals were the economists Radoslav Selucký and Eugen Löbl, the philosophers Ivan Sviták and Karel Kosík, Party official Jaroslav Šabata, the journalist Jiří Lederer, chess grandmaster Luděk Pachman, the historians Karel Bartošek and Jan Tesař, the authors Antonín J. Liehm, Pavel Kohout, and Ludvík Vaculík, and other well-known figures.

24 Jaroslaw A. Piekalkiewicz, *Public Opinion Polling in Czechoslovakia, 1968–1969. Results and Analysis of Surveys Conducted During the Dubcek Era,* New York 1972, p. 21.

25 Ibid., p. 24.

26 Alexej Kusák and Franz Peter Künzel, *Der Sozialismus mit menschlichem Gesicht. Experiment und Beispiel der sozialistischen Reformation in der Tschechoslowakei,* Munich 1969, p. 157.

27 Z. Mlynář, *Nachtfrost,* p. 183.

28 After the approval of the Party Presidium the draft of the statutes was published by the CPCz on 10 August 1968. For the original text see 'Návrh stanov Komunistické strany Československa' in *Rok šedesátý osmý,* p. 271 ff. The English translation can be found in R. A. Remington, *Winter in Prague,* p. 265 ff.

29 *Osteuropäische Rundschau* (Munich) XIV, 4 (1968), p. 9.

30 Otto Ulč, *Politics in Czechoslovakia,* San Francisco 1974, p. 137.

31 Osvald Machatka, 'Také jedno výročí', *Literární Listy,* 13 June 1968.

32 V. Kadlec, *Dubček,* p. 147.

33 Cf. reports in *Rudé Právo* of 2, 8 and 11 June 1968.
34 See Zdeněk Mlynář, *Československý pokus o reformu 1968. Analýza jeho teorie a praxe,* Cologne 1975, p. 138 ff. Cf. also Vladimir V. Kusin, *Political Grouping in the Czechoslovak Reform Movement,* London 1972, p. 170 ff. and S. Pošusta, 'Potřebuje náš demokratický socialismus dvě marxistické strany?' in *Rudé Právo,* 26 June 1968.
35 J. A. Piekalkiewicz, *Public Opinion Polling,* p. 227.
36 Ibid., p. 229.
37 A striking expression by Ladislaus Singer, *Der ungarische Weg,* Stuttgart-Degerloch 1978, p. 74.
38 J. Pelikán, *Ein Frühling,* p. 220.
39 Vasil Bilak, *Pravda zůstala pravdou. Projevy a články říjen 1967 – prosinec 1970,* Prague 1974, p. 305.
40 Z. Mlynář, *Nachtfrost,* p. 298.
41 Jiří Hájek, *Begegnungen und Zusammenstösse. Erinnerungen des ehemaligen tschechoslowakischen Aussenministers,* Freiburg im Breisgau 1987, p. 182.
42 V. Bilak, op. cit., p. 305. Cf. also J. Hájek, op. cit., p. 183.
43 See *Neues Deutschland* of 27 March 1968 and *Rudé Právo* of 28 March 1968.
44 *Rudé Právo,* 11 May 1968.
45 Memoirs of Smrkovský, *Listy* (Rome) V, 2 (1975), p. 8.
46 Cf. V. Kadlec, *Dubček,* p. 152 and 164; and Z. Hejzlar, *Reformkommunismus,* p. 233.
47 The Manifesto was signed by many prominent writers, artists, scientists, sportsmen and other well-known citizens. See *Literární Listy,* 27 June 1968. The English translation in Remington, *Winter in Prague,* p. 196 ff.
48 Boris Ponomarev to Waldeck Rochet, 15 July 1968. Quoted in V. Kadlec, op. cit., p. 154.
49 Ibid.
50 Cf. ibid., pp. 151 and 153. See also Smrkovský, *Listy* (Rome) V, 2 (1975), p. 15.
51 J. Hájek, *Begegnungen,* p. 187.
52 See *Rudé Právo,* 19 July 1968. (Also Remington, *Winter in Prague,* p. 225 ff.) Out of the Five of Warsaw only the Hungarian press cited a few passages from the Czechoslovak answer. The Soviet Union, the GDR, Poland and Bulgaria only published the Warsaw letter.
53 See Z. Mlynář, *Nachtfrost,* pp. 170–1.
54 Smrkovský, *Listy* (Rome) V, 2 (1975), p. 13; Mlynář, op. cit., pp. 193–4.
55 It concerned in any case the dismissal from their functions of František Kriegel (chairman of the National Front), Čestmír Císař (secretary of the Central Committee), Jiří Pelikán (director of Television) and probably also of Josef Pavel (minister of the Interior). Furthermore a ban on KAN and K-231, a curb on the mass media and other measures.
56 See the opinion of F. Kriegel, quoted in František Janouch,

Ne, nestěžuji si. Malá normalizační mozaika, Cologne 1985, p. 9. Cf. also Moravus, 'A. Dubček z dvojího pohledu' in *Listy* (Rome) I, 6 (1971), pp. 28–9.

5 MILITARY INTERVENTION AND THE NEW REALITY

1 See 'The Secret Report of the Meeting of the Parliament's Presidium' (probably of 22 August 1968) in *Listy* (Rome) VIII, 5 (1978), p. 53 ff.
2 Ibid., pp. 58 and 59.
3 Robert Littel (ed.), *The Czech Black Book. Prepared by the Institute of History of the Czechoslovak Academy of Sciences,* New York 1969, p. 34.
4 It is difficult to determine who exactly had been acquainted with the plan. In all probability they included the Presidium members Bilak, Kolder and Švestka; the Party secretary Indra; the politicians M. Jakeš and P. Auersperg; the head of the Czechoslovak Security Forces, the STB, V. Šalgovič; the director of the Czechoslovak press agency ČTK, M. Sulek; the minister of Post and Communications, K. Hoffmann and the ex-managing director of the Czechoslovak radio, M. Marko. See H. Gordon Skilling, *Czechoslovakia's Interrupted Revolution,* Princeton 1975, p. 761. Cf. also Zdeněk Mlynář, *Nachtfrost,* Cologne 1978, pp. 259 and 272.
5 What fate would have awaited Dubček, Smrkovský and the others, if the original version of the plan had been carried out, we do not know. The merciless liquidation of the Hungarian 'counter-revolutionary' leaders of 1956 speaks for itself. The imprisoned Czechoslovak leaders, with the history of communism in mind, entertained no hope about their future. Cf. Smrkovský about himself and about Černík in *Listy* (Rome) V, 2 (1975), pp. 17 and 19, and the statement of Černík about the attitude of Dubček during the negotiations in the Kremlin, in V. Horský, *Prag 1968,* Stuttgart 1975, p. 266. A trial in front of the 'revolutionary tribunal' at least, would have been in store for them. See Smrkovský about this in *Listy* (Rome) V, 2 (1975), p. 17 and a message from Dubček to the staff of the secretariat of the CC, 9 September 1968: 'Today it can already be said: they wanted to take me to court as head of a counter-revolutionary centre.' From a statement by the usually well-informed Z. Hejzlar, in Horský, op. cit., p. 265.
6 The text of the request for help that was never made can be found in *Pravda* (Moscow), 22 August 1968. For the English translation see R. A. Remington (ed.), *Winter in Prague,* Cambridge (Mass.) 1969, p. 295 ff. Three days later the request for help was no longer mentioned in the mass media of the 'Five'. Soviet propaganda had had to abandon this version.
7 See for the text Robert Littel (ed.), *The Czech Black Book,* pp. 21–2.
8 For more interesting details see Z. Mlynář, *Nachtfrost,* p. 191 ff. The invasion had not started on Tuesday evening by chance. This was the

night the Party Presidium regularly met, a fact well known to the Kremlin.

9 Ibid., p. 247.

10 It was especially due to this form of resistance that the number of victims under the civilian population remained relatively low, about 150. See Horský, *Prag 1968*, p. 235.

11 See Rober Littel (ed.), op. cit., p 233.

12 Cf. Franz Goëss and Manfred R. Beer, *Prager Anschläge. Bild-dokumente des gewaltlosen Widerstandes*, Frankfurt a.M. and Berlin 1969. For a photographic report from Prague in August, see J. Josten, *21-8-1968 Anno Humanitatis*, London 1968.

13 Some prominent confidants of Moscow suffered a curious - albeit temporary - mental conversion, which could be explained better by a psychologist than a historian. Zdeněk Fierlinger, for instance, who for years was the ambassador in Moscow, a member of the Party Presidium from 1948 till 1966, and chairman of the 'Union of Czechoslovak-Soviet Friendship' at the time of the intervention protested against the occupation at the Soviet embassy in Prague. The minister of Defence under Novotný, General B. Lomský, in full regalia, decked with numerous Soviet medals, issued orders to dumbfounded Soviet officers in front of the parliament building and ensured that the delegates could enter the building through the military cordon. In parliament he sharply condemned the occupation. General S. Kodaj, military commander in Slovakia during the intervention and one of the fiercest critics of the democratization in the ČSSR, refused all negotiations with the Soviet military authorities. These are only three examples of many.

14 For the documents of the XIVth Congress, see Jiří Pelikán (ed.), *The Secret Vysočany Congress. Proceedings and Documents of the Extraordinary Fourteenth Congress of the Communist Party of Czechoslovakia, 22 August 1968*, London 1971, p. 88 ff.

15 The following members were elected in the Presidium: A. Dubček, J. Smrkovský, O. Černík, J. Špaček, F. Kriegel, B. Šimon, Č. Císař, O. Šik, V. Šilhán, V. Slavík, L. Hrdinová, V. Matějíček, B. Kabrna, Z. Hejzlar, J. Litera, E. Goldstücker, B. Vojáček, M. Hübl, Z. Moc, V. Šimeček, G. Husák, J. Zrak, A. Ťažký, S. Sádovský, P. Colotka, J. Turček, V. Pavlenda, and A. Zámek. See J. Pelikán (ed.), *The Secret Vysočany Congress*, p. 254.

16 Cf. the memoirs of Smrkovský, in *Listy* (Rome) V, 2 (1975), p. 16. Dubček's decision to wait for the occupiers was seen by many as a tactical mistake and was criticized. Critics claim it would have been better for the future negotiations, if the leaders, backed by the XIVth Party Congress, had negotiated with the Soviets from Czechoslovakia. See e.g. J. Pelikán, *Ein Frühling*, Frankfurt a. M. 1976, p. 269 or V. Bernard, 'Na půl cestě', *Svědectví* (Paris) X, 38 (1970), p. 191.

17 Horský, *Prag 1968*, pp. 258–9.

18 Words of one of the formerly imprisoned leaders, quoted ibid., p. 263.

19 Memoirs of Smrkovský, op. cit., p. 20.

20 Ibid., p. 21. Z. Mlynář tells us stories in a similar vein about Svoboda in *Nachtfrost*, pp. 271–2.
21 For the text of this secret protocol see Remington, *Winter in Prague*, p. 379 ff.
22 Mlynář extensively reports about this in *Nachtfrost*, p. 295 ff. Not returning to Prague was the 'Head of the revolutionary government of workers and farmers', Alois Indra. He stayed behind in Moscow for some time because of a heart attack.
23 See 'Communiqué on Soviet-Czechoslovak Talks' in Remington, op. cit., p. 376 ff.
24 For Svoboda's speech see *Osteuropäische Rundschau* (Munich) XIV, 9–10 (1968), p. 19.
25 Ibid., pp. 20–1.
26 Ibid., p. 26.
27 Ibid., p. 30.
28 Jaroslaw A. Piekalkiewicz, *Public Opinion Polling*, New York 1972, p. 264.
29 Ibid., p. 27.
30 A. Müller, 'De 'normalisatie' in Tsjechoslowakije (1968–1971)', *Internationale Spectator* XXV (1971), p. 1718.
31 Piekalkiewicz, op. cit., p. 28.
32 G. Golan, *Reform Rule in Czechoslovakia. The Dubček Era 1968–1969*, Cambridge 1973, p. 243.
33 *Osteuropäische Rundschau* XIV, 9–10 (1968), p. 28.
34 Address by Husák at the Extraordinary Congress of the CPS, *Osteuropäische Rundschau* XIV, 9–10 (1968), pp. 27 and 29.
35 Horský, *Prag 1968*, p. 334. See also Mlynář, *Nachtfrost*, pp. 294–5.

6 THE PROCESS OF NORMALIZATION

1 The supporters of Dubček also strengthened the Central Committee. Eighty new members – all delegates of the Extraordinary XIVth Congress – were co-opted onto this body. In addition, forty-eight of them were members of the Vysočany Central Committee. Cf. J. Pelikán, *The Secret Vysočany Congress*, London 1971, pp. 96–7 and *Rudé Právo*, 3 September 1968.
2 *Pravda* (Moscow), 6 September 1968.
3 For interesting details about this visit see: Pavel Tigrid, *Why Dubcek Fell*, London 1971, p. 215 ff.
4 From an ideological-political point of view, the Soviet Union justified its military invasion with the theory later to become known to the west as 'the Doctrine of Limited Sovereignty' or 'the Brezhnev Doctrine'. Summarized in a few words, the doctrine runs more or less as follows: If the development of socialism in a country of the community of socialist states is threatened from within or without, the Soviet Union and its allies had the international duty to intervene by all means, including military help. The 'Brezhnev Doctrine' was first formulated by S. Kovalev in an article in *Pravda* (Moscow),

26 September 1968. For a translation see R. A. Remington, *Winter in Prague,* Cambridge (Mass.) 1969, p. 412 ff.

5 *Rudé Právo,* 5 October 1968.

6 For the original text of the treaty see *Rudé Právo,* 19 October 1968. The English translation can be found in Remington, op. cit., p. 420 ff.

7 Cf. G. Husák's address to the People's Militia in Bratislava, *Rudé Právo,* 14 November 1968.

8 The group of 'realists' included L. Svoboda, O. Černík, G. Husák and S. Sádovský; the other supporters of a firm approach to the normalization were the old leader of the Social Democrats, later to become a high official in the CPCz, E. Erban, who in those days was successor to F. Kriegel as chairman of the National Front, and L. Štrougal, for years minister of the Interior in Novotný's days.

9 The original idea was that the organizational structure of the CPCz should be matched by that of the state. This meant that, apart from the Slovak and the Czechoslovak Communist Party (the asymmetric model), there should also be a Czech Communist Party. The Soviet Union, however, objected to this. Štrougal's Bureau was meant to be a compromise, until the question of the Party structure could be definitely settled at the next congress. The Bureau was disbanded in 1971.

10 Cf. Z Mlynář, 'Normalization in Czechoslovakia after 1968', Research Project *Crises in Soviet-type Systems,* Study no. 1, Cologne (Index) 1982, p. 17.

11 Memoirs of Smrkovský, *Listy* (Rome) V, 2 (1975), p. 25.

12 *Rudé Právo,* 19 December 1968.

13 Smrkovský, op. cit., p. 25.

14 Ibid., pp. 24 and 25.

15 See for his address *Rudé Právo,* 6 January 1969. The new chairman was Peter Colotka, who was reputed to be a moderate progressive. Smrkovský became vice-chairman of the Federal Assembly and chairman of one of the two chambers. Colotka showed enough adaptability to maintain himself in high functions. Since May 1969 he had been prime minister of the Slovak government.

16 Vladimir V. Kusin, *From Dubček to Charter 77. A study of 'normalization' in Czechoslovakia 1968–1978,* Edinburgh 1978, p. 59.

17 Cf. *Pravda* (Moscow) and *Izvestia* of 30 January 1969.

18 See Z. Mlynář, *Nachtfrost,* Cologne 1978, pp. 312–13.

19 J. Hájek, *Begegnungen,* Freiburg im Breisgau 1987, p. 205.

20 P. Tigrid, *Why Dubcek Fell,* p. 161.

21 Z. Hejzlar, *Reformkommunismus,* Cologne 1976, p. 333. See also P. Tigrid, *Why Dubcek Fell,* p. 159.

22 These Soviet collaborators from August and other outspoken opponents of reforms at the time of the Prague Spring were cleared of any blame by a special order of the Executive Committee of 16 April 1969. In this way the road to top positions was reopened to them. Cf. *Rudé Právo,* 17 April 1969.

23 Z. Hejzlar, op. cit., p. 335.
24 Under the leadership of G. Husák the Party Presidium originally consisted of V. Bilak, P. Colotka, O. Černík, A. Dubček, E. Erban, J. Piller, K. Poláček, S. Sádovský, L. Svoboda and L. Štrougal. The Executive Committee was abolished.
25 See statements of František Pavlíček, the old manager of the well-known Vinohrady Theatre in Prague and former member of the Central Committee of the CPCz in Jiří Lederer, *České rozhovory*, Cologne 1979, p. 221.
26 For the complete text see *Rudé Právo*, 23 August 1969. The emergency laws, which, as was originally announced, were to be in force until the end of 1969, were later integrated into the Czechoslovak criminal code.
27 Even a humiliating self-criticism did not help Černík. A few months later he lost his place in the CC of the CPCz and in the same year he was thrown out of the Party. The vacant places (the trade union leader Polàček, an obliging 'normalizer' also had to leave) were taken by politicians who used to belong to the Novotný group: J. Lenárt, also first secretary of Slovakia; A. Kapek, a pronounced Stalinist; and J. Korčák, the new Czech prime minister.
28 Z. Hejzlar, *Reformkommunismus*, p. 353.
29 These figures were mentioned by Husák in an address held at the plenum of the CC of the CPCz, 10 December 1970. See *Rudé Právo*, 15 December 1970. There were two categories of ex-Party members: those who had been 'expelled' (according to Husák 67,147) and others who had simply been crossed off the Party register (259,670).
30 Cf. the statement of the chairman of the Control and Auditing Commission of the CC of the CPCz, Miloš Jakeš, at the XIVth Party Congress, 25 May 1971. See *XIV. sjezd Komunistické strany Československa*, Prague 1971, p. 91.
31 Cf. Jiří Hochman in *Svědectví* XIX (Paris), 76 (1985), p. 868. In 1966 the Party had 1,698,000 communists, 620,000 of whom had joined the Party before the February revolution. See Z. Hejzlar, 'K politice a vnitřnímu vývoji KSČ po roce 1948' in I. Bystřina, et. al. (eds), *Systémové změny* (Sborník), Cologne 1972, p. 79.
32 In protest against the intervention the editors renamed the journal *Literární Listy* as *Listy*. At the time of the ban this journal had a circulation of 200,000. In 1971 *Listy* was re-founded in Rome by Jiří Pelikán as 'Journal of the Czechoslovak Socialist Opposition'.
33 See J. Hochman, op. cit., p. 868 and V. V. Kusin, *From Dubček to Charter 77*, p. 101.
34 See for more information Peter Payne, 'The Academic Purge in Czechoslovakia', in *Index on Censorship* (1972), no. 2, p. 33.
35 Z. Mlynář, *Nachtfrost*, p. 170.
36 In 1967 299 writers and 158 translators were members of the Czech section of the Czechoslovak Union of Writers. In addition, there were 87 candidate-members. See V. V. Kusin, *Political Grouping*, London 1972, p. 70. The figure of 117 is based on the calculations of the

author of this book. Cf. J. Brabec (ed.), *Slovník českých spisovatelů. Pokus o rekonstrukci dějin české literatury 1948–1979*, Toronto 1982; V. Forst (ed.), *Slovník české literatury 1970–1981*, Prague 1985; and Petr Bílek, *175 autorů. Čeští prozaici, básníci a literární kritici publikující v 70. letech v nakladatelství Československý spisovatel*, Prague 1982.

37 See the document 'Kulturní politika v českých krajích 1970–1978', *Svědectví* XVII (Paris), 68 (1983), p. 828 ff.

38 Under Husák, numerous renowned intellectuals became simple labourers, but also windowcleaners, cleaners, dustmen or stokers. With a bit of luck they could work as doorkeepers, chauffeurs or gardeners, in some cases even as clerical staff in a library, museum or archive. The list with the names of 145 Czechoslovak historians who were removed from the universities and the Academy is revealing in this respect. In most cases, their new job is also mentioned. See *Acta Persecutionis. A Document from Czechoslovakia. Presented to the XIVth International Congress of Historical Sciences*, San Francisco, August 1975.

39 Up to the end of 1970 a total of 51,490 Czech and 13,740 Slovak officials were expelled. This concerned trade union officials of the central, as well as the provincial, district and the workplace organizations, both in paid and in unpaid functions. See *Československé odbory 1870–1970*, Brussels (International Confederation of Free Trade Unions) 1970, p. 46.

40 Z. Hejzlar, *Reformkommunismus*, p. 354.

41 Adolf Müller, 'Zur Lage in der Tschechoslowakei', *Osteuropa* (Stuttgart) XXIII (1973), p. 607.

42 Cf. V. V. Kusin, *From Dubček to Charter 77*, p. 173; and Rudolf Urban 'Sorgen um den Fortbestand der Nation. Zu den Säuberungen in der Tschechoslowakei', *Osteuropa* (Stuttgart) XXIII (1973), p. 119.

7 CZECHOSLOVAKIA IN THE LATE BREZHNEV ERA

1 First published in *Rudé Právo*, 14 January 1971.

2 See Z. Hejzlar, *Reformkommunismus*, Cologne 1976, p. 361.

3 Cf. *Listy* (Rome) I, 1 (1971), p. 12.

4 Hejzlar, op. cit., p. 361.

5 Ibid. See also V. V. Kusin, *From Dubček to Charter 77*, Edinburgh 1978, pp. 139–40. J. Piller and F. Barbírek finally became the scapegoats of the December session; these were two supporters of the hard line, but tainted by a sin of the night of the intervention, when they chose for Dubček, to their later deep regret. Piller, an extreme purger of the trade unions, lost his place in the Party Presidium, and both of them were also forced to give up their places in the Central Committee.

6 Kusin, op. cit., p. 142.

7 *XIV. sjezd Komunistické strany*, Prague 1971, p. 563.

8 Cf. also Leopold Grünwald, 'Vom XIV. zum "XIV." Parteitag der KPC', *Osteuropa* (Stuttgart) XXI, (1971), p. 873. Among the few survivors were, for example, Husák, Svoboda, Colotka, Erban and Defence minister M. Dzúr.The latter was the only one left over from the original government team of Černík who could stay on in this function under Štrougal.

9 *Rudé Právo*, 27 May 1971.

10 G. Husák, L. Svoboda, P. Colotka, J. Kempný, L. Štrougal and, in a sense, J. Lenárt, can all be said to belong to the first group. Another 'Husák man' was the Czech prime minister J. Korčák, whose successful career was due to the normalization efforts in the 'Bureau for Party Activities in the Czech Countries' mentioned before. The second group included V. Bilak, A. Indra, A. Kapek and K. Hoffmann.

Yet this division is not always true. It is known that there have been conflicts in Husák's Party leadership between some Czech Presidium members on the one hand (Indra and Hoffmann) and Slovak members (Husák together with Bilak) on the other. Cf. K. Kaplan, 'Anatomie einer regierenden kommunistischen Partei. Teil II: Das Politbüro (ZK-Präsidium)', *Berichte des Bundesinstituts für ostwissenschaftliche und internationale Studien*, Cologne, no. 26/1983, p. 63.

11 See Jan Příbram (pseudonym), 'Příběh s nedobrým koncem', *Svědectví*, (Paris) XIV, 55 (1978), p. 394. The 'origin' of the Czech society: I am referring to the thirties and forties of the nineteenth century.

12 Correspondence and interviews from my archives. The passage quoted dates from March 1974.

13 Among the first victims of the trials were the writer Ota Filip (1970), general Václav Prchlík (1971) and the extremely popular publicist and commentator Vladimír Škutina (1971). The latter had been imprisoned since September 1969 and was given four years because of a television broadcast in August 1968. For information about other trials and persecutions see chapter 8, concerning the opposition.

14 By comparison: during the same period personal consumption in the Federal Republic of Germany rose by 28 per cent.

The rise in consumption was mostly brought about in Czechoslovakia by decreasing investments and increasing the import of consumer goods, financed by the export of capital goods. This popular measure, taken on the basis of political considerations rather than the resulting economic consequences, was ultimately paid for in the production sector.

It is also assumed that the Kremlin allowed Czechoslovak military expenditure to be temporarily reduced, and foreign aid to Cuba, Vietnam and a few Arab states to be decreased. See Ota Šik, '15 let normalizace v ČSSR', *Listy* (Rome) XIII, 6 (1983), p. 43 ff. Cf. also Jiří Kosta, 'Ziele und Methoden der Wirtschaftspolitik in der Tschechoslowakei (1970–1978)', *Berichte des Bundesinstituts für ostwissenschaftliche und internationale Studien,* Cologne, no. 43/1979, p. 63.

It should be mentioned that this greater emphasis on consumption did not mean Husák's leadership was going 'its own way'. The Soviet Union of the early 1970s also made room in its economic policies for an increase in the standard of living.

15 Statement by Vasil Bilak, quoted in *Listy* (Rome) XIII, 5 (1983), p. 46.

16 The problem of the double moral standard and of the attitude of Czechs and Slovaks under the Husák regime is one which occupies the minds of many people both at home and under the emigrants. See amongst others Milan Šimečka, *The Restoration of Order. The Normalization d by the same author Kruhová obrana. Záznamy z roku hoslovakia 1969–1976,* London 1984, p. 122 ff. An1984, Cologne (Index) 1985, p. 81 ff. Also Evžen Menert in P. Tigrid (ed.), *Vývoj Charty. Záznam z konference ve Franken,* Cologne (Index) 1981, p. 121. These problems also form the central theme in the plays and essays of Václav Havel.

17 Cf. *Statistická ročenka ČSSR 1973* (Prague), p. 472 and *Statistická ročenka ČSSR 1982,* p. 550.

18 V. V. Kusin, 'Husak's Czechoslovakia and Economic Stagnation', in *Problems of Communism* (Washington DC) XXXI, May-June 1982, p. 28.

19 M. Šimečka, *The Restoration of Order,* London 1984, p. 162.

20 V. Kadlec, *Dubček–1968,* Cologne 1987, p. 137.

21 Z. Hejzlar 'K politice a vnitřnímu vývoji KSČ', in *Systémové změny,* p. 103.

22 [František Janouch], *Briefe aus der Tschechoslowakei. Der Untergrund berichtet über die Lage des Volkes,* ed. Jiří Stárek, Graz-Vienna 1974, p. 18.

23 Confidential communication by the Czechoslovak deputy prime minister R. Rohlíček at a closed meeting of high officials in Prague and of the then minister of the Interior J. Obzina at a plenum of the CC of the CPCz; both dating from the beginning of 1975. See *Listy* (Rome) V, 4 (1975), p. 5.

24 Cf. *XV.sjezd Komunistické strany Československa,* Prague 1977, p. 71 and *XVI.sjezd Komunistické strany Československa,* Prague 1981, p. 49.

25 *XV.sjezd KSČ,* p. 73.

26 *XVI.sjezd KSČ,* p. 49.

27 Adolf Müller, 'Der langweilige "Realsozialismus". Zur Entwicklung in der ČSSR', *Osteuropa* XXXII (1982), p. 911.

28 See *XV.sjezd KSČ,* p. 72 and *XVI.sjezd KSČ,* p. 49.

29 V. V. Kusin, 'Husak's Czechoslovakia', in *Problems of Communism* XXXI, p. 26.

30 V. Mastny, 'Tradition, Continuity and Discontinuity', in N. Lobkowicz and F. Prinz (eds), *Die Tschechoslowakei 1945–1970,* Munich 1978, p. 90.

31 Miroslav Šolc (ed.), *Stručný slovník teorie a praxe výstavby strany,* Prague 1982, p. 151.

32 Felix Gelbuch, 'Rozvinutý, zralý a reálný socialismus', *Týdeník aktualit*, no. 50/1982, p. 3.
33 Ibid.
34 Quoted in Miroslav Kusý, 'Charta 77 a reálný socialismus', *Svědectví* (Paris) XV, 59 (1979), p. 427.
35 Cf. Jan Vanous, 'East European economic slowdown', *Problems of Communism* XXXI, July-August 1982, p. 3.
36 Jiří Kosta, 'Neue Reformansätze im Wirtschaftssystem des ČSSR', *Berichte des Bundesinstituts für ostwissenschaftliche und internationale Studien*, Cologne, no. 21/1985, p. 46.
37 As can be seen from the table below, the debts of the ČSSR to the west were limited, compared to those of other east European countries.

East European hard-currency debts in billions of US$

	1970	*1980*	*1984*
ČSSR	0.6	3.4	4.1
Bulgaria	0.7	2.5	2.5
GDR	1.4	11.2	12.3
Hungary	0.6	5.8	8.2
Poland	1.1	22.0	27.0
Romania	1.6	9.3	8.4

See Charles Gati, 'The Soviet Empire: Alive But Not Well', *Problems of Communism* XXXIV, March-April 1985, p. 77.
38 Judging by the price level in 1974. See J. Kosta, 'Neue Reformansätze', p. 4.

After 1975 crude oil was to have further price increases. In 1982 the price of Soviet oil had risen by 255 per cent compared to that of 1975, with all the resulting consequences. See 'O dodávkách sovětské ropy do ČSSR' in *Listy* (Rome) XIV, 4 (1984), blz. 41.
39 By comparison: in the same period the market shares of the GDR and Hungary dropped by 20.8 per cent and 21.4 per cent respectively. See J. Kosta, 'Neue Reformansätze', p. 7. For more information see 'My a svět. Několik čísel o čs. ekonomice', *Listy* (Rome) XI, 2 (1981), pp. 13–14.
40 *Statistická ročenka ČSSR 1982*, p. 376; *Statistická ročenka ČSSR 1986*, p. 356.
41 *Listy* (Rome) XII, 2 (1982), p. 29.
42 Ibid. The situation in Prague is very precarious indeed, with over 13 per cent of apartments being shared by two families. The average size of a dwelling in Prague is 40m². See *Listy* (Rome) XIII, 5 (1983), p. 50. Regarding salaries: in 1984 a Czechoslovak employee earned an average of 2,837 Kčs per month. Salaries in the mining industry were considerably higher: 3,545 Kčs, while in the 'non-productive sector', the average salary earned in culture was only 1,836 Kčs, in education

2,622 Kčs and in health care 2,632 Kčs. *Statistická ročenka ČSSR 1985*, p. 202.

43 For this subject see the penetrating essay by Václav Havel 'The power of the powerless', in Jan Vladislav (ed.), *Václav Havel or Living in Truth. Twenty-two essays published on the occasion of the award of the Erasmus Prize to Václav Havel*, Amsterdam 1986, p. 36 ff.

8 OPPOSITION UNDER THE RULE OF GUSTÁV HUSÁK

* Part of this chapter has previously been published in Dutch in A. P. van Goudoever (ed.), *Oost-Europa in het verleden. Liber Amicorum Z. R. Dittrich*, Wolters-Noordhoff/Frosten, Groningen 1987.

1 Illustrative in this respect is Václav Havel's recollection of his long and open discussion with Alexander Dubček in early July 1968. Havel and a few other writers (amongst others L. Vaculík, P. Kohout, E. Goldstücker, J. Škvorecký and J. Procházka) were invited for an informal talk with the reformist leaders. Besides Dubček, the other people present were O. Černík, J. Smrkovský, J. Hájek, G. Husák and M. Galuška, then minister of Culture. See Václav Havel, *Dálkový výslech. Rozhovor s Karlem Hvížd'alou*, Edition Rozmluvy, (UK) 1986, pp. 115–16.

2 *Literární Listy*, special edition, 22 August 1968. This appeal was signed by the Union of Czechoslovak Writers, the Union of Journalists, the Union of Actors, the Union of Film and Television Artists, and the Union of Architects.

3 At that time the population was impressed by the addresses of the communist leaders František Kriegel and František Vodsloň at the session of the Central Committee of the CPCz in May 1969, of poet Jaroslav Seifert at a meeting of the representatives of the Union of Artists (May 1969), and of the communist journalist Karel Kyncl during the session of the Prague Party Committee (June 1969). Numerous copies of these addresses were circulated all over the country. (The texts are in my archives.)

4 Among other things citizens were asked to avoid public transport, not to go shopping, not to visit any public places such as restaurants, cinemas or theatres and to stop work for five minutes at the stroke of twelve.

5 See Vladimir V. Kusin, *From Dubček to Charter 77*, Edinburgh 1978, pp. 148–9. It was submitted by the writers V. Havel and L. Vaculík, the historian J. Tesař, the lawyer M. Lakatoš, the political scientist L. Kohout, the sociologist R. Battěk, the journalists J. Hochman and V. Nepraš, the chess grandmaster L. Pachman, and J. Wagner, a functionary in the youth movement during the Prague Spring. Battěk, Pachman and Tesař were promptly arrested in connection with this matter and disappeared into prison for over a year. For interesting details read Luděk Pachman, *Nu kan ik spreken ... Van Beneš tot Dubček. Over schaken en communisme*, Baarn-Antwerp

1975, p. 200 ff. The petition is also known under the name of Ten Points Manifesto. For the text see Jiří Pelikán, *Sozialistische Opposition in der ČSSR. Analyse und Dokumente des Widerstands seit dem Prager Frühling*, Frankfurt a.M./Cologne 1974, p. 119 ff.

6 Regarding the activities of the HRM and its previous history see Jaroslav Suk, 'Československá radikální levice', *Svědectví* (Paris) XVII, 67 (1982), p. 613 ff.

7 'Konstitutives Manifest der HRM' is to be found in Max Borin and Vera Plogen, *Management und Selbstverwaltung in der ČSSR. Burokratie und Widerstand*, (Rotbuch 4) Berlin 1970, pp. 118–20.

8 *Svědectví* XVII, 67 (1982), p. 622.

9 See reports in *Rudé Právo* of 4 January 1970 and 23 March 1971. Amongst the convicted were, besides the engineer Petr Uhl, who was regarded as the central figure (4 years jail), Jaroslav Suk, Pavel Šremer, Petruška Šustrová and the West German left-wing activist Sibylle Plogstedt. For particulars about this trial see *Listy* (Rome) I, 2 (1971), p. 8 ff.

10 Cf. 'Manifest des 28. Oktober 1970' in Pelikán, *Sozialistische Opposition*, Frankfurt a.M./Cologne 1974, p. 128.

11 Ibid.

12 Cf. 'Kleines Aktionsprogramm der sozialistischen Opposition' in Pelikán, op. cit., pp. 137–8.

13 In ten trials, held in July and August 1972, a total of 46 people were convicted, 33 of them unconditionally. They received a total of 102 years imprisonment. The heaviest sentences were given to Milan Hübl and Jaroslav Šabata, the author of the *Short Action Programme* (6½ years), Jan Tesař (6 years) and Jiří Müller (5½ years). Twenty-five people from this group of 46 were to be amongst the first signatories of Charter 77. Apart from those mentioned above, these also included, for instance, Rudolf Battěk, Ladislav Hejdánek, Karel Kyncl, the Šabata family, Antonín Rusek and others. For the complete list of people and sentences imposed see *Listy* (Rome) II, 5–6 (1972), pp. 32–3.

14 Pelikán, op. cit., pp. 78–9.

15 Zdeněk Mlynář estimated that of the 500,000 reformist communists purged during the normalization, no more than 10 per cent remained politically active in one way or another. Zdeněk Mlynář, 'Ideologische und politische Richtungen innerhalb der Bürgerrechtsbewegung in der heutigen Tschechoslowakei', *Sonderveröffentlichung des Bundesinstituts für ostwissenschaftliche und internationale Studien*, Cologne, October 1978, p. 26.

16 Kusin, *From Dubček*, p. 168.

17 Havel, *Dálkový výslech*, p. 137.

18 To mention only a few of such protests addressed to the Czechoslovak authorities: the open letters written in 1972 by Dr František Janouch, a prominent nuclear physicist and former chairman of the CPCz organization at the Institute for Nuclear Physics, *Listy* (Rome) III, 1 (1973), p. 52 ff.; the letter by the journalist Věra Šťovíčková (1973),

Listy IV, 4 (1974), pp. 45–6; the letter by Alexander Dubček to the Czechoslovak parliament (1974), *Listy* V, 3 (1975), p. 3 ff.; the letter by the former minister of Foreign Affairs Jiří Hájek to prime minister L. Štrougal (1975), *Listy* VI, 2 (1976) p. 44 ff. and the letter by the Party historian Karel Kaplan (1975), ibid., p. 42 ff.

19 See *Listy* (Rome) VI, 2 (1976), pp. 41–2. One of the many examples was a letter from three prominent Party veterans, former members of Parliament and future Charter 77 signatories František Kriegel, Mrs Gertruda Sekaninová-Čakrtová and František Vodsloň addressed to the Czechoslovak parliament (1975). In it they referred to the final act of the Helsinki Conference about Security and Co-operation in Europe and urged the parliament to do their best in the matter of withdrawal of the Soviet troops still in the ČSSR since 1968; to bring about the lifting of all repressive measures against adult citizens and their children; to rehabilitate all political prisoners, etc. See *Listy* (Rome) VI, 1 (1976), p. 44 ff.

20 V.V. Kusin, 'Dissent in Czechoslovakia after 1968' in Jane Leftwich Curry (ed.), *Dissent in Eastern Europe*, New York 1983, p. 49.

21 Mlynář, 'Ideologische und politische Richtungen', p. 37.

22 Cf. Havel, *Dálkový výslech*, p. 137.

23 For the official reaction see *Rudé Právo*, 16 December 1972 and *Tvorba*, 20 December 1972 and 7 February 1973. The text of the petition with the names of the original signatories can be found in *Listy* (Rome) III, 2 (1973), p. 3. The petition had been signed by, amongst others, the famous Czech poet Jaroslav Seifert. Among the well-known writers not belonging to the circle of dissidents, yet refusing to withdraw their support despite the pressure from the authorities were, for instance, Adolf Branald, Miroslav Holub, Bohumil Hrabal, Vašek Káňa, Václav Lacina and Jiří Šotola.

24 Quotation from the 'Letter to Dr Gustáv Husák' in Jan Vladislav (ed.), *Václav Havel or Living in Truth*, Amsterdam 1986, p. 4.

25 *Rudé Právo*, 14 June 1974.

26 *Listy* (Rome) IV, 4 (1974), pp. 12–13. Among the signatories, nearly all of whom later also signed the document Charter 77 (if they had not been forced to emigrate before that time), were, besides the majority of ex-communists and revolutionary socialists also some protestant activists such as the philosopher L. Hejdánek, the clergyman Jan Dus and the independent socialist Rudolf Battěk.

27 About the organization and the way of life in these communities (the word 'commune' is not used because of its obvious ideological connotations), see Zdeněk Vokatý, 'Sen o kole' in Václav Havel et al., *O svobodě a moci*, Cologne 1980, p. 345 ff.

28 The essay was published under a pseudonym in *Svědectví* XIII, 51 (1976), p. 571 ff. For the quotation see p. 586.

29 Havel, *Dálkový výslech*, p. 144.

30 Ibid., p. 145.

31 Václav Benda, 'Noční kádrový dotazník', *Svědectví* XV, 58 (1979), p. 274.

32 The complete text of this letter of 16 August 1976 can be found in H. Gordon Skilling, *Charter 77 and Human Rights in Czechoslovakia*, London 1981, p. 199 ff. The letter was also signed by Prof. Jan Patočka and Karel Kosík, two prominent Czech philosophers, Prof. Václav Černý, and by the writers Havel, Klíma and Kohout.
33 V. Prečan (ed.), *Kniha Charty. Hlasy z domova*, Cologne 1977, pp. 46–7. Of the 70 signatories we see 46 again under the Charter statement of 1 January 1977. The other messages of solidarity can be found in the same collection (Open letter from Mlynář, Open letter from ten legal specialists).
34 Cf. *Rudé Právo*, 2 September 1976.
35 Ivan Jirous was given the heaviest sentence of 18 months, Pavel Zajíček 12 months, Svatopluk Karásek and Vratislav Brabenec each 8 months suspended. The sentences were reduced on appeal. See H. Gordon Skilling, *Charter 77 and Human Rights*, p. 12.
36 Eight of them also signed the 'foundation declaration' of Charter 77: Prof. Zdeněk Jičínský, former vice-president of the Czech National Council; Dr Oldřich Kaderka, former head of the Department of International Relations and Politics of the Central Committee of the CPCz; Dr Vladimír Klokočka, former dean of the Faculty of Law at Brno; Dr Michal Lakatoš, former lecturer at the Institute of Law of the Czechoslovak Academy of Sciences; Dr Zdeněk Mlynář, former member of the Party Presidium and secretary of the CC of the CPCz; Dr Milan Richter, former chief public prosecutor at the Military Court of Justice; Dr Josef Rychetský, former head of the Department of Appeal of the Czechoslovak Attorney General; and Dr František Šamalík, lecturer at the Faculty of Law at the Prague Charles University.
37 Havel, *Dálkový výslech*, p. 149.
38 Mlynář, 'Ideologische und politische Richtungen', p. 39.
39 The spokesmen and signatories of the 'foundation declaration' referred to the international treaties signed by the government of their country, but not, in their eyes, honoured. The Charter declaration therefore started with a passage which was to provide the movement with a legal basis for its activities; activities which – as the chartists have since emphasized time and time again – are strictly within the limits of Czechoslovak law. The passage runs as follows:

> In the Czechoslovak Collection of Laws, no. 120 of 13 October 1976, texts were published of the International Covenant on Civil and Political Rights, and of the International Covenant on Economic, Social and Cultural Rights, which were signed on behalf of our Republic in 1968, were confirmed in Helsinki in 1975 and came into force in our country on 23 March 1976. From that date our citizens have the right, and our state the duty, to abide by them.
>
> The human rights and freedoms underwritten by these covenants constitute important assets of civilized life for which

> many progressive movements have striven throughout history and whose codification could greatly contribute to the development of a humane society.
>
> We accordingly welcome the Czechoslovak Socialist Republic's accession to those agreements.
>
> Their publication, however, serves as an urgent reminder of the extent to which basic human rights in our country exist, regrettably, on paper only.

For the complete text of this Charter document see H. Gordon Skilling, *Charter 77 and Human Rights*, p. 209 ff.

40 'Pure clean man', was what Jan Patočka was called by an ex-communist intellectual in *Svědectví* XIV, 54 (1977), p. 193. Prof. Patočka died of a cerebral haemorrhage on 13 March 1977 in a Prague hospital, where he was taken on collapsing after an 11-hour interrogation. It was not only the frequency and the length of the interrogations at the secret police headquarters which hastened his death. This old man, all his life an example of integrity and humanity, was the victim of a smear campaign by the mass media, who spread fabrications which touched him profoundly. Patočka's essays 'What Charter 77 Is and What It Is Not' of 7 January 1977 and 'What Can We Expect of Charter 77' of 8 March 1977, also called the 'Testament of Jan Patočka', can be found in H. Gordon Skilling, *Charter 77 and Human Rights*, p. 217 ff. For Havel's essay 'The power of the powerless. To the memory of Jan Patočka' see *Václav Havel or Living in Truth*, p. 36 ff.

41 Cf. Havel, *Dálkový výslech*, p. 151 and the interview with Jiří Hájek in *Listy* (Rome) XVI, 6 (1986), p. 46.

42 See Vilém Prečan 'K současné situaci Charty 77' in *Listy* (Rome) VIII, 3–4 (1978), pp. 4–5.

43 The disputes between Uhl and Hübl are confirmed by Mlynář in the same article in which he speaks critically of the ex-communist circle. See Zdeněk Mlynář, 'Charta 77 po dvou letech', *Listy* (Rome) IX, 1 and 2 (1979), pp. 1–6 and 5–12.

44 These two articles and a few other contributions to the discussion amongst which are two replies from Havel to Vaculík and particularly to Pithart are published in *Svědectví* XV, 58 (1979), p. 257 ff.

45 Ludvík Vaculík, *Český snář*, Toronto 1983. An abridged version of the original manuscript had earlier appeared in German under the title *Tagträume. Alle Tage eines Jahres*, Hamburg/Luzern 1981.

46 See *Svědectví* XV, 57 (1978), p. 105 ff. The contributions to the discussion of this theme were mostly published in *Svědectví* and *Právo Lidu* (journal of the Czechoslovak Social Democratic Party in Exile) in the years 1978–86.

47 'Charta 77 – Dokument č.22' in *Listy* (Rome) IX, 1 (1979), p. 55 ff. and 'Charta 77 – Dokument č.23 in *Listy* (Rome) IX, 2 (1979), p. 47 ff.

48 See 'Dokument Charty 77 č.11/84. Právo na dějiny', addressed to the presidium of the Czechoslovak Academy of Sciences, *Listy* (Rome) XIV, 5 (1984), p. 71 ff.
49 *Rudé Právo,* 12 January 1977.
50 A survey of articles from the press and texts from radio programmes of the first two months was published in Czechoslovakia as early as 1977 in two volumes. One (*Ztroskotanci a samozvanci*; 'The Has-beens and the Pretenders') was published by *Rudé Právo.* The other collection (*Ve jménu socialismu a šťastného života proti rozvratníkům a samozvancům*; 'In the name of socialism and life against saboteurs and the pretenders') appeared under the auspices of the 'Department of Agitation and Propaganda of the Central Committee of the CPCz'. The articles included in these volumes form a silent and permanent indictment against their makers, journalists such as Stanislav Oborský, Karel Douděra, Václav Doležal, Miroslav Kubín and others.
51 *Rudé Právo,* 29 January 1977.
52 A list of the names of these and other (later) signatories can be found in V. Prečan (ed.), *Křesťané a Charta '77, Výběr dokumentů a textů,* Cologne 1980, p.294 ff.
53 *Listy* (Rome) IX, 6 (1979), p. 10.
54 The numbers have been calculated on the basis of a statement by VONS no. 195, in *Listy* (Rome) X, 6 (1980), p. 67 ff.
55 Milan Šimečka, *Obnovení pořádku; příspěvek k typologii reálného socialismu,* Cologne 1979. (See Bibliography: *The Restoration of Order*).
56 See report by Marie Benetková in *Svědectví* XVII, 67 (1982), pp. 428–9.
57 In reality these 'foreign agents' were some foreign journalists. See *Info over Charta 77* VI, 5 (1987), p. 16 ff. The same charge was for instance brought against a young worker from Brno, Petr Pospíchal, signatory of Charter and member of VONS. He was imprisoned at the beginning of 1987 after a great deal of Charter material and *samizdat* publications had been found at his home. See *Listy* (Rome) XVII, 1 (1987), p. 52.
58 For a complete survey of Charter documents up to 1987 consult the 'Annotated list of Charter 77 Documents 1977–1986', in V. Prečan (ed.), *Ten Years of Charter 77,* Hannover 1986, p. 53 ff. Since 1977 documents by, and other news about, Charter 77 have regularly appeared in a special *samizdat* publication named *Infoch* (Informace o Chartě 77; Information about Charter 77) under the editorship of Petr Uhl and Anna Šabatová. Since 1978 *Infoch* also publishes the reports of VONS.
59 Václav Benda 'Paralelní polis' in Václav Havel *et al.*, *O svobodě a moci,* p. 101 ff.
60 Cf. Martin Hybler and Jiří Němec, 'Paralelní struktury, emigrace, Polské léto' in *Svědectví* XVI, 63 (1981), p. 468.
61 *Listy* (Rome) XI, 2 (1981), p. 20.

9 FROM HUSÁK TO JAKEŠ

1 See Husák's opening speech at the XIVth Party Congress in April 1981, in which he welcomed Brezhnev, *XIV. sjezd KSČ,* p. 7.

2 Regarding their own position, prudence was called for. It turned out that in the extensive corruption case, in which the chief of *Jednota,* a catering establishment in the north Slovak Dolný Kubín, Stanislav Babinský (who was arrested in 1984), took a leading role, also involved Pavol Kyman, the leading Party secretary of the district, and other local officials, the minister of Foreign Affairs B. Chňoupek and various high Slovak Party and government officials (Peter Colotka, Elena Litvajová a.o.). For any democratic government in the west, a scandal of such proportions involving embezzlement of state funds would have meant an immediate end to political careers. Not in socialist Czechoslovakia, however. For the highly placed people concerned the affair blew over; Babinský and others were punished, however, so as to set an example. Cf. 'Corruption Trial in Bratislava: Catering for the Elite', Czechoslovak Situation Report 10, *Radio Free Europe Research,* 14 August 1987, p. 21 ff and *Der Spiegel,* (Hamburg) 22 June 1987, pp. 108–9.

3 In 1984 there were 500,000 Hungarians living in the ČSSR out of a population of fifteen and a half million, mainly along the Slovak-Hungarian border, with the biggest concentration in West Slovakia. See *Statistická ročenka ČSSR 1986,* Prague 1986, p. 95 and for many official data regarding the Hungarians Gabriela Sokolová (ed.), *Soudobé tendence vývoje národností v ČSSR,* Prague 1987.

The circumstances in which the Hungarian minority in the ČSSR lived were incomparably better than those of the Hungarians in Romania, but certainly not optimal. This was mainly due to the political system in Czechoslovakia and the general oppressive atmosphere in Czechoslovakia and not so much to a conscious and systematic suppression of the rights of the Hungarians as a national minority. Of course, the Hungarian mother country, as the 'most cheerful barracks in the camp', exerted, and still exerts, a great attraction to the Slovak Hungarians, and the Czechoslovak authorities try to silence any opposition noises from this group. In November 1982, they imprisoned the well-known Hungarian activist from Bratislava, Miklos Duray, and only released him in May 1985.

4 Michal Štefaňák and Ivan Hlivka, 'Národní a internacionalní v politice KSČ' (The national and international in the politics of the CPCz), *Rudé Právo,* 30 March 1984.

5 For the development of the controversy and its background, see Jozsa Gyula, 'Ungarn im Kreuzfeuer der Kritik aus Prag und Moskau' Teil I (Die Aussenministerkonferenz der WP-Staaten (April 1984) und die Polemik gegen Ungarns Positionen), *Berichte des Bundesinstituts für ostwissenschafliche und internationale Studien,* Cologne, no. 5/1985 and no. 6/1985; and *East Berlin and Moscow: the Documentation of a Dispute, RFE* Occasional Papers no. 1, Munich 1985.

6 Cf. the address of L. Štrougal during the plenary session of the Parliament, *Rudé Právo,* 17 March 1983.
7 In this speech, on the occasion of the 40th anniversary of the Košice Programme Štrougal put himself unmistakably behind Gorbachev's plans for reform. He thereby became the first (and for the time being the only) member of the Czechoslovak leadership to do so. See the address entitled 'Významný dokument našich novodobých dějin' (An important document from the new era of our history) in *Rudé Právo,* 5 April 1985.
8 Zdeněk Mlynář, 'Stagnace končí', *Listy* (Rome) XV, 2 (1985), p. 1.
9 *Rudé Právo,* 17 February 1986.
10 See 'Zpráva o hlavních směrech hospodářského a sociálního rozvoje ČSSR na léta 1986–1990 a výhledu do roku 2000' (Report about the main lines of the economic and social development of the ČSSR for the years 1986–90 with an outlook to the year 2000), *XVII. sjezd Komunistické strany Československa,* Prague 1986, p. 63 ff.
11 The latter was particularly true of the then deputy prime minister of the Czech Republic, Ladislav Adamec, and the leading secretary of the provincial party committee in South Moravia, Vladimír Herman. Cf. *XVII. sjezd KSČ,* pp. 164–7 and 306–10.
12 This becomes abundantly clear when, for example, we compare the number of direct quotes from the classics of Marxism-Leninism in the speeches of Husák at the XVth (1976) and XVIth Congress (1981) with that of the XVIIth Party Congress (1986). Such a quantitative approach produces interesting results. At the XVIth (in brackets: XVth Party Congress) Husák cited:

Gottwald	2 x (1 x)
Marx	1 x (1 x)
Lenin	5 x (5 x)
Brezhnev	6 x (6 x)

The index of quotes at the XVIIth Congress looks entirely different:

Gottwald	-
Marx	-
Lenin	-
Gorbachev	3 x

Cf. *XV. sjezd KSČ,* pp. 27–95; *XVI. sjezd KSČ,* pp. 13–62; and *XVII. sjezd KSČ,* pp. 13–62.
13 Cf. Štrougal's speech in *Rudé Právo,* 29 January 1987.
14 'Závěrečné slovo soudruha Miloše Jakeše', *Rudé Právo,* 29 January 1987.
15 See 'Inspirující podněty i pro nás', *Rudé Právo,* 20 February 1987.
16 *Rudé Právo,* 3 March 1987.
17 Cf. *Rudé Právo,* 19 March 1987. The 'Principles of Restructuring' were quickly prepared at the end of 1986, when Prague realized that Gorbachev's reforms were not going to go away. The 'Principles'

were characterized by little daring and a lot of half-heartedness as a result of the compromises between the advocates and opponents of economic reforms. See for the complete text *Rudé Právo*, 9 January 1987; see for the explanation Zdeněk Mošna et al., *Zásady přebudování hospodářského mechanismu ČSSR*, Prague 1987. (A publication only for internal use at the Prague School of Economics).

18 See *Rudé Právo*, 20 March 1987. Cf. also AZ, 'Přestavba nebo přestrojení?', *Listy* (Rome) XVII, 4 (1987), pp. 11–12.

19 In a complaint directed at the Czechoslovak Attorney General, Václav Havel calculated that he had been watched by a total of 300 plainclothes detectives during an eight-day car trip in the summer of 1985. See the text of his letter in *Listy* (Rome) XV, 5 (1985), pp. 8 ff. The strength of the police force in the ČSSR is kept secret. It can be roughly estimated that, beside the ordinary police, it includes some 20,000 secret (political) police, the STB; furthermore, riot police units with over 10,000 men; auxiliary forces (paid volunteers) of about 23,000 men, in addition to an army of paid and unpaid informers from the population at the service of the STB. In 1978 Z. Mlynář estimated the numerical strength of the entire STB net to be about 150,000, or 'one policeman to every hundred citizens'. Jiří Ruml, however, was of the opinion that the number of people who are, professionally, part-time, or voluntarily, engaged in some form of checking the political behaviour of the Czechoslovak citizen, is even higher than 1 per cent: 2 to 5 per cent.

This estimate is not exaggerated, when the 120,000 men strong *Lidové milice* (People's Militia), a kind of private army of the Party, consisting of dedicated communist-volunteers, are also included in the 'controlling instruments' of the regime. This 'armed arm' of the Party is counted on to restore the rule of the CPCz over society by suitable means, if the occasion arises. The greatly privileged members of the *Lidové milice* are notorious for their plainly Stalinist mentality.

Cf. Z. Mlynář, 'Československo po deseti letech', *Listy* (Rome), December 1978 (a special issue), p. 37; Jiří Ruml in Václav Havel *et al.*, *O svobodě a moci*, pp. 290–1; and V. V. Kusin, 'Husak's Czechoslovakia and economic stagnation' in *Problems of Communism* (Washington DC) XXXI, May-June 1982, p. 26.

20 George Moldau, 'Diskusní příspěvek k semináři SL', *Listy*, (Rome) XIV, 6 (1984), p. 14.

21 It is not really possible to give the exact number of believers in the ČSSR, because no official census of the population according to religion has taken place since 1954. According to realistic estimates, the number of active religious believers varies between 4 and 5 million, including 1,300,000 non-Roman Catholics. See Czechoslovak Situation Report 4, *RFER*, 10 March 1986, p. 10.

Understandably, the authorities give lower estimates. In the non-specialist journal *Věda a Život* the number of believers in the ČSSR was estimated at a fifth of the population in 1987, which amounts to over 3 million people. Cf. 'Religion: the Repression Behind the Rhetoric' in Czechoslovak Situation Report 7, *RFER*, 12 June 1987, p. 11.

22 Some examples: In 1985 there were no more than 3,175 clergymen available for a total of 4,336 parishes in the ČSSR. At the same time there were over 400 priests without a licence, which meant that the state did not allow them to practise their profession any longer. If they ignored this ban, they risked imprisonment.

New priests could only be ordained in small numbers, so that year after year the number of deceased priests greatly surpassed the number of newly ordained ones. In 1985 the diocese of České Budějovice (South Bohemia) with 432 parishes had only 156 priests at its disposal, including those retired. During that year 14 priests died, while only 4 new ones took their places. In 7 Slovak dioceses the situation was not much better. Between 1979 and 1987 the number of Roman Catholic priests decreased from 1,773 to 1,396 and the average age increased to 62 years.

At the top of the ecclesiastical hierarchy the situation was, if anything, worse. Since 1973 it had not been possible to appoint a new bishop in the ČSSR, with the result that in the beginning of 1988, 8 out of 10 bishops' sees and 2 out of 3 archbishops' sees were vacant. The youngest bishop was 75, the other was 78, and the archbishop of Prague was 89 years old. The problem was that the state wanted to fill these positions with their own candidates, the pro-regime clergymen of the official organization *Pacem in Terris*, which numbered about 500 members. The authorities feared they would otherwise lose control of the Church.

See Czechoslovak SR/7, *RFER*, 2 May 1986, pp. 19 ff.; SR/9, *RFER*, 18 June 1986, p. 14.; SR/15, *RFER*, 14 October 1987, pp. 13 ff.; and SR/19, *RFER*, 30 December 1987, pp. 15 ff.

23 Cf. 'Religion: Persecution and Resistance', Czechoslovak Situation Report 9, *RFER*, 18 June 1986, p. 11 and *Svědectví* XIX, 76 (1985), p. 776.

24 See Background Report 250, *RFER*, 30 December 1987, p. 16.

25 From an opinion poll carried out in the ČSSR in 1985/1986 by a group of 'independent sociologists' (scholars who do their research outside the official structures), it appeared that of the younger generation born after 1951 hardly anybody considered himself a Marxist and less than 1 per cent a communist. Cf. Zdeněk Strmiska, 'Výsledky nezávislého průzkumu současného myšlení v Československu', *Svědectví* XX, 78 (1986), p. 291.

26 Karl Srp, Vladimír Kouřil and other leaders of this organization (which took up the cudgels for non-conformist musicians, writers and artists, and had 7,000 members and 100,000 sympathizers), were arrested in September 1986, and convicted, despite international protests. In March 1987 Srp was sentenced to 16 months and Kouřil to 10 months imprisonment. The others got away with suspended

sentences. For more details see Czechoslovak Situation Report 4, *RFER*, 6 April 1987, pp. 17 ff., and *East European Reporter*, II, 4 (1987), pp. 2 ff.

27 *Rudé Právo*, 28 January 1987.

28 Cf. 'Stanovisko k rozhovoru Rudého Práva s Vasilem Bilakem' sent to the Presidium of the CPCz and published in *Listy* (Rome) XVII, 2 (1987), pp. 56–7. An amazing appeal to the Czechoslovak leadership to resign was made by the famous Czech actor Miloš Kopecký, (definitely not a dissident), in his speech at the Fourth Congress of the Theatre, Cinema and Television Artists, May 1987. Of course the papers did not publish the controversial passages from his speech. As a great sensation, numerous copies of the complete text circulated throughout the country. See 'Actor Urges the Regime to Resign', Czechoslovak Situation Report 7, *RFER*, 12 June 1987, pp. 17–21. Cf. *Listy* (Rome) XVII, 4 (1987), pp. 5 ff.

It was not only the constantly active ex-communists from Charter 77 and other chartists who made themselves heard. Alexander Dubček, too, directly addressed Mikhail Gorbachev in several letters. It was remarkable that the dispatch of Dubček's message in November 1987, on the eve of the anniversary of the October Revolution, was openly announced by the official Soviet spokesman, and also mentioned in radio broadcasts from Budapest and Warsaw. See V.V. Kusin, 'Gustav Husák's Strange Absence from the Moscow Parade', Background Report 219, *RFER*, 12 November 1987, p. 1.

29 Although Ladislav Adamec, a supporter of Štrougal's, entered the Presidium, succeeding the incompetent Josef Korčák as member of the Presidium and prime minister of the Czech republic (Korčák resigned 'at his own request for reasons of health'; *Rudé Právo*, 20 March 1987), the dogmatic wing was also strengthened. Presidium member Karel Hoffmann also became Party secretary, thus moving up to the top of the power elite, beside Husák, Bilak, Štrougal and Jakeš. Neither could another reinforcement of the secretariat in the person of Miroslav Zavadil, previously ambassador in Moscow, be considered as a gain for Štrougal.

30 Cf. Jiří Ruml 'Vše při starém', *Listy* (Rome) XVI, 4 (1986), p. 19.

31 *Rudé Právo*, 8 April 1987. It was also remarkable that in the *Rudé Právo* of 9 April 1987 there was still mention of a 'four-day official friendly visit'. However, in the late afternoon of the third day Gorbachev left for Moscow again from Bratislava. The 'final programme was shortened by mutual agreement' without reason given. 'Nevertheless comrade Gorbachev has finished the complete planned program', according to *Rudé Právo*, 13 April 1987.

32 *Rudé Právo*, 18 December 1987.

BIBLIOGRAPHY

PERIODICALS

Berichte des Bundesinstituts für ostwissenschaftliche und internationale Studien, Cologne.
Der Spiegel, Hamburg.
East European Reporter, London.
Internationale Spectator, The Hague.
Listy, Prague (banned in 1969).
Listy, Rome.
Literární Listy, Prague.
Osteuropa, Stuttgart.
Osteuropäische Rundschau, Munich.
Právo Lidu, Wuppertal.
Problems of Communism, Washington DC.
Radio Free Europe Research (RFER), Munich.
Research Project *Crises in Soviet-type Systems.* Directed by Z. Mlynář, Vienna.
Rudé Právo, Prague.
Statistická ročenka Československé socialistické republiky, Prague.
Svědectví, Paris.

LITERATURE

Beneš, E., *Demokracie dnes a zítra*, Prague 1946.
Bilak, V., *Pravda zůstala pravdou. Projevy a články říjen 1967–prosinec 1970*, Prague 1974.
Bílek, P., *175 autorů. Čeští prozaici, básníci a literární kritici publikující v 70. letech v nakladatelství Československý spisovatel*, Prague 1982.
Brabec, J. (ed.), *Slovník českých spisovatelů. Pokus o rekonstrukci dějin české literatury 1948–1979*, Toronto 1982.
Brahm, H., *Der Kreml und die ČSSR 1968–1969*, Stuttgart 1970.
Brisch, H., and Volgyes, I. (eds), *Czechoslovakia: The Heritage of Ages Past. Essays in Memory of Josef Korbel*, Boulder 1979.

Bystřina, I., *et. al.* (eds), *Systémové změny* (Sborník), Cologne 1972.
Dějiny Komunistické Strany Československa, Prague 1961.
Flégl, V., *Ústavní základy Československé socialistické republiky*, Prague 1981.
Forst, V. (ed.), *Slovník české literatury 1970–1981*, Prague 1985.
French, A., *Czech Writers and Politics 1945–1969*, Boulder 1982.
Frolík, J., *Špion vypovídá*, Cologne 1979.
Golan, G., *Reform Rule in Czechoslovakia. The Dubcek Era 1968–1969*, Cambridge 1973.
—*The Czechoslovak Reform Movement. Communism in Crisis 1962–1968*, Cambridge 1971.
Gottwald, K., *Deset let. Sborník statí a projevů 1936–1946*, Prague 1949.
Hájek, J., *Mýtus a realita Ledna 1968*, Prague 1970.
Hájek, J. (ex-minister of Foreign Affairs), *Begegnungen und Zusammenstösse. Erinnerungen des ehemaligen tschechoslowakischen Aussenministers*, Freiburg im Breisgau 1987.
Havel, V., *Dálkový výslech. Rozhovor s Karlem Hvížďalou*, Edition Rozmluvy (UK) 1986.
Havel, V. *et. al.*, *O svobodě a moci*, Cologne 1980.
Hejl, V., and Kaplan, K., *Zpráva o organizovaném násilí*, Toronto 1986.
Hejzlar, Z., *Reformkommunismus. Zur Geschichte der Kommunistischen Partei der Tschechoslowakei*, Cologne 1976.
Hoensch, J. K., *Geschichte der Tschechoslowakischen Republik 1918–1978*, Stuttgart 1978.
Horský, V., *Prag 1968. Systemveränderung und Systemverteidigung*, Stuttgart 1975.
Hrubý, P., *Fools and Heroes. The Changing Role of Communist Intellectuals in Czechoslovakia*, Oxford 1980.
Hvížďala, K., *České rozhovory ve světě*, Cologne 1981.
[Janouch, F.], *Briefe aus der Tschechoslowakei. Der Untergrund berichtet über die Lage des Volkes*, ed. J. Stárek, Graz-Vienna 1974.
Janouch, F., *Ne, nestěžuji si. Malá normalizační mozaika*, Cologne 1985.
Josten, J., *Oh my Country*, London 1949.
Kabrhel, J. (ed.), *Zemědělská politika KSČ*, Prague 1977.
Kadlec, V., *Dubček - 1968*, Cologne 1987.
Kaplan, F. L., *Winter Into Spring: The Czechoslovak Press and the Reform Movement 1963–1968*, Boulder 1977.
Kaplan, K., *Der kurze Marsch. Kommunistische Machtübernahme in der Tschechoslowakei 1945–1948*, Munich 1981.
—*Die Entwicklung des Rates für gegenseitige Wirtschaftshilfe (RGW) in der Zeit von 1949 bis 1957*, Ebenhausen 1977.
Kolman, A., *Die verirrte Generation. So hätten wir nicht leben sollen. Eine Biographie*, Frankfurt a.M. 1979.
Kosta, J., *Abriss der sozialökonomischen Entwicklung der Tschechoslowakei 1945–1977*, Frankfurt a.M. 1978.
Král, V., *Historické mezníky ve vývoji Československa*, Prague 1978.
Krejčí, J., *Social Change and Stratification in Postwar Czechoslovakia*, London 1972.

Krystufek, Z., *The Soviet Regime in Czechoslovakia*, Boulder 1981.
Kusák, A. and Künzel, F. P., *Der Sozialismus mit menschlichem Gesicht. Experiment und Beispiel der Sozialistischen Reformation in der Tschechoslowakei*, Munich 1969.
Kusín, V. V., *From Dubček to Charter 77. A Study of 'Normalisation' in Czechoslovakia 1968–1978*, Edinburgh 1978.
—*Political Grouping in the Czechoslovak Reform Movement*, London 1972.
—*The Intellectual Origins of the Prague Spring. The Development of Reformist Ideas in Czechoslovakia 1956–1967*, Cambridge 1971.
Lederer, J., *České rozhovory*, Cologne 1979.
Littel, R. (ed.), *The Czech Black Book. Prepared by the Institute of History of the Czechoslovak Academy of Sciences*, New York 1969.
Lobkowicz, N., and Prinz, F., (eds), *Die Tschechoslowakei 1945–1970*, Munich 1978.
Löbl, E., and Grünwald, L., *Die intellektuelle Revolution. Hintergründe und Auswirkungen des 'Prager Frühlings'*, Düsseldorf 1969.
Memoirs of Dr Eduard Benes. From Munich to New War and New Victory, London 1954.
Mlynář, Z., *Československý pokus o reformu 1968. Analýza jeho teorie a praxe*, Cologne 1975.
—*Nachtfrost. Erfahrungen auf dem Weg vom realen zum menschlichen Sozialismus*, Cologne 1978.
Opat, J., *O novou demokracii 1945–1948*, Prague 1966.
Ostrý, A., *Československý problém*, Cologne 1972.
Pachman, L., *Nu kan ik spreken ... Van Beneš tot Dubček. Over schaken en communisme*, Baarn-Antwerp 1975.
Pelikán, J. (ed.), *Das unterdrückte Dossier. Bericht der Kommission des ZK der KPTsch über politische Prozesse und 'Rehabilitierungen' in der Tschechoslowakei 1949–1968* (the so-called Piller-report), Vienna 1970.
Pelikán, J., *Ein Frühling, der nie zu Ende geht. Erinnerungen eines Prager Kommunisten*, Frankfurt a. M. 1976.
—*Sozialistische Opposition in der ČSSR. Analyse und Dokumente des Widerstands seit dem Prager Frühling*, Frankfurt a.M./Cologne 1974.
—*The Secret Vysocany Congress. Proceedings and Documents of the Extraordinary Fourteenth Congress of the Communist Party of Czechoslovakia, 22 August 1968*, London 1971.
Piekalkiewicz, J. A., *Public Opinion Polling in Czechoslovakia, 1968–1969. Results and Analysis of Surveys Conducted During the Dubček Era*, New York 1972.
V. Prečan (ed.), *Kniha Charty. Hlasy z domova 1976/1977*, Cologne 1977.
—*Acta Creationis. Independent Historiography in Czechoslovakia 1969–1980* (Presented to the XVth International Congress of Historical Sciences, Bucharest, August 1980), Hannover 1980.
—*Křesťané a Charta ' 77. Výběr dokumentů a textů*, Cologne 1980.
—*Ten years of Charter 77*, Hannover 1986.

Průcha, V., *Hospodářské dějiny Československa v 19. a 20. století*, Prague 1974.
—*30 let budování socialistické ekonomiky Československa*, Prague 1978.
Reden zum IV. Kongress des Tschechoslowakischen Schriftstellerverbandes Prag, Juni 1967, Frankfurt a.M. 1968.
Remington, R. A. (ed.), *Winter in Prague. Documents on Czechoslovak Communism in Crisis*, Cambridge (Mass.) 1969.
Rok šedesátý osmý v usneseních a dokumentech ÚV KSČ, Prague 1969.
Šejna, J., *We will bury you*, London 1984.
Šimečka, M., *Kruhová obrana. Záznamy z roku 1984*, Cologne 1985.
—*The Restoration of Order. The Normalization of Czechoslovakia 1969–1976*, London 1984.
Shawcross, W., *Dubček*, London 1970.
XIV. sjezd Komunistické strany Československa, Prague 1971.
XV. sjezd Komunistické strany Československa, Prague 1977.
XVI. sjezd Komunistické strany Československa, Prague 1981.
XVII. sjezd Komunistické strany Československa, Prague 1986.
Skilling, Gordon H., *Charter 77 and Human Rights in Czechoslovakia*, London 1981.
—*Czechoslovakia's Interrupted Revolution*, Princeton 1976.
Snítil, Z., *Československá revoluce 1944–1948*, Prague 1979.
Sokolová, G. (ed.), *Soudobé tendence vývoje národností v ČSSR*, Prague 1987.
Šolc, M. (ed.), *Stručný slovník teorie a praxe výstavby strany*, Prague 1982.
Szulc, T., *Czechoslovakia Since World War II*, New York 1971.
Taborsky, E., *Communism in Czechoslovakia 1948–1960*, Princeton 1961.
Tigrid, P. (ed.), *Vývoj Charty. Záznam z konference ve Franken*, Cologne 1981.
Tigrid, P., *Why Dubček Fell*, London 1971.
—*Únor 1948 očima vítězů i poražených o třicet let později*, Cologne 1979.
Ulč, O., *Politics in Czechoslovakia*, San Francisco 1974.
Vaculík, L., *Český snář*, Toronto 1983.
Valenta, J., *Soviet Intervention in Czechoslovakia, 1968. Anatomy of a Decision*, Baltimore-London 1979.
Veselý, L., *Dubček Biografie*, Munich 1970.
Vladislav, J. (ed.), *Václav Havel or Living in Truth. Twenty-two essays published on the occasion of the award of the Erasmus Prize to Václav Havel*, Amsterdam 1986.

INDEX